The New Geopolitics of Central Asia
and Its Borderlands

The New Geopolitics of Central Asia and Its Borderlands

EDITED BY

ALI BANUAZIZI AND MYRON WEINER

INDIANA UNIVERSITY PRESS
BLOOMINGTON AND INDIANAPOLIS

Published by arrangement with I.B.Tauris & Co Ltd

Manufactured in Great Britain

Library of Congress Cataloging-in-Publication Data
The New geopolitics of Central Asia / edited by Ali Banuazizi and Myron
Weiner.
    p. cm.
    ISBN 0-253-31139-X — ISBN 0-253-20918-8 (pbk.)
    1. Asia, Central—Politics and government.   2. Geopolitics—Asia,
Central.   3. Asia, Central—Relations—Middle East.   4. Middle East—
Relations—Asia, Central.   I. Banuazizi, Ali.   II. Weiner, Myron.
    DS329.4.N48   1994
    320.958—dc20   94-11996

            1   2   3   4   5   00   99   98   97   96   95   94

Contents

Acknowledgements

The papers for this volume were prepared for and initially presented at a series of workshops held at the Center for International Studies at the Massachusetts Institute of Technology. The editors would like to acknowledge, with great appreciation, the financial support given the project by The Fund for Peace and the active encouragement and support of its Executive Director, Dr Nina Solarz. We would also like to thank the following scholars who helped in the initial planning for the project: Thomas Barfield (Boston University), Donald Blackmer (MIT), Stephen Burg (Brandeis University), Donald Carlisle (Boston College), Paul Goble (Carnegie Endowment for International Peace), Beatrice Forbes Manz (Tufts University), Stephen Meyer (MIT) and Mark Saroyan (Harvard University). Our gratitude goes as well to William Fierman (Indiana University) and Ashraf Ghani (The Johns Hopkins University), who served as discussants at two of our workshops. Ms Lois Malone (MIT) contributed to every phase of this endeavour, from the initial planning stages to the completion of this volume, with her unique combination of managerial talents and discerning editorial skills, for which we are deeply grateful. Finally, we would like to thank our editor at I.B. Tauris, Ms Anna Enayat, for her encouragement, advice and support in bringing this project to fruition.

Ali Banuazizi
Myron Weiner

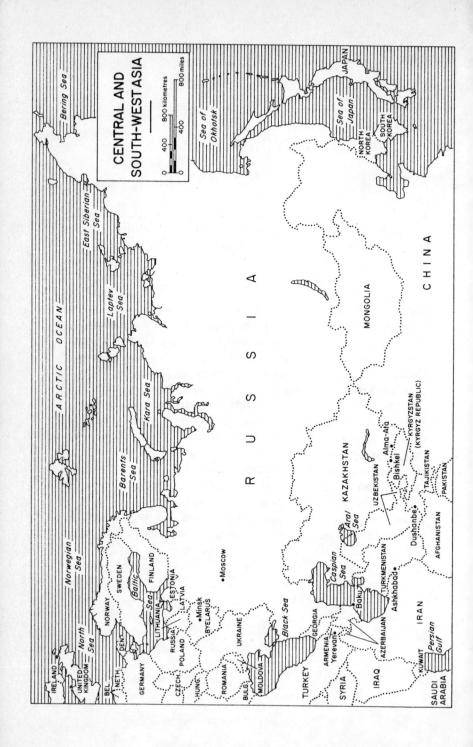

Introduction

ALI BANUAZIZI AND MYRON WEINER

I

No major empires have dissolved in this century without their successor states undergoing civil wars or regional conflicts. The breakup of the Ottoman empire was accompanied by the Balkan wars and by internecine conflicts among the successor Arab states. The dissolution of the Austro-Hungarian Habsburg empire triggered conflicts within both the Balkans and Central Europe. After the Second World War, the withdrawal of the British, French, Dutch, Americans and Portuguese from their overseas colonies left unstable states and regional conflicts. The departure of the British from South Asia left two successor states, India and Pakistan, in conflict, and Sri Lanka a deeply divided society. The withdrawal of the British, French and Portuguese from Africa left dozens of countries torn by civil conflicts, guerrilla warfare, refugee flows and declining economies in the midst of rapid population growth. The French and Dutch withdrawal from Indochina and Indonesia was, in both cases, followed by civil conflicts. What is it about the breakup of empires that leads to civil wars and regional conflicts among successor states?

It is first necessary to recognize that ethnic conflict within and between successor states is not merely the result of the reemergence of historic enmities that had been suppressed by the imperial centre. It is tempting to argue that the conflicts between Hindus and Muslims, Serbs and Croats, Bosnian Muslims and Serbs, Armenians and Azeris, Russians and Estonians are ancient battles that reflect fundamental clashes between peoples of different cultures, even different civilizations. While historic memories do play a role in ethnic conflict, imperial states typically create conditions which generate conflict among and within their successor states. Under imperial rule, non-indigenous peoples migrate into the region under colonial authority, where they often assume positions of political, social and economic superiority. The migrants often belong to the ethnic community of the imperial states, but they can also come from elsewhere. Under British and French rule, for example, Chinese or Indian migrants settled in various parts of the empire; under Ottoman rule Turks, but also Albanian and Bosnian Muslims, settled throughout the Balkans. These migrations were sometimes simply the result of the emergence of new opportunities; at other times they represented a systematic effort by the imperial power to relocate peoples for political reasons.

The governments of newly established states, and their supporters, often regard migrants and their descendants as an alien people whose very presence is illegitimate. Successor states may take away citizenship from the migrant communities, expel them, or impose restrictions on language use, education and employment which induce them to leave. Thus, Uganda and Burma expelled Indians; Indonesia massacred Chinese; Algeria forced out the French *pieds noirs*; Bulgaria expelled the Turks; and Romania pushed out the Hungarians.

Massacres and expulsion are by no means inevitable, because there are constraints upon nationalist élites. Although the nationalists' capacity for economic self-destruction should not be underestimated, nationalist leaders may be aware of the economic importance of the migrant community and the losses incurred if entrepreneurs, professionals, financiers and skilled workers are forced to leave. Nationalists may also be constrained by fears of intervention by the country from which the migrants originate, or by a concern that discriminatory policies may result in civil conflict. How nationalist élites deal with the demographic legacy of imperial rule is a complex matter, often shaped by historic memories of overlordship, by deep cultural notions of jealousy, or by egalitarian levelling sentiments, rather than by concerns over economic growth or even of avoiding violent conflict.

A second feature of empires that generates conflict in successor states is that the internal borders of empires rarely coincide with linguistic, religious or racial boundaries. Empires are built by accretion, so that their administrative boundaries often reflect the manner of absorption of new territories. Moreover, imperial authorities often govern by pitting one community against another; they prefer, and therefore may create, administrative divisions that divide ethnic and religious communities so as to impede their mobilization. Each of the administrative units within an empire often contains minorities who form majorities in a neighbouring state. Azerbaijan's Nagorno-Karabakh, Romania's Transylvania, Serbia's Kosovo and Burma's Arakan are not unusual examples. When empires dissolve, it is common for the successor states to be based upon existing administrative divisions. Rarely is self-determination accompanied by redrawing of boundaries so as to be inclusive of an ethnic community, with minority-dominated regions transferred to another state. The presence of minorities from a neighbouring state combined with irredentist disputes over boundaries is a dangerous mix.

While successor states ever proclaim the general principle that state boundaries are inviolable, the fact is that irredentist wars have been commonplace – between Ethiopia and Somalia, between India and Pakistan over Kashmir, between Bulgaria, Yugoslavia and Greece over Macedonia, between Italy and Austria over Trieste, etc. The breakup of empires also often leaves some peoples without states of their own – Kurds, Baluch, Macedonians, for example.

In any event, multi-ethnicity in the successor states may be unrelated to migration under colonial rule or to the way in which administrative boundaries were established. Tamils and Sinhalese occupied Sri Lanka long before the Europeans arrived; in Africa tribes lived side by side, and sometimes fought one another, long before imperial rule. Under imperial rule some groups coalesce, and new alliances are formed, but also new cleavages are created. Some groups do relatively well under imperial rule, as they become disproportionately more educated and move into the professions and into the civil or military bureaucracy while others are left behind. At the end of imperial rule, some groups are in a stronger position than others to exercise political power or to control the major economic institutions. If a demographically hegemonic community assumes power, minorities are sure to be uneasy, especially when majorities assume political power, but minorities have a strong hold upon the economy. The removal of foreign domination creates a new political arena within which groups once subordinate to the imperial rulers now contend for power.

A third feature of successor states is that they are often weak. Under imperial rule the major institutions – the civil administration, the police, the military, the financial institutions, the universities, the corporations – were dominated by the imperial power. The successor states often lack the experienced manpower to manage these institutions;

Table 1 Basic Demographic and Economic Indicators for the Central Asian Republics and Azerbaijan

Country	Area (1000 km²)	Population[a] (million)	Urban population[b] (%)	Titular nationality (%)	Main minorities (%)	Per capita GNP[b] (US$)
Kazakhstan	2717	16.8	57	40	Russians (38) Ukranians (5) Germans (5)	2470
Kyrgyzstan	199	4.5	38	52	Russians (22) Uzbeks (12)	1550
Tajikistan	143	5.5	32	62	Uzbeks (23) Russians (7)	1050
Turkmenistan	488	3.8	45	72	Russians (9) Uzbeks (9)	1700
Uzbekistan	447	20.9	41	71	Russians (8) Tajiks (5)	1350
Azerbaijan	87	7.1	54	83	Armenians (6) Russians (6)	1670

[a] mid-1991
[b] 1991

Source: World Development Report 1993. New York: Oxford University Press, 1993. Figures for titular nationality and main minorities are from *The Economist*, 26 December 1992–8 January 1993, pp 44–6.

in some instances, the institutions themselves have become discredited and their legitimacy eroded by their nationalist opponents; and in still other instances these institutions continue to be dominated by the same individuals who controlled them during the era of imperial domination. It is also sadly not uncommon for emerging élites to regard these institutions as a source of personal gain for themselves and their families, and as a way in which they can now exercise autocratic authority over others. The result is a further erosion of these institutions and of public regard for them.

The successor governments may also find that their economies were in some fundamental ways warped by imperial domination, as they became suppliers of raw materials for the imperial centre, and their transport systems structured to meet the needs of a distant metropole.

A fourth and final feature of successor states is that violent conflicts within and quarrels among them readily become internationalized as each party to a dispute seeks external allies. Minorities within states often turn for support to a neighbouring country with whom there are ethnic bonds. As states dispute their borders, make claims upon each other's territory, or support secessionist or irredentist movements within a neighbouring state, they often turn to outsider powers for support. Weaker states need military and political support from others and, in turn, stronger states often respond by creating alliances with those who are enemies of their neighbour's allies. And so, in time, countries that have little intrinsic interest in the internecine quarrels of smaller states soon find themselves embroiled in large balance-of-power conflicts. Examples abound: during the interwar period, for example, Albania, in dispute with Yugoslavia, allied with Italy; Hungary joined with Germany; Bulgaria with Russia, then subsequently with Germany; the Serbs with the allies and the Croatians with the Germans; the Greeks with Britain, while Turkey flirted with the Germans. Similarly, in the postwar period, Sudan, Somalia, Ethiopia, Mozambique, Angola, India and Pakistan each turned to one or another of the great powers to help them in their regional disputes.

II

The six Muslim republics of Central Asia and the Transcaucasus on which this volume focuses – Kazakhstan, Kyrgyzstan, Tajikstan, Turkmenistan, Uzbekistan and Azerbaijan – largely fit this model of successor states to empires. Their ethnic composition was transformed by settlers from Russia and other Slavic republics of the former Soviet Union, as well as population movements and resettlements across their own boundaries. Today, among their 60 million inhabitants, there are an estimated 10 million ethnic Russians, many of whom hold important positions in the economy, the professions and in the state apparatus itself. As Table 1 shows, the proportion of Russians in these republics ranges from 6 to 9 per cent in Azerbaijan, Tajikstan, Turkmenistan and Uzbekistan, to 22 per cent in Kyrgyzstan and 38 per cent in Kazakhstan. Indeed, ethnic Russians comprise more than three fifths of the population in north and east oblasts of Kazakhstan and significant majorities in the capital cities of Almaty and Bishkek. Socio-economic disparities between the Russians and the local populations, differences in cultural values and modes of behaviour, and the inability of the vast majority of the resident Russians to communicate in the local tongues lead to considerable resentment by the indigenous populations. At the same time, with the current surge of ethnic nationalism in Russia itself, the fate of Russian communities in Central Asia and elsewhere within the Commonwealth of Independent States (CIS) has become a highly charged political issue and is likely to have a major effect in shaping Russia's future policies towards the Soviet successor states.[1]

The boundaries of these states, drawn originally in the mid-1920s by the Commissariat of Nationalities under Stalin to favour some nationalities, to isolate others, and to ensure Moscow's domination, are arbitrary and rarely coincide with any historic boundaries or with the linguistic and cultural affinities of the different subpopulations within each of them. The result is that each country shares one or more ethnic groups with its bordering republic, with bordering states to the south, or with other republics of the former Soviet Union.

The conquest of Central Asia by Russia in the latter part of the nineteenth century created a relationship of dependency between the peoples of this region and tsarist Russia that changed only in form under Soviet rule. The major institutions of these states were Soviet creations, dominated by Russians or Russified (or, more accurately, 'Sovietized') Central Asians, with few opportunities for the emergence of local élites prepared to assume control over the state institutions and the economy. Thus, as Martha Brill Olcott points out in her contribution to this volume, before the collapse of the Soviet Union in December 1991, 'none of these republics planned or supported a

formal break with Moscow....When the three Slavic republics unilaterally dissolved the USSR on 8 December 1991, effectively expelling Central Asia, the Central Asians were left with an independence
for which they had not prepared, which they did not want, and which
was not likely to bring them any tangible benefit for a long time, if
ever.'

The economies of these states were made into adjuncts of the Soviet
economy. Primarily producers of raw materials for the Russians, these
economies were warped by Soviet domination, cut off from opportunities for independent development, and unable to engage in free
trade with their immediate neighbours or others beyond the Soviet
borders. The Russians also left behind a devastated environment,
including the well-known ecological disaster of the Aral Sea as well as
the loss of irrigated lands, chemically contaminated water supplies
and polluted rivers. In the absence of real and expanding employment
opportunities, and given the youthful and rapidly growing populations
of these republics, there is likely to be increasing competition for
jobs, economic deprivation and frustration – i.e. the all-too-familiar
conditions in newly independent states that lead to social conflict and
political instability.

Can we then expect that the successor states of Central Asia will
experience the internal turmoil and external conflicts that have characterized so many other post-imperial successor states? Will they fall
victim to ethnic strife and civil disorder? Will minorities be attacked
and forced out? Will rivalries and conflicts develop among the Central
Asian states and will these states in turn seek external allies to inter-
nationalize their disputes? Will this region, so obscure to most of the
world in the twentieth century, become in the next a maelstrom of
political turbulence which will spill over to its southern neighbours?
Would the growth of an Islamic identity draw these states closer to
other Islamic countries in South-west Asia and the Middle East? The
answers to these questions depend not only on the developments
within each of the republics, but also on a complex set of influences,
rivalries and conflicts involving them, the major regional powers and
their neighbours to the south.

The eleven contributors to the present volume review the post-
Soviet developments in these republics and address the above questions with special emphasis on the religious, ethnic and cultural ties
that have historically bound these republics to the four neighbouring
Muslim countries of Turkey, Iran, Afghanistan and Pakistan. The

three contributors to Part I, Graham E. Fuller, Martha Brill Olcott and Boris Z. Rumer, provide an overview of the emerging geopolitical situation in Central Asia, the background and political orientations of their élites, and some of the potentials for political instability and conflict in the region. In Part II, our contributors focus on Uzbekistan (Henry Hale), Tajikistan (Muriel Atkin) and Azerbaijan (Tadeusz Swietochowski) as case studies, illustrating the dynamic interplay between the domestic political developments in each republic and their stance *vis-à-vis* their 'southern tier' Muslim neighbours. The contributions to Part III, on Turkey (Sabri Sayari), Iran (Seyed Kazem Sajjadpour) and Pakistan and Afghanistan (Tahir Amin), view the same relationships from the other side of the borders, describing both the ambitions of and the constraints upon these four countries as they try to forge new economic, political and cultural ties with their northern neighbours. And finally, in Part IV, the new geopolitical situation and its ramifications are analysed from the viewpoint of Russia (Mikhail Konarovsky) and the United States (Nancy Lubin).

III

This volume assesses the recent developments in the six post-Soviet Muslim republics of Central Asia and Transcaucasus within a geopolitical rather than a national framework. Its basic premise is that both the internal developments and the international relations of these states need to be seen in the context of the larger Turko-Islamic and Iranian civilizations, to which they once belonged and with which they have now once again begun to interact, as well as in the still broader Eurasian context that includes Russia, China, Pakistan, India, Japan and the neighbouring Middle Eastern states.

There are three reasons for studying these states within such a geopolitical framework. The first and foremost is the obvious fact of geography. It is but a short distance from Azerbaijan to the border of Turkey; Azerbaijan and Turkmenistan border on Iran; Turkmenistan, Uzbekistan and Kyrgyzstan border on Afghanistan; and Tashkent, Samarkand, Dushanbe, Bukhara and Almaty are closer to Kabul and Peshawar than to any Russian cities. Even putting aside cultural and religious ties, proximity alone ensures that developments in one state will impinge upon others. Strife within any country in the region is likely to spill across the borders as refugees flee, as indeed has already been demonstrated in Tajikistan and Afghanistan. The ecological disasters that have afflicted the Central Asian states are not confined by national boundaries. The need to develop workable schemes for access to scarce water resources, oil and gas pipelines, and building common routes to ports link these landlocked countries to one another and to their southern neighbours.

Central Asian trade, now routed primarily through Russia, can move through the Arabian Sea only if the neighbours to the south are willing to cooperate. If Pakistan is to open trade with its new near neighbours, it needs a stable Tajikistan *and* Afghanistan to serve as a trade corridor. Thus, both Pakistan and the Central Asian states have an interest in a peaceful resolution of the present civil conflicts in these states. For its part, Pakistan has reorientated its Afghan policy from one of supporting the most militantly fundamentalist Mujahedin faction (the Hizb-i Islami of Gulbuddin Hekmatyar) to one of supporting the more moderate elements within the highly fractious Afghan leadership that are likely to be more acceptable to the secular leaders of Central Asia and conducive to its own goals of regional stability. In short, increased commercial relations, expansion of communications and transport routes, and a desire to avoid political upheavals that could easily cross international boundaries are creating common interests among these geographically linked neighbours.[2]

The second factor is that all six successor republics have historic, ethnolinguistic and/or religious ties to the 300 million people who reside in the four neighbouring Muslim countries of Afghanistan, Pakistan, Iran and Turkey. These ties, largely ruptured under Soviet rule, are in the process of being reestablished, as much through the efforts of their neighbours as by the Central Asian states' own inclinations. Besides their common faith in Islam, there are many other ethnic and cultural bases for closer relations between the peoples of Central Asia and the populations of Turkey, Iran, Pakistan and Afghanistan.[3] Thus in language (Azeri–Turkic) and religion (Shi'ite Islam), for example, the 7 million Azerbaijanis in the Republic of Azerbaijan are nearly identical with the 15 million Azerbaijanis across the Aras River in Iran, where they constitute Iran's largest linguistic minority. The Uzbeks, who comprised the third largest ethnic group in the former Soviet Union (after Russians and Ukrainians), count over 1 million Afghan Uzbeks as their ethnic kinsmen and also share the language and many cultural traditions of the Anatolian Turks. The Tajiks are a Persian-speaking people with historic roots in Iranian culture and even closer ties to 4 million Tajiks in Afghanistan. The

2.5 million Turkomans have ethnic brethren, though in much smaller numbers, in Iran and Afghanistan. Significant cultural, linguistic and religious ties exist also between some of the communities in the eastern parts of the Central Asian states and communities in China's Xinjiang province.[4]

All of the major states in the region, including Turkey, Iran and Pakistan, as well as China, Saudi Arabia and India, have taken an active interest in recent developments in Central Asia – each seeking to promote its own cultural, political and economic interests, while being wary of the intentions and initiatives of others. They have negotiated new trade agreements, expanded consular arrangements, and created cultural and academic exchanges. In the cases of Turkey and Iran, locked in a rivalry for status as regional powers, their competition has an important ideological dimension as well: a pro-Western Turkey versus a radical anti-Western Iran with its revolutionary Islamic identity.

Besides its expanding economic and cultural ties with the republics of Central Asia and the Transcaucasus, Iran has a special interest in the internal political developments of the Republic of Azerbaijan. The Azerbaijani minority in Iran constitutes one quarter of the population, and the prospect of a strong Azerbaijan orientated towards Turkey can have both internal as well as external repercussions for Iran. Similarly, Iran has an interest in the internal political developments of Tajikistan, especially the relationship that develops between the Persian-speaking Tajiks and whatever government finally emerges in Afghanistan.

For Turkey, the opening of Central Asia provides both opportunities and risks: opportunities for becoming a communications and transport link between Central Asia and the West and for serving as a successful liberal-secular model for the former; risks because any decisive support for or intervention on behalf of Azerbaijan is likely to create conflicts with Armenia, its closer neighbour, and its supporters in the West. Furthermore, too deep an involvement in the potentially turbulent politics of Central Asia could adversely affect Turkey's efforts to become part of Europe.

In the case of Afghanistan, which has common borders with three of these republics, as well as with Iran and Pakistan, the various factions currently contending for political power there recognize that their own struggles can be shaped significantly by Pakistan, Iran, Tajikistan and other Central Asian states. The key military battles in early 1994 shifted from Kabul to the international highways, particularly between Kabul, Kunduz and points north, from which supplies come.

The third reason for analysing Central Asian developments within a geopolitical framework is that the way in which each republic defines its own identity – separately from or in common with one or more of its neighbours, or its coethnics in the neighbouring countries – is likely to have significant ramifications for the geopolitics of the entire region. Emphasis on separate ethnolinguistic identities by Azerbaijanis, Kazakhs, Tajiks, Uzbeks, Kyrgyzes and Turkomans can lead to both consolidation and conflict within states and between them. Alternatively, any moves towards the creation of a pan-Turkic identity within the framework of a new union or confederation on the basis of a common language would not only isolate and threaten the Persian-speaking Tajiks, but would also be perceived as potentially threatening to China.[5]

IV

When the Soviet state disintegrated and newly independent predominantly Muslim states emerged in Central Asia, a simple model for understanding their role in international politics was widely put forward. According to this model, the peoples of the Central Asian states will be drawn to an Islamic identity, long suppressed by Soviet rule, which might take a militant anti-Western form and thereby increase the regional power of Iran and the world-wide influence of fundamentalism. This 'clash of civilizations' between fundamentalist Islam and the West will attract other Muslims who, although not drawn to fundamentalism, are antagonistic to the West. In this struggle, both the West and Russia, for different reasons, are handicapped, but Turkey as a state largely populated by secular-minded Muslims is in a position to exercise influence upon the new states because of its linguistic and cultural affinities for the majority of the Central Asians and the desire of their urban élites to prevent the rise of militant Islam. According to this view, Turkey and Iran will compete for influence in Central Asia and it is therefore clear who should receive Western backing. This is a new version, of course, of the nineteenth-century 'Great Game' model, with Turkey and Iran replacing Russia and Great Britain for influence in Central Asia.

This model was soon recognized as overly simplistic, in part because it failed to recognize the differences between Islam in Central Asia and elsewhere in the Middle East, as well as the many significant differences among these republics with respect to the nature, depth and impact of Islam on their national life and consciousness. In Kazakhstan, for example, Islam is of relatively recent origin (the conversion to Islam took place in the seventeenth and eighteenth centuries, i.e. a thousand years after the rest of Central Asia), and today some three fifths of the population is made up of non-Muslims; there is no established clerical hierarchy with a knowledge of the classical languages of Islam, i.e. Arabic or Persian. On the other hand, in Uzbekistan, with a more urbanized culture, Islam has much deeper roots; there are great mosques, libraries, and madrasas and a revival of Islam is clearly under way. In all republics, several decades of secularization and official atheism have confined Islam, for the most part, to the arenas of spiritual faith, rituals and cultural identity, rather than a basis for communal associations and political organization. The only exceptions have so far been in Tajikistan, where Islamic groups in coalition with nationalist and democratic forces have been fighting the authoritarian control of the former communist élite (now supported by Moscow and the Uzbek government), and in the economically deprived Ferghana Valley (which straddles Uzbekistan, Tajikistan and Kyrgyzstan), where economic hardships and grievances have already led to a militant Islamic resurgence movement.

Furthermore, in spite of their initial enthusiasm in approaching these republics, it has become increasingly apparent that both Turkey and Iran lack the economic resources that would enable them to exercise a dominating influence in this region. Neither have pan-Turkism or pan-Islamism had much appeal to populations of these states up to now. Artificial as they may in some sense be, they are no less 'artificial' than other states whose ethnic composition is diverse and whose borders are not, from an ethnic point of view, 'natural'.

As this 'old' but very short-lived model has given way, a new model has emerged, one that points to the role Russia can play in helping to stabilize the region. Developing, in part at least, as a response to the bloody ethnic conflicts in former Yugoslavia and political turmoil in Somalia, Sudan and elsewhere in Africa, this second model stipulates that political order among the weak states in the Third World (to which Central Asia now belongs) depends upon the willingness and capacity of regional superpowers to intervene. The USA has demonstrated that it is unwilling to intervene in regional conflicts or to intercede in internal civil conflicts unless its own interests are at stake or where it can be part of a collective action legitimized by the United Nations, NATO or other regional grouping. According to this view, the USA and the European powers have some stake in developments in the Baltic states and in Ukraine, and possibly in nuclear-wielding Kazakhstan, but not in the other Muslim republics of Central Asia. Thus, according to this model, it is best to permit and indeed encourage Russia to play an active role in mediating disputes within and between the Central Asian republics, even when it involves the exercise of military power, as it already has in Tajikistan.[6] In our view, this model has two major weaknesses. It fails to recognize that nationalist Russians and sections of the Russian military have an interest in promoting conflicts in the region precisely in order to extend their influence, as they apparently did in Georgia. And, secondly, it ignores the possibility that the reestablishment of Russian hegemony in Central Asia is likely to strengthen the non-democratic tendencies that already exist within Russia. As Zbigniew Brzezinski put it recently, 'any effort to recreate some form of empire, repressing the awakened national aspirations of the non-Russians, would surely collide head-on with the effort to consolidate democracy within Russia. The bottom line here is a simple but compelling axiom: Russia can be either an empire or a democracy, but it cannot be both'.[7]

A third model is aspired to by the states of the region, one which emphasizes their independent character and seeks to strengthen this independence through membership in a variety of regional groupings, including the Economic Cooperation Organization (ECO) consisting of the five Central Asian states, Azerbaijan, Turkey, Iran, Afghanistan and Pakistan. The new states are eager for investments from the USA, Korea, Japan and Western Europe to enable them to diversify their economies and to reduce their dependence upon Russia. The protection of minorities, including Russian settlers, is critical to their efforts to create stable political systems and to avoid external intervention. Fiscal stability, supported by the World Bank and the International Monetary Fund (IMF), also remains an essential need. It is not difficult to formulate the outlines of such a model, but again the reality is more complex. Inter-ethnic antagonisms and rivalries among the republics seem likely. There have already been conflicts among the Tajiks and between Uzbeks and Meskhetian Turks. And there remains a high potential for conflicts between Russians and Central

Asians, especially in Kazakhstan. The present governing élites and the institutions they control are, with few exceptions, legacies of the Soviet regime and it seems unlikely that they will continue in their present form for very long. And as the economies remain weak, the governments have been unable (and unwilling) to control the rising traffic in drugs or contain the growing bureaucratic corruption. As Nancy Lubin points out in her chapter, the prospects for sustaining law and order in Central Asia are further jeopardized by the flow of small arms from Afghanistan and from Russian soldiers, with resources coming from the narcotics trade. Moreover, conflicts within the CIS military, whose rank and file are Central Asians but whose officers are predominantly Russian, also remain a distinct possibility.

The creation of independent states in the region, with viable economies and stable political systems, is still a distant ideal. There are modest opportunities for constructive involvement by outside powers to facilitate trade and flows of technology, promote educational development, and attend to some of the ecological disasters in the region. But should conflicts within the region grow, as seems likely, outsiders' temptation to intervene is likely to be great, with destructive and unpredictable consequences.

As we have suggested earlier, the breakup of empires has often led to conflicts by successor states over claims to each other's territories, and conflicts over the treatment and expulsion of minorities. As groups within successor states violently contend for political power, the prospects for creating legitimate institutions and political processes erode and, in the worst case, central authority may lose its capacity to maintain even rudimentary law and order. Thus far, two major violent conflicts have erupted among the states of Central Asia and the Transcaucasus, the war between Armenia and Azerbaijan over the disputed territory of Nagorno-Karabakh and the civil war in Tajikistan. In both instances the efforts of local groups to solicit external support have raised the risk that a local conflict could escalate into a larger struggle. In the Armenia–Azerbaijan dispute, however, the major external powers with an interest in the outcome, Turkey, Iran and Russia, have been prudent in recognizing the risk that military intervention by one could provoke intervention by another. Nonetheless, Turkey has backed Azerbaijan by supporting an embargo on imports to land-locked Armenia, preventing the entry of oil, natural gas, food and even relief supplies, and one cannot rule out the possibility that other neighbouring states may also actively take sides.

In the Tajikistan conflict, the Russians have sent troops to provide support for the regime, while their armed Islamic opponents reportedly have established bases in Afghanistan and Iran. Warring factions within Afghanistan have also taken sides in the Tajikistan conflict, with one Afghan warlord (General Abdul Rashid Dostam) allied with the pro-Russian group in Dushanbe and another (Akhmed Shah Masud) backing Tajik rebels. The government of Uzbekistan has also sided with the Dushanbe regime in what some Central Asian leaders regard as an Uzbek–Russian coalition intended to enhance Uzbekistan's stature as a regional power backed by the Russian military.

Those two examples highlight the wider dangers posed by local conflicts within the region. While it would be a gross oversimplification to regard Central Asia's future as a mere replication of the Balkans' past (or present), nonetheless there are parallels that should not be summarily dismissed. For much of the twentieth century, the Balkans have been regarded by Western Europeans as a remote corner of Europe whose fate was of little significance to the major powers, but that assessment has time after time proven to be inaccurate. Similarly, the Central Asian states seem geographically remote, and for so long have been far removed from the concerns of major powers. But it is not difficult to see how in the next few decades the Central Asian states could become visible on the world stage. With significant resources in oil and minerals, several Central Asian states are already attracting investments from the USA, Western Europe and Japan. And just as the walls between Eastern and Western Europe have fallen, so have the walls been removed that separated Central Asia from the southern tier and from China. It is in no one's interest, except perhaps that of Russia, that any single power exercise control over the Central Asian states, and in everyone's interest, including that of Russia, that the states avoid violent conflict with one another. It is also in everyone's interest that intra-state ethnic conflicts do not adversely affect their neighbours, as is surely the case if minorities at risk flee across international borders. Perhaps it is too much to hope that the new political leaders in these states realize that independence depends upon their capacity to reduce ethnic conflicts within their borders, avoid quarrels with their neighbours over disputed territories, and establish cooperative economic and political relations with one another and with their neighbours. Should they fail to do so, they will not only jeopardize the independence of their own states, but they will also increase the possibility of wider regional conflicts.

Notes

1. For an analysis of the potential impact of the 25 million Russians residing beyond the borders of the Russian Federation – what the Russian media refer to as the 'near abroad' – on the development of interventionist and new-imperial policies, see William D. Jackson, 'Imperial temptations: ethnics abroad', *Orbis*, xxxviii/1 (Winter 1994), pp 1–17.

2. For a discussion of the potential geopolitical consequences of the emerging patterns of communications and transport in Central Asia and the four southern tier countries, see Robert L. Canfield, 'Restructuring in Greater Central Asia: changing political configurations', *Asian Survey*, xxxii/10 (1992), pp 875–87.

3. For a comparative analysis of recent developments in the last-mentioned three countries, as politically related parts of a region, see Ali Banuazizi and Myron Weiner, eds, *The State, Religion, and Ethnic Politics: Afghanistan, Iran, and Pakistan* (Syracuse, NY: Syracuse University Press, 1986); and Myron Weiner and Ali Banuazizi, eds, *The Politics of Social Transformation in Afghanistan, Iran, and Pakistan* (Syracuse, NY: Syracuse University Press, 1994).

4. See William Peters, 'Central Asia and the minority question', *Asian Affairs*, xxii/2 (1991), pp 152–7.

5. For an analysis of the Chinese perceptions of this threat, see J. Richard Walsh, 'China and the new geopolitics of Central Asia', *Asian Survey*, xxxiii/3 (1993), pp 272–84.

6. Such a role for Russia, as its 'manifest destiny', has been advocated increasingly since 1992 by Russian officials and commentators from a wide political spectrum. Addressing a Western audience, one prominent Russian analyst offered the following rationale for Russia's new 'oriental policy': '[T]here are two extremes in the west's attitude towards Moscow's oriental policy. Some people there hastily suspect Moscow of neo-imperial ambitions, while others, on the contrary, are ready to entrust Russia with the role of a barrier, protecting Christian civilization from the "jihad" of the East. In the meantime, facts leave no doubt that world civilization as a whole equally needs both military protection against Islamic (and any other) extremism and the laying of bridges between the Christian world and the world of Islam, one of the great religions, determining the image of civilization. The peculiarity of Russia's geopolitical situation and her historical experience dictate to Russia precisely this role.' (Denis Volkov, 'Whom and how does Islamic fundamentalism threaten?', *New Times* [Moscow], January 1994, p 26).

7. Zbigniew Brzezinski, 'The premature partnership', *Foreign Affairs*, March–April 1994, p 72.

PART I

Central Asia's Catapult to Independence

The New Geopolitical Order

GRAHAM E. FULLER

The collapse of the Soviet empire is indisputably one of the most astonishing geopolitical events of the century, comparable only to the collapse of the Ottoman and Habsburg empires during the First World War. Where for 75 years the world had grown accustomed to the presence of a Soviet monolith, suddenly independent states with unfamiliar names have emerged on to the political scene. Massive chunks of territory have been torn away from the largest political landmass in the world, leaving geopolitical confusion in their wake. Central Asia and the Caucasus alone are faced with the emergence of eight new states, six of them Muslim.

The emergence of multiple new successor states to the former USSR has already both literally and figuratively changed the map of Asia, but the impact on the surrounding regions is just beginning to be felt, all the way from the Arab world to Beijing. At least a decade will be required before the full effect of these events on the politics of Asia can be tentatively determined. For Central Asia is just that: it lies at the very centre of the Asian continent, inevitably extending its impact over large numbers of states in the region.

Change has not come only with the emergence of many new independent states, but also in the global political environment in which they have emerged. International politics have been dominated for 70 years by a massive ideological struggle between communism and the democratic world in which the interrelationships of states were often gauged by their impact on the global balance of forces between East and West. With the death of communism, that obsessive factor in geopolitical thinking is now gone. While none of us can fail to welcome the end of the global ideological struggle, international politics have now grown immeasurably more complex than at any time since the end of the First World War.

The new character of international politics in Asia – described by some as the 'back to the future' of nineteenth-century politics – is rendered particularly complex by the presence of many new players on the scene: the new-born republics of the former Soviet Union. More importantly, not one of the new Central Asian states has yet been able to develop an understanding of the nature of its own national interests. The national interests of the USSR were well defined, even if grossly distorted by Marxist–Leninist ideology and the Cold War. That same contagion also affected – in mirror image – America's own perception of its national interests, a crisis from which that country has not yet emerged. Before any observer can understand, then, the new geopolitics of Central Asia and the 'Northern Tier' countries (i.e. Turkey, Iran, Afghanistan and Pakistan), these new states must generate their own sense of national identity and national interests, friends and foes, a process upon which they have scarcely embarked.

Their problems are legion. Most of them have never before existed as independent modern states – with the exception of a brief interlude for the three states of Transcaucasia after the First World War. For the Central Asian states the very concept of Uzbek, Turkoman, Kazakh, Kyrgyz or Tajik as the basis of statehood was entirely new under early Leninist policies, and was also somewhat artificial since the essential elements of genuine sovereignty were almost totally denied them during the whole period of the Soviet empire. And however gratifying their new independence is to the fulfilment of their national aspirations, the basic fact is that independence came far earlier than anyone could have expected, and probably faster than most would have wanted, forcing them – without political, economic or psychological preparation – to face a brand new world.

Thus the states of Central Asia are now emerging in search of an understanding of the most fundamental elements of statehood. What are their state borders and what do those borders imply? What is the cultural character of the new state? Who are its inhabitants, and who should be its citizens? How permanent is the ethnic mixture of the state? Who are likely allies, and who are likely rivals? Is the state's future best fulfilled in independent national policies, or in some kind of federation, confederation or union? What are the intentions and attitudes of the states surrounding them outside the former Soviet

Union? How will they survive economically? What are the most immediate external and internal threats to their national existence? These questions are extremely complex, but at least tentative answers must be attempted if the new geopolitical realities of the region are to be accommodated.

I propose to examine the new geopolitics of the region in three sections: the internal factors that will influence the policies of these new states, the likely new interrelationships of the new states among themselves; and the impact of external players on the new states and the new geopolitical factors affecting the region as a whole.

The character of political life in the new states

National identity vs nationalities

The most urgent internal problem confronting the new Muslim states is to survive the sudden shock of total independence and to establish the fundamentals of a new national policy. That means that no government wants to take on any more problems at the outset than it must in order to preserve order, protect its borders, meet the daily needs of its population – and to stay in power. Not surprisingly, policies have taken on an ad hoc character as each regime seeks to cope with the new circumstances thrust upon it. Administrative reliance upon the old communist structures is still widespread.

Yet the unspoken agenda, the critical issue facing all of these states in Central Asia, is ultimately to determine the national character and identity of the new states and to understand the policy implications that flow therefrom. Five of the six new republics – all except Tajikistan – are ethnically Turkic in character. Yet this tells us little. What does it mean to be Kyrgyz or Uzbek? Who should be granted citizenship in the new states? How will each of these 'new' nationalities fulfil its own political and cultural aspirations? In the communist past the 'independent' character of each Central Asian republic had little practical meaning since all key internal policies were determined by Moscow; regional problems were also adjudicated by Moscow. But today the process of developing traditional nationalist aspirations is well under way in each republic as it seeks fulfilment of its nationalist aspirations. So far these aspirations are largely formulated by a small élite, as is usually the case in the development of Third World nationalism.

But even if not all the trappings of nationalism are understood by the population, they are well aware of the existence of traditional tribal and ethnic differences and understand that very concrete economic stakes are involved. Every single state, apart from its titular nationality, contains literally dozens of other nationalities including Russians, other Central Asian nationalities, and nationalities from other parts of the former empire, especially from the Caucasus. Only 73 per cent of Uzbekistan is Uzbek, for example, while only 40 per cent of Kazakhstan's population is Kazakh. In every case the titular nationality almost invariably sees its interests as poised against the interests of all other nationalities within the republic, regardless of whether those nationalities are fellow Muslim or even Turkic. While these views are unstated, and often run counter to official policy, they are a reality and will be the source of considerable ethnic conflict in the future. For nationalism in each of the states is growing after nearly a century of distortion and repression of nationalist impulses. Indeed, in the multi-national composition of all of these states there can be no domestic issue or policy that does not immediately affect relations among the internal national groups and their foreign policies.

While the former communist leaders of each of the republics moved quickly to preempt the nationalist cause of separatism when it became possible to do so, the leaderships are still conservative in nationalist terms. In most cases leadership is appropriately concerned that ethnic conflict not break out in the republics. No national leadership in Central Asia today wishes to take on the complex nationalities problem at this juncture. Such a policy runs counter to the long-inculcated 'internationalism' and 'friendship of the peoples' of the Soviet era; it invites potential problems with Moscow even today, and, worst of all, it will create internal friction, possible violence, and perhaps even military conflict with neighbours. Yet each regime is under pressure from growing nationalist fronts and movements that were formerly underground in the old system but who today are demanding that the leadership adopt more nationalist policies. Over time nationalist forces will increasingly compel each government to base its policies on the specific interests of the titular nationality of each republic rather than on the overall ethnic mixture of the republic. Kazakhs will thus inevitably seek to perpetuate the best interests of the Kazakh people in specifically nationalist terms, as will the Uzbeks, Turkomans, Azerbaijanis and others.

The concept of 'rodina' ('homeland') lies at the heart of the nationalist vision. Nearly all of the dozens of other nationalities who live within each of these republics have their own ethnic 'homelands' elsewhere in the former Soviet Union. Russians can go to Russia, Armenians to Armenia, Chechens to Chechenya. But there is only one homeland for Kazakhs, Kyrgyz or Tajiks in which their national aspirations can be fulfilled. Binational or highly diverse multinational states do not fulfil those aspirations, however narrowly outsiders may consider them to be formulated. Thus the titular nationalists in each republic recognize the precariousness of their own national movements. Not only are they of recent vintage, but the local culture and language had been denied opportunity for true flowering within an independent national state throughout the Soviet period. True, 'independent' national languages were established by Soviet authorities and in principle encouraged to develop, but this was in part a 'divide and conquer' policy. Russian was invariably the language for all official intercourse, and local languages often had little more than folkloric value. In most cases they were not encouraged to rise and meet the needs of contemporary political, economic and technical culture in the modern world. Thus every nationalist will declare that the local language is 'sick', and in the case of Kazakh perceived as almost dying.

Language, not surprisingly, is perhaps the supreme vehicle of nationalist expression; language policy in Central Asia is thus of major importance to the perpetuation of local nationalism and interests. The local languages will almost surely be increasingly encouraged and developed by each state; no national leader will be able to resist this course of development, especially as local nationalists grow more shrill on the issue. Local language laws now mandate the local language as the official language of state, even though the law is unevenly applied, often almost not at all as in Kazakhstan. But the growing sentiments of nationalism and the demand for policies that favour the titular nationality will increasingly alienate other nationalities that live in the republics, probably creating a gradual *de facto* trend towards homogenization of population as minorities seek to leave.

The problem of Russians

The presence of large numbers of Slavs – mostly Russians – in each republic is the single most provocative element of the nationalities problem. For the Russians represent not only a distinctly different cultural and religious group, but also the 'masters' of the now crumbled empire. Their control of so much of the state political and economic apparatus, as well as many of the best 'perks' of local life makes them a prime target for the nationalists. While the Russians remain a critical element in the local economy, whose skilled labour and know-how is still vitally important to the republics, most nationalists seek to remove both their presence and influence from the republic. Disagreement comes only over timing and method. All but extreme nationalists recognize that the process cannot be rapid or violent, but they wish to hasten the process as much as is feasible in order to eliminate all former vestiges of colonialism, to prepare their own people to move into more skilled and responsible jobs, to inherit Russian housing in conditions of severe shortage, and to help build the new nation under the control by the titular nationality. Nearly all other non-titular nationalities in practice identify their fate with the Russians in the sense that the new nationalist nation state aims to deprive them too of significant political, economic or demographic power in the new state. The problem of local Russians is compounded by the fact that many have lived in Central Asia for long periods – sometimes for generations – have no family ties in Russia, and at this point have literally nowhere else to go. Some 25 million Russians live outside Russia; at this stage, Russia can hardly accommodate them.

Problems of economic integration and reform

Economic issues are equally pressing, for the traditional web of economic relations within the former union, however negatively interpreted by many, provided a predictable if unsatisfying framework. Today nearly all those relationships have been ruptured, requiring urgent and radical rethinking of the economic requirements of each state and how they can be met through new bilateral relationships based on a new, more demanding market. These economic requirements may provide some of the most positive stimuli for regional cooperation as opposed to the shoals of autarky and economic conflict.

Yet economic development is intimately and inevitably linked with issues of economic reform, liberalization and privatization. As complex as these problems are in their own right, they are immeasurably complicated by ethnic relations within each of the republics: reforms invariably create winners and losers. Nationalist governments cannot afford to preside over 'rational' economic reforms in which the titular nationality is the prime loser. Naturally, conditions differ considerably from republic to republic, but in many the dominant position of Russians, particularly in industry and agriculture, places serious restraints upon local governments in fostering privatization where the Russians will emerge the economic winners. In Kazakhstan, for example, the Kazakhs are not only not significantly represented in industry but also are weak in both the agricultural sector and the bazaar/market sector where other minorities have a dominant role. Privatization in Kazakhstan at this point poses extremely negative consequences for the Kazakhs in their own republic. The same problem exists to a lesser extent in other republics.

State power

Apart from the turmoil created by independence, domestic politics are deeply caught up in the throes of transition from totalitarian to 'softer' authoritarian or more democratic regimes. The process of political reform, so far advanced only in Russia itself, has been slowest of all to reach Central Asia. Traditional Communist Party leaders still dominate the government in all republics except Kyrgyzstan and Azerbaijan. While these leaders very early on learnt that the road to survival lay through full embrace of nationalist policies *vis-à-vis* Moscow and Russia, the structures of power still remain those established by the party over many years. Yet the totalitarian flavour of past decades has also weakened. Nearly every national leader runs a fairly tight ship in terms of internal controls, but the question is one of varying degrees of authoritarian rather than totalitarian leadership. Although the local press is still censored and unable to engage in frank discussion of all aspects of government policy, people are no longer afraid to meet freely with foreigners and privately criticize policies and leaders. External news does filter in via the Moscow press; other external publications are rarely formally prohibited, but they are not readily available. Local opposition groups often face severe problems in publishing their views, but they are not silenced outright. Unlike totalitarian regimes in which the government tells people what to think, today the regimes merely seek to discourage serious criticism of existing leadership and policy issues.

Thus the character of Central Asian politics will be marked by increasing demands for popular participation and by the opening of the political system to more nationalist and more democratic parties (not necessarily synonymous). This too will create instability in the evolution of the region. Political demands may in turn create greater repressiveness, or possibly greater instability. Economic conditions will also inevitably tell on the political stability of the republics and will have a direct impact on interethnic relations.

Islamic politics

After the issue of nuclear weapons, no other problem in Central Asia rivets international attention as much as the potential spread of 'Islamic fundamentalism'. There is no doubt that an Islamic revival is under way in all the republics of Central Asia to one degree or another. Yet this should not be surprising, for Islam has been a key feature of Central Asian civilization starting in the eighth century AD. While the more distant nomadic cultures of Kazakhs and Kyrgyz were far less touched by settled urban Islamic culture, Islam is still the primary cultural force of the region. Communism was never able to destroy the unofficial and private practice of Islam, therefore it is natural that religious practice should reemerge vigorously once freed from official repression. Nor does Islam necessarily conflict with nationalism. To be a Muslim is to be a Turk (except in Tajikistan) and to be a Turk is to be a Muslim. The two concepts tend to be self-reinforcing, enabling Islam to serve as a vehicle for nationalist expression as well, especially against non-Muslim populations such as Slavs.

Yet the national leaderships of each republic, however nationalist they have become, are deeply worried about the force of Islam or Islamic fundamentalism, for it represents, along with radical national-ism, one of the major challenges to the existing power structures. 'Official Islam', or the Islamic structures that were permitted by the state during the long years of communist darkness (in Muslim eyes), has been compromised by its subservience to the state in the eyes of many. Official Islam to this day strongly supports the new national leaderships and is outspokenly hostile to unofficial or popular Islamic movements and parties; state Islam says that 'Islam has no need of parties' – indeed, the very idea is un-Islamic in their eyes.

Yet unofficial Islam is emerging, most vividly in the form of the Islamic Renaissance Party, which is strong in Tajikistan and develop-ing now unofficially in other republics. More fundamentalist leaders are also emerging, especially in Tajikistan and in the densely popu-lated Ferghana Valley in Uzbekistan. Their presence is potentially a serious challenge to the state since they tend to question the legitimacy of existing state governments and call for 'Islamic government' and 'Islamic morality' in daily life. While these movements may be kept in hand through strict police measures, they are potential vehicles for popular national dissatisfaction. This dissatisfaction is most likely to spring from either deteriorating economic conditions, serious inter-ethnic conflict in which the government may be seen as 'soft' on local Slavic populations, or in conditions of government repression of the people, in which case its legitimacy can be challenged in the most damning of all terms: Islamic.

This, then, is the character of the Islamic challenge to the new regimes of Central Asia. So far these regimes evidence little sophistication in terms of understanding Islamic politics, so new is the phenomenon in the post-Soviet context. They seem ill equipped to distinguish between the 'natural' rise of Islam in the post-communist ideological vacuum on the one hand, and the emergence of more radical Islamic forces on the other. They may well be inclined to suppress Islamic activism rather than to attempt to integrate it into the state in some fashion. Most importantly, if 'official' or 'establishment' Islam continues to show total subservience to the state, then it too will be fully discredited in the public eye, with the effect of ceding all religious power to new Islamic forces not under the control of the state. (Islamic politics is also integral to foreign policy, see chapter 4 below.)

The above internal factors therefore have direct bearing on the conduct of external relations by the states involved: uncertain national identity, unpredictable relations with Russia and Russians, internal ethnic rivalry and conflict, the uncertain legitimacy of the new regimes and the growth of the Islamic factor. These factors of uncertainty render the determination of national interests and foreign policy difficult, especially in the absence of long-evolved and well-understood political relations among modern states. To witness the evolution of the geopolitics of this region is to 'be there at the creation', as it were.

Regional factors and interrelationships

The republics of Central Asia differ sharply one from another in many respects. These differences cannot be set forth in detail here, but a few key features must be characterized because they are critical to the behaviour of these republics in the context of future foreign policy.

Kazakhstan

Kazakhstan is the most distinct republic in the Central Asian context, often not even included within the traditional definition of 'Central Asia' in Russian parlance. Yet it cannot be ignored in discussing Central Asia because of its undeniable Turkic and Muslim character and a historical experience shared with the rest of Central Asia. Its size, its aspirations to being characterized as a 'nuclear state', the burning character of its ethnic grievances and its richness in resources all contribute to its major importance.

The Kazakhs are deeply anguished by their position as a minority in their own republic (40 per cent). They feel they lack basic control over the industrial, agricultural and market forces of the state, which are in the hands of the Russians, Koreans and other Muslim nationalities in the bazaars – although their political control over the state is growing. As a people they feel wronged by massive population losses during collectivization – reportedly up to a quarter of the population – and the corrupting character of Russian colonialization that stripped them of their land, their dignity and to a considerable extent even their language and culture.

To understand Kazakh anguish it would not be amiss to make certain comparisons with the feelings of American Indians in the USA who similarly feel their culture and society to have crumbled. Yet unlike them, the Kazakhs have political power, and they will be increasingly intent upon using it. But at the same time the Kazakhs are hostage to another terrible geopolitical reality: the fact that vast portions of northern Kazakhstan, and great portions of its industries and vital resources, are in areas populated overwhelmingly by Russians. If Kazakh nationalism should come into sharp confrontation with the Russian population within the republic, the Russians explicitly threaten to secede from Kazakhstan, taking the northern and. eastern lands and resources with them and dwarfing the remaining part of the republic.

The Kazakh situation is potentially the most volatile of all ethnic situations in Muslim Central Asia. The intensity of wounded Kazakh pride and nationalism, coupled with the desperation of their search to save their culture, nearly guarantees eventual confrontation with Russia. Loss of northern Kazakhstan to Russia would almost certainly push an angry and vengeful Kazakhstan into closer relations with other Central Asian states, as well as with Ukraine if that state should maintain hostile relations with Russia.

To redress its severe demographic problems *vis-à-vis* more powerful neighbours in Russia and Uzbekistan, the Kazakh government has an unspoken policy of encouraging the Kazakh diaspora of perhaps several million people to return to Kazakhstan from China, Mongolia, Uzbekistan, Russia, Turkey, Europe and elsewhere. Kazakhstan also has potential grounds for ethnic or territorial disputes with Uzbekistan, given the large number of Uzbeks who live in the southern region of Kazakhstan along the Uzbekistan border. The Karakalpak autonomous region of Uzbekistan is also ethnically closer to the Kazakhs than to the Uzbeks, a potential trouble spot if borders in the region begin to be rearranged along more ethnic lines. Kazakhstan, along with Uzbekistan, is one of the giants of Central Asia whose destinies and national characters are just beginning to be shaped. The obstacles to the fulfilment of their national destinies are immense.

Uzbekistan

Uzbekistan is the other giant of Central Asia in terms of weight and influence and home of the great cities of traditional Central Asian culture. The Uzbeks have a profoundly clear sense of national self-identity and possess a self-assurance that stems from an awareness of their historical importance. The population, vastly exceeding that of any other Central Asian people, and the role of Tashkent as the 'Asian capital' of the Soviet Union in past decades, give the Uzbeks a dominant position in Central Asian politics. Russians make up only some 11 per cent of the population, and their skills are still needed by the new Uzbek republic. Nonetheless Uzbeks themselves possess a higher educational level, technical know-how and advanced scientific and technological institutes that guarantee their dominance as a people within the region. Because of the weight of Uzbek political and social culture, other smaller states in the region tend to feel intimidated by the Uzbeks and often refer to the threat of 'Uzbek chauvinism'. Uzbekistan is the chief rival to Kazakhstan for regional influence.

Conflict between Uzbekistan and its neighbours is most likely with Tajikistan. Given the large number of Tajiks (20.5 per cent of Tajiks in the former Soviet Union live in Uzbekistan), who perhaps even constitute a majority in the city of Samarkand, there are increasing demands from the Tajiks for greater cultural autonomy and more widespread use of the Tajik language. Equally significant is the large Uzbek population in Tajikistan (1.5 million according to Uzbeks and

7 per cent of the overall Uzbek population), mainly concentrated in the northern part of the republic, who exert considerable influence within the Tajik government. If ethnic conflict should break out between Tajiks and Uzbeks, the possibility of secession of northern Tajikistan and its consolidation into the Uzbek republic can hardly be excluded. Overall Uzbek–Tajik frictions are potentially the most serious of all in Central Asia (after the potential Russian–Kazakh conflict), despite the extreme cultural closeness of the two peoples as the twin inheritors of the urban tradition of Central Asia.

Tajikistan

Tajikistan is the single non-Turkic republic among all the newly emergent Muslim states of Russia. It is also the most isolated from the centre of the old empire and is surrounded by a sea of Turks on all sides except the south. Not surprisingly, a new sense of nationalism has been growing in this republic over the past several years, conspicuously directed towards Iran and the common cultural–linguistic heritage of the two countries, even though Tajiks are mostly Sunnis by faith. The foreign policy implications of this orientation are discussed later in this chapter.

Tajikistan also distinguishes itself by having the most active movement of political Islam within the former USSR. The Islamic Renaissance Party is firmly registered and deeply embroiled in politics, while the overall Muslim movement falls under the active leadership of the charismatic Kazi Hoja Akbar Turajonzoda, head of the Spiritual Administration of Tajikistan. The republic has already been beset by extremely serious internal conflicts among northern and southern clans, between Uzbeks and Tajiks, between communists and reformers, and between the poor and the establishment. This volatile political situation is unlikely to find ready resolution and has great potential for spilling over into other parts of Central Asia, particularly since this is the centre of political Islam.

Kyrgyzstan

This republic distinguishes itself by the fortuitous placement in 1990 of a genuinely democratic technocrat at its helm, who has sharply limited the power of the old Communist Party, opened up the political system, and who is striving for a multi-party, liberal, free-market, democratic system. President Askar Akaev is making major efforts to introduce his country to the West as an enlightened state where co-operation with foreign states is welcome. Despite its good fortune in possessing the only democratic regime in Central Asia, Kyrgyzstan too is heavily mountainous and somewhat isolated, with limited economic prospects. It has already had one very serious ethnic clash with Uzbekistan in 1990 in the oblast of Osh in the Ferghana Valley and expresses fear of 'Uzbek expansionism'. A considerable Uzbek minority exists in Kyrgyzstan. Ethnically and linguistically the Kyrgyz are closest to the Kazakhs, but mutual ethnic relations are not as cordial as they might be; Kazakhs tend to think disparagingly of Kyrgyz as 'mountain Kazakhs'.

Turkmenistan

Turkmenistan is physically isolated from the other Central Asian republics by a vast desert expanse. Linguistically its residents form the Oghuz (Western Turkish) language group, along with the Azerbaijanis and Turks of Turkey. Turkmenistan has historically been somewhat aloof, and to this day continues a somewhat aggressively independent stance in working with the other republics of the region. It is well aware that geopolitically it is in a dominant position, astride the sole land corridor leading into Iran and on to the Persian Gulf and Turkey; it is in a position to exploit this geopolitical advantage in future bargaining. Turkmenistan also possesses major oil and gas reserves that make it the richest per capita state of Central Asia. So far Turkmenistan has demonstrated the smallest degree of political evolution away from the former communist order; 'law and order' tend to prevail and there are as yet few significant political movements to challenge the old structure.

Azerbaijan

While Azerbaijan is not part of Central Asia, it is an important player among the Muslim states of the former Soviet Union. It is strategically located next to Turkey and Iran and shares water access to Turkmenistan and Kazakhstan across the Caspian. It sympathizes with the political positions of Central Asian states in many respects and likewise courts their support for Baku's fierce struggle with Armenia over the enclave of mountainous Karabakh. Some potential friction exists between Azerbaijan and the Central Asian republics since Azerbaijani merchants are heavily represented (and resented) in the bazaars of the region, often at the expense of the titular nationalities (especially in Kazakhstan and Kyrgyzstan) who lack a mercantile tradition. Azerbaijan's oil expertise can be important to Central Asia.

Common problems

All the republics face a number of common problems with which they must deal jointly. Regular meetings of the Central Asian leadership have taken place, with some limited progress. Central Asian cooperation takes on a much more urgent profile as the prospects wane for significant multi-lateral relations among the former republics of the USSR. The future of the Commonwealth of Independent States (CIS) as a meaningful institution is increasingly in doubt, forcing the Central Asian republics to work more with each other. The most immediate common problem is the lack of any Central Asian control over financial management of the Russian-controlled ruble zone, placing severe difficulties upon their own economic independence. Other common problems include coping with the extremely limited water resources of the region. Many states share in the fate of the shrinking Aral Sea, which threatens widespread ecological disaster in the region. The states also have a common interest in the completion, expansion and maintenance of rail links from Beijing to Tehran, as well as other road links to encourage regional trade. Arrangements are also urgently needed for the sharing of power resources (electricity, gas and oil). Common policies are also urgently required on immigration and emigration (particularly as they relate to the movement of Russians) and adjudication of the problems of the status of minorities within each republic.

Lastly, the Turkic states need to work towards common cultural policies, especially as they relate to the selection and implementation of a common Turkic alphabet (probably Latin, but conceivably Cyrillic, or – even less likely – Arabic script) which would facilitate the mutual intercomprehension of written languages in the region; the present alphabets in use were deliberately designed under Bolshevik policy to stress differences and still serve to hinder mutual comprehension of written languages. Choice of the Latin alphabet, as used in Turkey, would carry political implications of facilitating cultural exchange with Turkey, while the less likely choice of the Arabic alphabet would signify a strong leaning towards the Muslim heritage of the region –

with political consequences. It is noteworthy that Tajikistan, whose language is very close to the Farsi of Iran, almost surely will go over to the Arabic/Persian alphabet used in Iran (and in Afghan Persian).

External influences upon Central Asia and Azerbaijan

The emergence of Central Asia has already exerted a major impact upon other states of the region.[1] Accustomed to the nearly century-long absence of Soviet Central Asia from any interaction with the Muslim world, most external states were slow to grasp the implications of the appearance of six new Muslim states on the political stage – a process that inevitably promised to alter traditional geopolitical balances of the region. Since then, however, these neighbouring states have gradually begun to develop their own geopolitical calculations *vis-à-vis* Central Asia. A new struggle for the political soul of Central Asia is now under way, partly reflecting aspects of the nineteenth-century geopolitical 'Great Game' that played itself out between the tsarist and British empires along similar fault lines of Asia. All border states have been affected.[2]

Turkey

Turkey has been the most profoundly influenced of all the states in the region by recent Central Asian events; the five new independent Turkish states of Central Asia have launched a series of changes with possibly far-reaching repercussions within and around Turkey. Indeed, the very foundations and primal assumptions of the Turkish world view have been shaken, perhaps bringing about a fundamental shift in the character of Ankara's modern foreign policy.

The founder of the modern Turkish republic, Kemal Ataturk, early on made the geopolitical decision that modern Turkey must eschew any kind of pan-Turkic or pan-Islamic policies that would lead it into foreign policy imbroglios, especially with the burgeoning Bolshevik power in Russia. For decades, therefore, Turkey's foreign policy rigidly excluded any kind of interest in the Turks of the Soviet Union. Growing prospects for genuine autonomy in Central Asia towards the end of the 1980s, however, caused these republics to look first to Turkey as an external ally. Slowly at first, the Turkish press, public and leading politicians also began to evince interest in the extra-ordinary emergence of the hitherto closed world of Turks – quickly forcing change upon a reluctant Turkish Foreign Ministry and the Ataturkist-orientated élite. Both the late President Turgut Ozal and Prime Minister Suleyman Demirel soon undertook visits to all the new republics and to explore new economic, political, cultural and even military relationships with them.

For Turkey the emergence of a new political order in the Balkans, the Caucasus and Central Asia has opened new opportunities, but also presented new dilemmas. Ankara has consistently orientated itself towards the West since very early in the history of the republic. Its membership in NATO has been its strongest institutional anchor in the West. With the end of the Cold War and the development of a new geopolitical climate and institutions in western Europe, however, Turkey's possible entrée into the EC has grown more problematic. Turkey in fact no longer finds its diplomacy and national interests limited primarily to Western Europe, but expanding into the newly independent areas of the Balkans, the Caucasus and Central Asia. But Europe has also shown increasing doubt about the appropriateness of Turkish membership in the EC at this time; several NATO states, especially Germany, are concerned about the implications of potential 'new' NATO borders on such trouble spots as Azerbaijan, Georgia and Iraqi Kurdistan.

The emergence of a whole new Turkish world also raises fresh identity questions for Turkey itself. Once isolated as the sole accessible Turkish state in the world, Turkey had few other options for alliance; an ethnically orientated policy was not a viable alternative. Today the forces of Turkish nationalism on a broader plane have grown in Turkey, suggesting in some political circles consideration of a policy orientated towards leadership of the new Turkish world. While such a policy need not be mutually exclusive with a strong European orientation, in fact a 'Turkic orientation' that seeks to exert significant influence in Central Asia and the Caucasus could tend to alter Europe's perception of Turkey and the appropriateness of Turkish membership in the EC.

A possible new trend towards pan-Turkish nationalism in Turkey raises some internal problems as well, most notably with the Kurds. Although the Kurds have essentially been denied the expression of their own culture and existence as a separate ethnic element within Turkey, the country has never employed racial identity as a criterion for full Turkish citizenship. Today the potential rise of a strong pan-Turkish-orientated nationalism could create a counterforce of reinforced Kurdish nationalism and even augment separatist forces among the Kurds. The greatest risk that Turkey might run would be the development of a new kind of 'great Turkish chauvinism' – made possible only by the emergence of the new Turkish states of the world – that could make Turkey a less constructive or moderate state in a volatile region. There is no reason to assume that Turkey will take this course, but for the first time it is at least a conceivable development never before possible as long as the Turkish world of the Soviet Union was closed.

In the Caucasus a strongly Turkish nationalist policy could well push Turkey in the direction of full support for Azerbaijan against Armenia. Turkey initially took a neutral stand in Armenia's struggle with Azerbaijan over mountainous Karabakh, offering its good offices and initiating a policy of reconciliation with Armenia after the long legacy of hostility stemming from the massacre of Armenians in Turkey after the First World War. Such a neutral stand would have been very important in giving Turkey the role of a great power or power-broker in the region, standing above the local disputes that rend the Caucasus. Subsequently, however, intensified fighting between Armenia and Azerbaijan, and rising Turkish public opinion sympathetic to the Azeri side, has much compromised Turkey's neutrality and may over time force it to form alliance with its 'Azeri brothers'. A strong anti-Armenian posture will inevitably have negative effects upon Turkey's relationship with the West and with the USA in particular.

A possible alliance based on Turkish nationalism between Turkey and Azerbaijan would have an even more negative impact upon Turkish–Iranian relations. Ankara and Tehran have, in fact, enjoyed a long period of excellent relations beginning with the creation of modern nation states in both countries after the First World War. Those long-term relations are now for the first time extremely likely to deteriorate as the two states move into deep rivalry for influence in Central Asia and the Caucasus. In Central Asia rivalry is not necessarily damaging, but in the Caucasus it will be, for newly independent Azerbaijan threatens to stimulate breakaway trends among the Azeri population of northern Iran, nearly twice as great as that of Azerbaijan itself. The population of Iranian Azerbaijan, in fact, still maintains considerable ambivalence as to whether they are really Persians who happen to speak a Turkic language, or whether they are in fact ethnically identical with the Azeris of independent Azerbaijan to the north.

While in past years there was little likelihood of a strong Azeri separatist movement in Iranian Azerbaijan, today, given the character of ethnic separatist movements elsewhere in the world, Iranian Azerbaijan may also undergo new aspirations towards union with independent Azerbaijan that will be deeply destabilizing to the region. This trend would not have been possible without the emergence of an independent Azerbaijan in the north. If the territorial integrity of Iran is threatened, Iran will undoubtedly see Ankara's hand behind these events and will probably react violently. Iran's chief resources under such circumstances would be to support Kurdish separatism in Turkey, to make common cause with Armenia internationally against Turkey, and to cooperate with Iraq or Syria against Turkey. The independence of Iranian Azerbaijan would unquestionably also spark the separation of Iranian Kurdistan.

Rivalry between Ankara and Tehran in the former states of the Soviet Union and Central Asia is less mutually damaging to both states. Both states have created new regional structures, at least on paper. Turkey has established the Black Sea Consortium that will link all the Black Sea riparian powers of Eastern Europe as well as Ukraine, Russia, Georgia and Armenia. Iran has created a Caspian Sea organization that will create ties among Iran, Azerbaijan, Turkmenistan, Kazakhstan and Russia. Both powers are included in a tentative new bloc that will link the states of old Soviet Central Asia with the old 'Northern Tier' states of Turkey, Iran, Afghanistan and Pakistan. Turkey has also spoken of creating a 'Turkic commonwealth' that will obviously exclude Iran. Only time will tell which, if any, of these organizations will be viable and what the scope of their mutual interests will be. The chances are that only the broadest of organizations will be attractive to all members because none wishes to see itself excluded and none of the new states will wish to limit its own range of international options for the future.

However, Turkey's increasingly ambitious diplomatic moves into Central Asia have begun to produce some initial disquiet in Russia. The concept of 'pan-Turkism' was of course anathema to Soviet power and was ruthlessly stamped out in Central Asia during the Soviet empire; it was the very symbol of un-Marxist nationalist revivalism and ethnically fissiparous separatism. After the fall of the empire, 'pan-Turkism' in principle lost most of its menace. After all, as many Russians noted, Turkey is a moderate, democratic, secular and stable state that would probably serve as a stabilizing force in Central Asia, especially against the inroads of Islamic fundamentalism as propagated by Iran.

Nonetheless, Turkey's newly stated interests in creating a Turkic commonwealth, and even its suggestions that Central Asia might wish to abandon the ruble zone, now strike many Russians as a more direct challenge to Russian interests, both in terms of serving to break up the CIS, and in creating a new ethnic bloc. Turkey's offer to provide military training to the new states creates greater concerns among Russians that Turkey might in fact succeed in creating a bloc which, if not hostile to Russia, might at least see its interests defined along very new and different lines that are less in Russia's interests. Lastly, some Russian strategists are asking whether in fact Turkey has not now become 'America's instrument' in Central Asia, given the strong support Washington has given it. While Russia should have no specific reason to suspect Turkish–American motives in the area, the legacy of the Cold War has not yet faded completely, and in any case no one can be sure what course the new Russian state will be able to follow in the long run.

Russia may therefore grow cooler towards Turkish ambitions in Central Asia. In similar terms, Russia very definitely sees a need to maintain the important natural, industrial and agricultural resources of Kazakhstan close to Russia and not to 'lose them' to a Turkic commonwealth. Russia thus may come to evince greater coolness towards Turkey over time and may look increasingly to Iran as a counterweight, especially since Washington's policies have so explicitly pushed the Turkish model in Central Asia and so clearly denounced the role of Iran there.

Many of the Central Asian élite also express doubts about a too-rapid embrace of Turkey, pointing out that Turkey is limited in its own resources and has so far been unsuccessful in winning access to the EC. They wonder, therefore, whether hitching their wagon to the Turkish star might not in fact serve to prejudice their relations with western Europe. India, too, has reportedly expressed some coolness at strong Central Asian interest in ties to a Turkic bloc, a political formulation that smacks too much of Muslim solidarity to be congenial to Islamophobic India. In the end, many in the Central Asian republics recognize that it would be unwise to take any political steps that might close geopolitical doors in any direction useful to their future strategic and economic interests.

Iran

If there is a new Turkish belt stretching from Mongolia to the Balkans, Iran is interested in strengthening its own Persian-orientated ties in Central Asia, a region that had long been under the sway of Persian culture during the heyday of Central Asian Islamic civilization, even when political power was in the hands of Turkic tribes. Iran, further-more, is contiguous with Central Asia while Turkey is not; and it was the Persian Empire, never the Ottoman Empire, that permeated the region. Iran has thus actively sought to establish ties with the new states as rapidly as Turkey has done. Tajikistan, as a Persian-speaking state, is naturally of special interest to Iran, an interest strongly recip-rocated by the Tajiks who otherwise see themselves isolated in a sea of Turks. Iran is making strong cultural and even religious inroads into Tajikistan, even though the republic's population is largely Sunni rather than Shi'ite.

Iran shares Russia's concerns over a possibly dominant Turkish influence in the region. Indeed, Iran may well be of interest to Russia precisely as a counterweight to excessive Turkish influence in Central Asia, assuming that Russia comes to feel that it is losing influence to Turkey. While Iran still promotes a vision of political Islam that is anathema to the rulers of Central Asia (and to Russia too, with its own many millions of Muslims within the Russian republic), Iran cannot be ignored as the critically indispensable land-corridor to the West and the Persian Gulf. Iran is especially active in providing workers to neighbouring Turkmenistan, whose natural gas and oil can be exploited with Iranian know-how in both those fields. (Iran's ideology, however, has caused Western states interested in investing in Turkmenistan to seek to avoid any dealings or even pipelines through Iran.) Iran is also critically interested in the geopolitical role of Afghanistan, described below.

Afghanistan

Afghanistan was suspended for 14 years as a geopolitical player in the region because of its status as a battleground for other players in the region starting with the communist revolution in April 1978 and end-ing with the collapse of the communist regime in 1992. Afghanistan now stands at a critical geopolitical crossroads in its traditional inter-nal ethnic rivalries. There is a real possibility that the northern half of Afghanistan – the area north of the Hindu Kush historically inhabited primarily by Tajiks and Uzbeks – could choose to separate from Afghanistan and join their coethnics in the northern Muslim republics. The Pashtuns who founded and dominated the Afghan empire for several hundred years have traditionally granted little political power to the Tajiks and the Uzbeks, while the latter, especially after their major role in the mujahedin movement against the Soviet Union, are no longer willing to be relegated to a subordinate position.

Any breakaway of northern Afghanistan could lead to a consolidation of the Tajiks and create a continuous Persian-speaking belt from the borders of China to the Persian Gulf, a belt that would rival the Turkish belt to the north. If Russia were to feel uncomfortable with Turkish power immediately to its south, including in the important republic of Kazakhstan, it might well look to strengthening the Persian belt at the expense of the Turkish. It is premature automatically to posit the existence of a united and consolidated Turkish belt, much less a Persian belt, or even Russian hostility to it; yet the geopolitical possibility cannot be ruled out, especially in the present fluid circumstances.

Pakistan

The chain reaction of events involving the evolution of the Persian-speaking belt of Central Asia has had a direct impact on the territorial integrity of Pakistan. The breakup of Afghanistan would bring serious geopolitical consequences in its wake, such as the strong likelihood of a remaining Pashtun residual state in Afghanistan seeking to join with the more numerous Pashtuns in Pakistan to form 'Greater Pashtunistan', long sought by Pashtun nationalists. A collapsing Pakistan would also lose the Baluch in the south-west, whose coethnics also spread into Iran and Afghanistan, further affecting the territorial integrity of Iran. In the event of Pakistan's loss of the critical Northwest Frontier Province and Baluchistan, the viability of the rest of the state would come into serious doubt, especially as India has long claimed that the very creation of Pakistan was artificial.

The remaining two provinces, Sind and Punjab, would be weak and probably unable to maintain an existence entirely separate from their coethnics across the border in India, especially in Indian Punjab. While religious differences between Hindus and Muslims have long divided the massive Punjab region, Indian Punjab itself is now rent by Hindu–Sikh differences; the appearance of a free-floating Pakistani Punjab could have incalculable consequences on the relationship of Punjab to the rest of India. Thus the breakup of Pakistan could have serious impact on the overall integrity of India itself, already seriously under assault in Kashmir and Punjab. One would hope that the democratic character of India would serve to insulate it from the processes of ethnic collapse that affect the totalitarian regimes of the Soviet Union and China, and from the 'unequal' ethnic relationships and authoritarian character that have long dominated Afghanistan and even Pakistan to some extent.

In the hope that none of the above disastrous trains of development take place affecting the states of Afghanistan, Pakistan and India, Pakistan remains intensely interested in the emergence of newly independent Central Asia. Feeling itself isolated as a vulnerable Muslim state on the borders of massive Hindu India, Pakistan perceives the possibility of a new 'Muslim strategic depth' that Central Asia could lend to Pakistan. Indeed it was Pakistan that coined the expression 'Islamistan' to denote the huge expanse of Muslim states that now stretch north-west from Pakistan. It was the Pakistani desire to gain direct access to these new states that prompted it to shift its policy in Afghanistan in 1992 to try to bring about rapid resolution of the Afghan struggle.

The Pakistani role in Central Asia cannot at present be fully gauged; at the least it offers Central Asia an alternative route, via Afghanistan, to the Indian Ocean. To date, however, the Central Asian leadership has been cool in its relations with Pakistan, recognizing the strong Islamic component in Pakistan's geopolitical thinking and in the character of its own government. The Central Asian states are also more accustomed to dealing with India during the long years of Soviet empire and recognize that India has more to offer economically than does Pakistan. Lastly, Pakistan's interest in 'pan-Islamic' regional solidarity will conflict in the future with China's determination to suppress any separatist tendencies among their own Muslim Turks, as discussed below.

China

The independence of the Turkic republics in the former Soviet Union is certain to affect ethnic politics within China, where some eight million Uighur Turks live in Xinjiang province – the old Chinese

Turkestan. The Uighurs already seek cultural autonomy and are more likely now to be impelled towards independence. More than a million Kazakhs also live in China. The peoples of these Turkic border areas of China are well aware of the struggle of the Tibetans, and of the people of Inner Mongolia, to achieve independence. The Chinese are very unlikely to escape the prospects of separatism in the north, especially as the Chinese communist regime weakens and eventually joins other communist parties of the world on the ash-heap of history.

China will also face a dilemma in squaring its foreign policy with its domestic policies. Beijing has long been interested in furthering its markets and its diplomatic support in the Middle East. Repressive policies against its own Muslims will have a negative impact on its policy interests in the Middle East, although China will almost surely give priority to its domestic security requirements.

The role of the Central Asian republics in this process cannot now be fully foreseen. The republics will in part be torn by the desire for good economic relations with China. (Kazakhstan, at least, is nervous about Uighur independence because it could involve claims on Kazakh territory along the Chinese border, where a large Uighur minority lives.) Other republics face no such threat from the breakup of China. How will the forces of nationalism and shared ethnicity mix with economic interest? Whatever posture the Central Asian republics adopt towards ethnic separatism in China, they lie between two great powers, Russia and China, and they have historically been the objects of manipulation by both these states at different times. How will the republics respond if Sino-Russian rivalry should once again develop? Will they opt to support Russia against China, or China against Russia? Or will some support Russia while others look more towards China? The new geopolitics of this region are still very much in the process of defining themselves.

The Arab world

The Arab world was basically comfortable with the Cold War and the role of the Soviet Union in the Middle East. For radical Arab regimes the Soviet Union was a direct source of support; even for Arab moderates Moscow served as a counterweight to unlimited American freedom of unilateral action in the region. When the Soviet Union collapsed, the Arabs were at first slow to realize that they needed to involve themselves in this new segment of the Muslim world. Since then the Gulf states in particular have sought to establish influence in Central Asia, especially through financial and banking policies. Saudi Arabia has also conducted Islamic-orientated policies there, designed primarily to build mosques, provide religious education and literature, to strengthen the institutions of establishment Islam, and to encourage adoption of the Arabic alphabet in place of Cyrillic for the writing of local languages.

The emergence of Central Asia and a new Turkic world has shifted the balance of power in the Muslim world away from the Arabs. Whereas Turkey was once on the periphery of the Muslim world, today it is the spiritual centre of a large Turkic world; the importance of the Arab world has been accordingly proportionally diminished. Iran's power has probably also grown, despite the threats to its integrity, but new strategic preoccupations to the north may distract some of its attentions from traditional involvement in the Persian Gulf. The longer-term consequences of this readjustment of the Arab–Turkish equation means that a more moderate Central Asian group of states – probably not particularly anti-Western in character – will now have a greater voice in the Muslim world. This factor has been underlined by the establishment of formal relations between Israel and several Central Asian states and Azerbaijan.

Western relations

Western interest in Central Asia is essentially preventive in character. While there is interest in investments in the region, there is nothing that is uniquely economically attractive about the region that will especially attract Western capital to it any more than to any other area. On the other hand, Western governments are very anxious that certain negative developments not take place that would seriously destabilize the region. The highest-priority issue, of course, is the question of a nuclear Kazakhstan and the further proliferation of nuclear weapons in the region in general. President Nursultan Nazarbaev's calculated ambiguities about his intentions to possess nuclear weapons have so far cleverly worked to Kazakhstan's own interests in that they have placed Kazakhstan on the map and caused the West to grant it considerable attention and even to discuss its security needs. Over time, however, any serious effort to gain permanent possession of and control over nuclear weapons will raise strong Western opposition and could lead to sanctions against Kazakhstan. It is unlikely that Nazarbaev in fact intends to parlay the presence of former Soviet nuclear weapons on Kazakh soil into a genuine permanent nuclear status. Any regional proliferation of weapons will be countered by Russian as well as by Western and international powers.

The West will also be concerned for human rights and the status of minorities in the region, especially as it affects the Russian population in Central Asia. Any persecution or bloodshed among the Russians could have the potential of unleashing neo-colonialist trends in Russia that would involve the reentry of Russian troops into former areas of the empire. Anti-Russian campaigns could also spark the emergence of extreme Russian nationalism and xenophobia that would be seen as potentially hostile to the West as well.

In addition, the kind of breakup and regrouping of nations described earlier will obviously be deeply destabilizing for the entire world; Western policies will try to avoid ethnic convulsions that can have disastrous consequences far beyond the realm of Central Asia itself.

Notes

1. For an early geopolitical assessment of this phenomenon see Graham E. Fuller, 'The Emergence of Central Asia', *Foreign Policy* (Spring 1990), pp 49–67.

2. For a more recent view of these events, see Graham E. Fuller, 'Russia and Central Asia: Federation or Fault Line?' in *Central Asia and the World*, ed. Michael Mandelbaum (New York: Council on Foreign Relations Press, 1994).

2

Emerging Political Elites

MARTHA BRILL OLCOTT

To study the élite of Central Asia today is a particular challenge. Elite identity studies are essentially attempts to divine the direction in which a given society is likely to be led, based upon the personalities and characteristics of the elites being identified. The society under analysis is usually undergoing a dynamic of growth, either physically, as in territorial expansion, or, more frequently, economically, culturally or politically. Throughout the former Soviet Union, but even more especially in the case of Central Asia, there is now the opposite – a dynamic of collapse, of societies shrinking. Although the collapse of the USSR makes plain that the Soviet economic and social system was unworkable, the fact remains that for Central Asia at least it *did* work, providing funding and social services which the republics will now find it difficult to provide for themselves, and the poorest of them, countries like Tajikistan and Kyrgyzstan, may never be able to do so.

Central Asia's leaders understood how closely their republics' economic well-being was tied to that of the USSR as a whole, and most Central Asians did as well. This helps explain why, with the sole exception of Uzbekistan's Erk (Independence) movement,[1] there were no indigenous independence movements, no national liberators active in Central Asia before the abortive coup of August 1991.

Even after that, with the exception of Tajikistan, in which the opposition had a broad but unfocussed political agenda which included a call for independence, Central Asia's new independence movements were all stage-managed by local republic communist parties in the aftermath of the failed coup, and the call for independence was a slogan intended to keep the old élite in power. Before the collapse of the USSR in December 1991, the governing élite in Central Asia

44

wanted the terms of the centre-periphery relationship redefined, but none of these republics planned or supported a formal break with Moscow.

Moreover, none of the ruling Central Asians expected the type of redefinition that was ultimately offered. When the three Slavic republics unilaterally dissolved the USSR on 8 December 1991,[2] effectively expelling Central Asia, the Central Asians were left with an independence for which they had not prepared, which they did not want, and which was not likely to bring them any tangible benefit for a long time, if ever.[3]

What independence brought instead was acute élite awareness that the social 'pie' would soon begin shrinking, which greatly intensified a struggle which had begun even before the dissolution, under the guise of a fight over sovereignty, about control of existing natural and man-made resources. Although there have been some efforts, even valiant ones, to take up the burdens and responsibilities of true nation-hood, for the most part élite studies of Central Asia present a picture of patrons and clients of a suddenly defunct empire, now scrabbling to secure for themselves benefits and pleasures they had until recently taken for granted.

However, it is inaccurate to assume that there is no support for independence, now that it has come. Soviet history and political discourse is full of references to 'the masses', for whom all sorts of claims are made, but never substantiated. In fact the nature and dynamic of mass opinion is largely a cipher everywhere in the former USSR, but doubly so in Central Asia; there the masses are twice removed from the Russian or Russified élites who claim to interpret them, or to speak in their name.

The élites: an overview

However little is known about the masses, who ultimately will be the shapers of Central Asia's future, considerably more is known about the élites upon whom they will be pressing, and who will be attempting to shape and use them. There are five existing élite groups in Central Asia today. These are: the *nomenklatura*, former functionaries of the Communist Party; functionaries of the military-industrial complex, and the Russian élite more generally; members of the arts and intellectual communities; the religious establishment; and partici-pants in the 'shadow economy', or black- and grey-markets.

Although these groups have distinct identities and agendas, both their membership and their interests can and do overlap, often within single republics, and not infrequently from republic to republic. None of the groups is tightly disciplined or closely controlled; nor are the subgroups monolithic – there are distinctions which must be made for the generation and nationality of each group's members, and for the functions they fulfil.

There are striking differences in behaviour between generations. Take for example the behaviour of former Communist Party apparatchiks. Those who spent substantial parts of their career working in the Brezhnev, Andropov and early Gorbachev years still remain firmly orientated to Moscow, while those who came to power in the late Gorbachev years and 'post-independence' have sought to create their power bases closer to home.

Moscow remains an important crutch to the senior members of the Central Asian élite. Many spent long periods of their career working in Moscow – the most prominent example is President Askar Akaev, of Kyrgyzstan, who spent all but a decade of his adult life in Moscow or Leningrad; others, like President Sapurmurad Niazov of Turkmenistan, were promoted to first secretary immediately after completing a 'training' period in Moscow. Even those whose careers did not take them to Moscow often spent their time serving Moscow-based bureaucracies, such as Uzbekistan's President Islam Karimov, who worked for Gosplan (the USSR state planning agency).[4]

In times of crisis they still have a natural tendency to turn to Moscow for help. This tendency has become particularly pronounced since President Rakhmon Nabiev of Tajikistan was deposed. Nabiev himself pleaded for help from the Russians. Since May 1992, when Nabiev was forced into a power-sharing relationship with Tajikistan's combined 'democratic' and Islamic opposition, each of the Central Asian republic presidents has signed a security agreement with Russia.[5]

Among the intellectual élite, which is predominantly of local nationality, there is an entire spectrum of affiliations, ranging from those who were completely intertwined with the old establishment, through those who were 'sanctioned' nationalists and mild dissidents, to some who are genuinely independent of other élites.

Here too generational differences are quite profound. Take the case of Olzhas Suleimenov, Kazakhstan's most prominent poet, who became a national political figure during the late Gorbachev years. Suleimenov was elected to the USSR Congress of People's Deputies and used this as a platform to launch his anti-nuclear movement, Nevada-Semipalatinsk, an organization which among other things succeeded in getting the nuclear test sites closed in Kazakhstan.[6]

As a result of this popularity, in October 1991 President Nursultan Nazarbaev approached Suleimenov to form a People's Congress of Kazakhstan, which was intended to serve as a pro-government political movement.[7] Suleimenov, whose writings are exclusively in Russian and who himself speaks only pidgin Kazakh, found himself unable to translate his Soviet-period status as a national hero into the post-Soviet period.

This organization never developed into a mass political force, and in November 1992 Nazarbaev tried again. He created a 'new' organization, calling it the Congress of the Nationalities of Kazakhstan (SNEK), and asked Erik Abdurahmanov to head it. Abdurahmanov, a former Komsomol secretary-turned-ecologist, is in his early 40s, some 15 years younger than Suleimenov, and speaks fluent Kazakh.[8] It is obviously too soon to know whether this ploy will succeed, and Suleimenov himself has become a critic of Nazarbaev's new political organization.[9] SNEK is now headed by Kuanysh Sultanov.

The religious élite also covers a wide spectrum, but here the greatest divide is not generational, but between those people who served in the local branches of the Central Asian Spiritual Directorate of Muslims (SADUM), the all-USSR governing body for official Islam created by Stalin,[10] and who worked as clerics in local communities, generally without official approval, and Islamic 'fundamentalists' or revivalists. However, the gap between the positions of these two groups is gradually narrowing.

The party élite

Each of Central Asia's presidents is from the *nomenklatura* of the Communist Party of the Soviet Union (CPSU) – even the seemingly mild-mannered former academic Askar Akaev was a member of the Central Committee of the CPSU, and served as president of the academy of sciences of his republic, a post that was always restricted to trusted party members. Karimov (Uzbekistan), Nazarbaev (Kazakhstan) and Niazov (Turkmenistan) were all first secretaries of their respective republics when their supreme soviets chose them as president, in the aftermath of Gorbachev's election as President of the USSR by the Congress of People's Deputies in March 1990. Absamat

Masaliev, first secretary of the Communist Party in Kyrgyzstan, initially declined to seek the post of president; when he finally did so in October 1990, an intra-party putsch within the legislature brought Akaev to power instead.[11]

Qahhor Makhkamov, first secretary of Tajikistan, was also initially elected that republic's first president by his Supreme Soviet, only to be ousted by his predecessor as first secretary, Nabiev, who received popular election to the post.[12] Currently, Tajikistan has no president, and the head of the Supreme Soviet, Imamali Rahmonov, also a former member of Tajikistan's *nomenklatura*, is functioning as head of state.[13]

Masaliev, Niazov and Makhkamov all came to power as first secretaries to do Moscow's bidding in the party purges of the post-Brezhnev and early Gorbachev years. Nazarbaev and Karimov were not named to be first secretaries of their respective republics until June 1989, nearly five years later. But Nazarbaev in particular gained political position through advocating a pro-Moscow reform line.

Central Asian leaders have all tried to compensate for these political liabilities by trying to cast themselves as national leaders. The model chosen varies according to local circumstances and the temperament of the president himself. The most common tack is for the leaders to define themselves as what they are *not*. Thus Karimov is *not* an Islamic fundamentalist, while he leaves it unclear what it means to be a secular reformist in independent Uzbekistan.[14] Similarly Akaev's political rhetoric asserts that a democrat is someone who is *not* a partocrat, rather than defining democracy in the context of Kyrgyzstan.[15] Positive definitions are much scarcer. Nazarbaev depicts himself and Kazakhstan as a bridge between Europe and Asia, but without making obvious whether his country will cease to be a bridge without him.[16] Niazov has taken a different approach, creating for himself a plethora of new medals and honours to celebrate his personality and presidency, but this does no more to answer the question of why he, and not some other, should be president. Even Akaev's reputation as hero of 'the silk revolution', while still untarnished, becomes less effective with time, because of growing ambivalence to the blessings that revolution conveyed.[17]

The most extreme case is that of Sapurmurad Niazov, who has created a personality cult akin to the crude Stalin-era style to honour his own achievements. He became the first recipient of two new state 'orders', and presides over a national portrait commission which is charged with quality control and the nation-wide dissemination of his official photograph. Newspapers in the republic now begin with quotations from his daily mail in praise of his accomplishments.[18] Large photographs of him were a mainstay of the lavish public display put on for Independence Day 1992 in Ashkhabad.

Islam Karimov was also eager to take official credit for gaining and sustaining Uzbekistan's independence during its first anniversary celebrations in September 1992. Among the events to mark this occasion was the publication of a pamphlet-size book of his speeches, which was distributed free to all schoolchildren, published in full in the press, and then offered for sale in republic bookstores and kiosks for a fraction of what it cost to print.[19]

While Karimov has shied away from establishing his own full-scale personality cult, he is encouraging the small-scale 'cult-making' of others, notably that of Sharif Rashidov; his reputation as Brezhnev-era first secretary was reduced to posthumous ignominy when Moscow's investigative teams revealed the existence of a republic-wide scheme for falsifying cotton statistics that was netting its participants tens of millions of (pre-inflationary) rubles.[20] One of the main streets in Tashkent has been named 'Rashidov Prospect', and the 75th birth-day of the deceased leader was marked throughout the republic. This is something which is making Uzbekistan's 'democratic forces' nervous. To them Rashidov is not the 'Uzbek national hero' who is currently being depicted, but the representative of a more corrupt and even less democratic political administration than the one currently in power.

Uzbekistan's political opposition has objected to the ways in which Karimov is manipulating nationalist themes. The leaders of Erk (whose leader, Muhammad Salih, a prominent poet-turned-legislator, ran against Karimov in the December 1991 elections) and Birlik (Unity) claim that Karimov's policies are mere sloganeering. They argue that renaming streets after previously suppressed historical figures does not constitute the development of a national history, that eliminating Russian-language announcements from public-address systems is not synonomous with the advancement of the Uzbek language. It is a sad irony, they have argued, that though the democratic opposition is being attacked for exacerbating inter-ethnic tensions, it is the poorly thought-out policies of the government that are exacerbating the fears of local Russian, Tajik and other minorities (nearly a quarter of Uzbekistan's population).[21]

The language issue is a highly politicized one throughout Central Asia. Each of the republic presidents now makes public addresses in his native language and, where appropriate (i.e. frequently in both Kazakhstan and Kyrgyzstan), in Russian as well. For Karimov, this meant that he was not infrequently making blunders on nation-wide television, for until he began working with a tutor he had only 'kitchen' Uzbek.

Karimov, like Niazov, was brought up in a state orphanage (with Central Asian society rife with family-based patronage systems Gorbachev apparently considered orphanhood an ideal qualification for a potential reformer). Nazarbaev and Akaev, however, both come from traditional rural families and each speaks his national language fluently. Furthermore, Nazarbaev really has played the *dombra* (the Kazakh national instrument, a two-string lute) since childhood, so he is not just faking a skill to impress Kazakh television audiences.

Central Asia's leadership has also sought to carry out its institution-building in a 'Central Asian context'. Immediately after the collapse of the Communist Party, successor 'socialist' (in Kazakhstan) and 'national democratic' (in Turkmenistan and Uzbekistan) parties were formed, but none has become a strong republic-wide organization, nor do any of them control the former CPSU property, which reverted to the respective republic governments. This property, everywhere in the region, has been turned over to local 'hakim', appointed by the republic presidents to be simultaneously their personal representatives and the repository of local executive power. Each 'hakim' heads a 'hakimet' which has replaced the functions of the local party committee.

The return to the vocabulary of the pre-conquest period is more than a mere symbolic exercise. The same party leaders who previously publicly decried Central Asia's 'vestiges' of its traditional society now praise the fact that Central Asia has managed to preserve parts of its traditional society. Moreover, they go to great lengths to demonstrate their own links to it.

Tajikistan and clan politics

A complex of clan and regional ties has always underlain power in Central Asia, before the Soviet period, during it, and on into the present. Forbidden to be mentioned during the Soviet period, and in some republics discussed reluctantly even now, these ties of family, clan and region of birth dictate patronage patterns in rural Turkmenistan, Kyrgyzstan, Kazakhstan and Uzbekistan.

Kyrgyz and Kazakh leaders now make open reference to their own ties, and those of others, and are pleased to accept the additional political loyalty that clan membership confers on them. After a World Congress of Kazakhs, held in Almaty in September–October 1992, one of the most desirable items in that city became the family tree of all the Kazakh clans, which people proudly hang on their walls with their own ancestry traced.

The current state of near civil war in Tajikistan is a much less pleasant demonstration of the power of clan and regional politics. Many see the war in Tajikistan as little more than an inter-clan struggle, which has been exacerbated by the presence of a large Islamic opposition. For most of the Soviet period, politics in Tajikistan were dominated by three large clans, from Khujand (Leninabad), Qurghonteppe and Kulob, with the Pamiri Tajiks barred even from competing.[22]

The current crisis has been slow to build. It began in February 1990 with small demonstrations when rumours spread that thousands of Armenians would be settled in Dushanbe;[23] mass demonstrations then brought down the Makhkamov government in the September 1991 coup; three months of nation-wide disturbances in the spring of 1992 were prompted by Nabiev's refusal to grant political concessions to the secular and religious opposition groups which had helped him come to power the preceding autumn; three months followed of even greater mass disorder after the May 1992 accord between Nabiev and the opposition, which made Nabiev into a virtual puppet;[24] then an all-out civil war was touched off by Nabiev's ouster in September 1992.[25] In late November Dushanbe was conquered by pro-Nabiev forces from Kulob, Imamali Rahmonov came to power and the Islamic forces returned to armed opposition.[26]

Throughout the whole drama, ties of clan and region have played a critical role. Nabiev, who died in April 1993, was from Khujand, the province adjoining Uzbekistan from which the republic of Tajikistan has long been ruled. This is the most developed of the provinces, the centre of what industry exists in Tajikistan (most of which was formerly run by various branches of the USSR defence ministries). These are the enterprises that the Russian army was sent in to protect. Obviously, it is the wealthiest of Tajikistan's oblasts. The poorest was Kulob, whose party organization had been the major rival of the Khujand group. It is their forces who retook Dushanbe and who put Rahmonov, a former minor communist official from Kulob, in control.

The centre of the opposition was Qurghonteppe, a region of dis-
parate Tajik and Uzbek family groups. For most of the Soviet period,
it was the part of Tajikistan in which forcibly resettled peoples were
placed. This has been the centre of the Islamic opposition. There has
been a loose alliance between those in Qurghonteppe and those from
the Pamirs (the democratic opposition leader Davlat Khudonazarov is
from the Pamirs).[27]

There is no reason to see the current situation in Tajikistan as a
stable one. The strength of the 'Kulobtsy' was substantially weakened
with the death in March 1993 of Sangak Safarov, the commander of
their irregular forces. Similarly, Nabiev's death also leaves the path
clear for new leadership to emerge in Khujand.

Most local observers do not see clan struggles as definitionally
unhealthy, and similar struggles are to be expected throughout Central
Asia. Turkmenistan also has three powerful tribally based groups.
Uzbekistan has four or five major regional (and partially kin-rein-
forced) groupings, and seven families are said to control the political
and economic life of Tashkent.

Kazakhstan has three hordes, but two clans in the Great Horde
dominated old *nomenklatura* lists and post-independence appoint-
ments, although Nazarbaev himself does not come from either.[28] This
fact has undoubtedly contributed to his independence of mind, but it
has also made it harder for him to implement his policies, particularly
at the more local level where patterns of personal loyalty are more
important than a commitment to abstract policies of reform.

Clan politics have also reasserted themselves in Kyrgyzstan. In the
decades before perestroika, Kyrgyzstan was dominated by a clan from
Naryn oblast; Masaliev's people came disproportionately from a Talas
oblast clan; and President and Mrs Akaev are said to be related to
both groups, although the Akaev government includes representatives
from every major clan in the republic.[29] Although Akaev is working to
ensure the 'representativeness' of the republic's government, he has
acquiesced to the need to play clan politics at the oblast level.

New oblast 'hakims' all come from prominent families of the region.
In fact, in Dzhelalabad, there was nearly a 'battle of the families'
when the Usmanov family took over virtually all posts of prominence
in the republic. In order to oust Usmanov, Akaev had to bring in
someone also with strong family connections, which necessitated
moving the head of privatization (Tagaev) to Dzhelalabad as hakim.[30]
Though this may have been a good solution for Dzhelalabad, it has

not eliminated the former hakim as a political actor in the republic, for he remains a deputy in Kyrgyzstan's parliament, where in the spring 1993 session he was reported to be cultivating his image as a populist.

The younger generation of partocrats

Less firmly entrenched than their elders when the Soviet Union collapsed, the younger generation of party élites is now in a precarious situation. They too have lost their former inter-republic ties, while their ties to their respective local populations are weak. Not having the lucrative Moscow connections their elders enjoy, these younger apparatchiks have no choice but to attempt to form new political, economic and structural links for themselves.

They face three choices: they can mortgage themselves to the old family structures and work to serve their family interests above all; or they can become strong advocates of economic reform and aspire to dominate a new competitive market economy; or they can try to strike a balance between the two. Generally speaking, few young people born to privileged families are willing to oppose the family/clan structure in its entirety.

However, it is also true that throughout Central Asia, it is the 'young partocrats' who have pushed hardest for economic reforms, provided they emerge in economic control. They are most in evidence in Kazakhstan and Kyrgyzstan, in both the agricultural and industrial sectors, but they also exist in good number in Uzbekistan, particularly among the emerging 'foreign trade' élite. In fact in Uzbekistan, two distinct foreign policy élites have emerged, one tied to the Ministry of Foreign Affairs and the other to the Ministry of Foreign Economic Relations. The former is dominated by the partocrats and the latter by the 'golden youth'. The two briefly came together in January 1993 with the appointment of Sadyk Safaev (formerly deputy prime minister of foreign relations) as foreign minister, but Bahtiar Hamidov, a vocal representative of the 'partocrat' wing, was left deputy prime minister in charge of foreign policy.

The shadow élite[31]

The only élite which can truly be called age-indifferent and nationality-blind is that which staffs and controls the shadow economy; this élite also is the least tied to any particular region, having ties and contacts throughout each republic, all across Central Asia, and all across the former USSR. There are enormous differences by nationality, which are discussed below in the section on Russians.

Like the dissident intellectuals, the élite of the shadow economy is an 'alternative' élite as well. However, unlike the anti-establishment élite, most of this group emerged from the local traditional leadership, and represent a conservative, traditional view. They are closely and directly tied to the masses, but they are equally well connected to the other élites. In the Soviet period the shadow economy essentially subsumed the kolkhoz structure, which now leaves this élite in firm control of agriculture, particularly in the branches most closely tied to direct market sales. The subject of most direct concern to this group is land; they support continued public ownership of agricultural land, with rights for themselves to rent or lease the best available land, and to collect a tax-in-kind through arranging the marketing of common crops.

The ex-party élite to some degree overlaps with the shadow economy, with which it is said to have strong and growing ties, at the all-union level and at the republic level. At the republic level the degree of interconnection varies according to the background of each republic's leader.

In Uzbekistan, for example, initially ties between party élite and members of the Tashkent shadow economy were weak because of a personal feud between President Islam Karimov (whose roots are in Samarkand) and former Vice-President Shahrullah Mirsaidov (a former mayor of Tashkent). This was an intolerable situation for Karimov, who was not content with Mirsaidov's withdrawal from the government but pushed Mirsaidov out of the legislature and placed him under virtual house arrest, allegedly in part for having 'incited' students to demonstrate against the president in January 1992.[32] Karimov is said to have been simultaneously offering strong financial incentives to Mirsaidov family members and former business partners to serve the president.

The Russian élite

The key constituent group of the Russian élite is attached to the military-industrial complex, which is prominently represented in the economies of Kazakhstan and Uzbekistan. Of nearly equal importance is the Russian-dominated management of the remaining (civilian) heavy industries still present in the respective republics; these are of unclear ownership now, but are uniformly under the control of local Russians, who remain in close contact with the Russian ministerial and industrial associations which replace the all-union ministries, or through the military directly.

The ex-party élite also shares an interest in controlling a perceived 'Islamic threat' with members of the industrial-military élite, but in most other issues the industrialists are orientated towards Moscow and all-union concerns, not towards their immediate surroundings.

There is some overlap in most of the republics between the old party élite and the military-industrial élite, and in Uzbekistan this overlap also encompasses a portion of the all-union élite of the shadow economy. Some of its members, though, are 'local' (far more frequently local-born Russian than local nationals), while others have no ties at all to the region where their factories or troops happen to be located. It was that sort of connection which probably kept Nabiev in office through the summer of 1992; throughout his career he was said to have been closely connected to people in the military-industrial plant in Khujand.

Karimov has obvious close ties with the military-industrial complex in general, and Uzbekistan's aircraft industry in particular. In addition, both he and Niazov in Turkmenistan have turned over control of their 'national' armies to the Russians stationed locally.[33]

Of all the republic leaders in the region, Nursultan Nazarbaev of Kazakhstan probably enjoys the strongest ties with the old USSR military-industrial complex. Before the beginning of the conversion process in the late 1980s, some 80 per cent of industry in northern (and Russian-dominated) Kazakhstan was tied to the Soviet defence industries – this notwithstanding that Nazarbaev had few Russians in prominent places in Kazakhstan's government. But in December 1992 his deputy prime minister charged with supervising the defence sector (Soskovets) went from his government into Yeltsin's, and in April 1993 Soskovets was appointed a deputy prime minister of the Russian government.

The military-industrial élite is but one of the various Russian groups in the region. It must be remembered that the Russians of Central Asia are almost as various as are the Central Asians among whom they live. The most obvious group to differentiate is the Cossacks, who claim large territory in six separate regions of north-east, north-west, central and south-east and south-west Kazakhstan, based on their descent from tsarist frontier troops who were first sent into the area 400 years ago. Suppressed by the Soviets in the 1920s, the Cossacks secretly maintained their military formations and ranks, carefully preserving records of the lands given to them for communal usage by various Russian tsars, which they now claim for their exclusive control.[34]

However there are also distinctions to be made among non-Cossack Russians. The descendants of Stolypin-era 'homesteaders', found throughout Kazakhstan and in central Kyrgyzstan, see Central Asia as Russia's 'Wild West', the frontier their ancestors helped to 'civilize'. Though none has assimilated, such Russians know something of the local history, many respect the local culture, and some even speak the local language. The descendants of the next wave of Russian migration, the children of exiled kulaks and Second World War evacuees who are now to be found throughout Central Asia, also have few remaining ties to mainland Russia. Many consider themselves to be Uzbekistanis or Kazakhstanis, and live on good terms with their Central Asian neighbours. Most of Central Asia's Jewish residents spring from this group, although there are Bukharan (Sephardic) Jews who have lived in Central Asia since the time of the Arab conquest. Most of the Russians in the universities, academies of sciences, and other 'white-collar' and intellectual professions come from this emigration.

The generally positive attitudes towards Central Asians of these two groups contrast sharply with the views of the Khrushchev-era Virgin Land 'enthusiasts' and Brezhnev-era 'industrial refugees'. Like the ex-kulaks and evacuees, these are also to be found throughout the region, especially in the cities; economic 'marginals' who left Russia in search of economic opportunity, these consider themselves to be ex-Soviet, now Russian, citizens, now stranded in a foreign country dominated by an alien culture which they fear. The generally quiescent Russian population is leaving Central Asia at a rate of over 5 per cent per year, with much greater numbers leaving from Tajikistan.[35]

In general, Russians have had few national political parties. An exception is Edinstvo (Unity) and its successor LAD (Harmony) in Kazakhstan, which are alleged to have ties with similar Russian nationalist groups outside Central Asia. Branches of the various Russia-based democratic groups are also present in the region, but their influence is rather insignificant.

The intellectuals

Independence has also wrought havoc among the Central Asian intelligentsia. All products of a system which specialized in social engineering, the Central Asian leaders continue to use intellectuals to assist in creating stable popular support, believing in the efficacy of political image building. Now the goal is to create 'democratically rooted' nationalist ideologies, and it is hoped that the national intellectuals can play a constructive role in the process.

Thus many of the intellectuals who always depended upon republic patronage to survive, even if largely discredited because of their past associations, continue to occupy the posts they always did, as can be demonstrated by a simple comparison of the tables of contents of pre- and post-independence editions of social science publications from local academies of science.

The group which disdained local support and found it instead in Moscow from an all-union audience, and that which once seemed to be a nationalist 'loyal opposition', articulating national concerns during the Soviet period, have now both fallen into the classic dilemma of post-colonial intellectuals. Educated and shaped by Russians, often unable even to read or speak their putative 'native' languages, let alone use them for scholarly purposes, these intellectuals inevitably view the future through the eyes of the Russians who shaped and once supported them; their former teachers and audience, consumed by other worries and concerns, now tend to see these intellectuals as foreigners, not fellow Russians.

In reality, most of the intellectuals in these groups are neither Russian nor native; their interests scarcely coincide with those of the masses with whom they share only nationality. A good example is the much-discussed 'Turkish model' of Central Asian development, which Russianized intellectuals embrace in the hopes of re-creating in their homelands a Europeanized, market-driven version of the Russian society in which they once comfortably lived, one in which, importantly for them, Islam does not predominate.

The former 'loyal oppositionists' are particularly visible in the new governmental bodies, the parliaments and the press, where they hope to create new identities, neither Soviet nor traditional, for citizens of the Central Asian republics. In this way they hope as well to forge new links between themselves and their non-élite countrymen. Some of these figures have become figures of real political prominence. They include Olzhas Suleimenov, former USSR deputy and leader of the anti-nuclear Nevada-Semipalatinsk movement, who is fighting to retain independent political influence in Kazakhstan's current political scene, because in the aftermath of his declaring Nazarbaev to have 'Bonapartist' tendencies the Kazakhstan procuracy charged irregularities in the financial dealings of Nevada-Semipalatinsk.[36]

They also include Davlat Khudonazarov, the former head of the USSR Union of Cinematographers, who ran as the opposition candidate in Tajikistan's presidential elections of 1991, receiving less than full support from the Islamic opposition. He was a key supporter of the anti-Nabiev coalition government in Tajikistan, and along with other democratic leaders is now a 'fugitive from justice' and living in exile.[37]

The opposition has also fared poorly in Uzbekistan. Karimov has asserted that the democratic opposition in his republic is responsible for exacerbating political tensions in Uzbekistan, although he disavows any personal responsibility for beating Abdulrahim Pulatov, co-chairman of Birlik, in the summer of 1992,[38] or his fellow co-chairman Shukhrat Ismatulaev in the spring of 1993.[39] Muhammad Salih, leader of Erk, fled the republic in early 1993 after having been called in for questioning, and has gone from being an establishment stalwart to an opposition figure.

The situation is far more peaceful in Kyrgyzstan and Kazakhstan. Of much more moment to intellectuals in these republics are laws mandating obligatory use of the native language, and they are eager for regulations calling for the switch from printing their national languages in a Cyrillic-based alphabet to a Turkish-style, Latin-based one, to be implemented rapidly.[40] Uzbekistan and Turkmenistan also plan to shift their languages to Latin script.

The fights over language law are potentially extraordinarily divisive issues in societies with large Russian minorities, like Kyrgyzstan and Kazakhstan. Both Nazarbaev and Akaev are more sensitive than the other leaders to the fact that they rule multi-national societies, and that they must strike a balance between the aspirations of local nationalists with the sensibilities of Russians and other minority populations. One problem is that neither community views the situation wholly rationally. This is especially true in Kazakhstan, where there is currently a major fight over the language provisions of the draft constitution. Kazakhs demand that their language be recognized as the sole official language; Russians demand that both languages have identical legal status. In reality, both languages have virtually identical status if Kazakh remains the official language and Russian remains the language of inter-nationality communication (which is the state of current legislation), but the new constitution recognized Kazakh as the exclusive national language while guaranteeing that Russian has near equal rights.[41]

Russians would have to develop some minimal linguistic competence in Kazakh. But the Kazakh nationalists are prepared to modify current provisions requiring all potential government employees to be able to demonstrate this by 1995. Modifications in the language law designed to meet some Russian demands have been promised for 1994 in both Kyrgyzstan and Kazakhstan. Russian nationalists argue that the Russian population need not learn Kazakh at all; the Kazakhs maintain that Kazakhstan is their homeland, and so their language, culture and history must be accorded a place of prominence in the republic.

Kazakh history has already conquered the streets of the republic capital of Almaty. All the old Soviet street names are gone, and the new names honour the great figures of Kazakh pre-revolutionary history, including those who organized the anti-Russian uprisings of the nineteenth century. However, most local Russians know so little Kazakh history that these names are not threatening, merely unpronounceable. Moreover, in the current free-for-all that is post-Soviet education, it is not clear how soon Russian children (enrolled in Russian-language schools) will have to learn a new pro-Kazakh history. With local school officials gaining greater discretionary authority, Russian-language schools will either retain the old Soviet-era curriculum or adopt experimental programmes 'imported' from the Russian republic. However, any efforts to do this on a formal basis are sure to be controversial.

Askar Akaev discovered this in October 1992, when he announced plans for the opening of a Slavonic University in Bishkek.[42] This project was designed to address the concerns of Central Asia's large Russian population (some 12 million people across the five republics), that their children would not be able to get a 'proper' Russian-language university education. The local state universities had all introduced state-language competence provisions of varying severity for admissions, and access to Russia's universities was no longer free or automatic for residents of Central Asia. Plans for the new Slavonic University became an immediate *cause célèbre* in Bishkek, as Akaev was pilloried for 'selling-out to Russia' in *Respublika*, Kyrgyzstan's popular opposition newspaper.[43] Given the vituperative nature of the criticism, the university soon changed from being Slavonic to being 'Kyrgyz-Russian', and the whole project became less of a priority for the government.

More serious, though, is the growing trend for former communists to make common cause with the nationalists, which has been happening with greater frequency in both Kyrgyzstan and Kazakhstan. These groups joined together in Bishkek in the summer of 1992 to block passage of Akaev's draft constitution, which would have formalized the existing presidential system. Both allied against Akaev to push for a document which would introduce a parliamentary government in Kyrgyzstan; each of the two groups was calculating that their group would outdo the other in parliamentary elections. Moreover, the democrats (from the Democratic Movement of Kyrgyzstan, now an umbrella for nearly 50 different parties and groupings) continue to believe that they will have greater political influence after new parliamentary elections. This is true even though the last three by-elections have resulted in the victory of prominent former communists, including two of the three surviving first secretaries of the Communist Party of Kyrgyzstan.

The final document, which was passed on 5 May 1993, provides for a weakened presidency, to be introduced after the next presidential and parliamentary elections (to be held in 1995). It also names Kyrgyz as the sole state language, without the provision of special rights for Russian.[44] Political observers in Moscow report that as a result of the 1993 legislative session, disaffection was already rising among the Russians of Kyrgyzstan.[45] In June 1994 President Akaev introduced a programme designed to keep local Russians from leaving the republic.

In Kazakhstan, local nationalists may also prove to be a powerful pressure group. Those close to Nazarbaev confide that they are nervous about the 'nationalist potential' of former partocrats. The scenario they project is that some of the old *nomenklatura* will usurp the nationalist agenda of the secular opposition (the Azat [Freedom] movement and the Republic Party) and charge Nazarbaev with selling out Kazakh patrimony through an economic reform package which largely benefits distant capitalists as well as local Russians and Jews. The recent electoral victories of partocrats-turned-opposition figures in two predominantly Kazakh oblasts (Taldy Kurgan and Jambyl) is cited as proof that this scenario is not wholly imaginary.

The religious élite

Connections between the party élite and the religious élite vary from republic to republic. In Uzbekistan, both generations of partocrats have strong ties to SADUM; all three groups are interested in controlling a popular 'Islamic threat', not because such a threat necessarily exists, but because suppressing it gives them a reason to exert control. Neither generation of partocrat has much other contact with the Central Asian masses, but to some degree no other is necessary, because Central Asians are also enmeshed from birth in local traditional power structures.

However, even in Uzbekistan, relations between President Islam Karimov and the local religious establishment have become strained. He was on very good terms with Mufti Muhammad Yusuf in 1991 and much of 1992; he even kept the head of SADUM in power at a point (in mid-1991) when it seemed that the mufti's opponents would oust him.[46] But in the wake of the unrest in Tajikistan, relations between the two became strained, and on 30 April 1993 it was announced that the mufti had been removed for reasons of health.[47]

Karimov has found the activities of the non-SADUM élite wholly alien, agreeing with the Russians about the 'fundamentalist threat' to Central Asia, and he has consistently refused to register the Islamic Renaissance Party (IRP) in his republic. Nazarbaev has also refused to register the IRP (which unlike in Uzbekistan is an insignificant group) as well as the pro-Islamic Alash (a much larger movement with the potential to become politically significant).

The only intellectuals who have good contacts with the religious opposition are the dissident or anti-establishment figures who began to appear when it first became possible publicly to discuss republic sovereignty in the last years of Gorbachev's rule. In Tajikistan the anti-establishment intellectual élite was able to enter into a long-term political alliance with the IRP, and because of that they are now being persecuted by the Rahmonov regime. Ties between Birlik (Unity), Uzbekistan's major opposition group, and local religious élites are more informal but certainly seem to be pervasive. Their relationship to the locally banned IRP is harder to ascertain, however as a rule the dissident intellectuals have good connections with the non-SADUM clerics and, in many cases, ties with the local members of the shadow economy. In Tajikistan this opposition was able to join with the local power structures, which could happen in Uzbekistan as well.

The role of SADUM has changed since the collapse of central authority. The Spiritual Directorate no longer enjoys even a formal monopoly on the religious life of the Central Asians, and Nazarbaev has formed a separate Kazakhstan Religious Board to usurp the functions of SADUM in his republic. On a practical level the local communities themselves now play a much greater role in regulating and funding local religious life. On the other hand, the role religion plays in society has significantly expanded, which gives the formal religious establishment a whole range of new responsibilities. SADUM is responsible for distributing *hajj* pilgrimage trips to Mecca, and receives funds from foreign governments for religious education and the construction, renovation and repair of mosques.

The 'government' clerics have also begun to play a certain role in government. In Uzbekistan and Turkmenistan there is formal, if limited, clerical participation in the government. Both Kyrghyzstan and Kazakhstan are determinedly secular in their government philosophy, but the Akaev government's draft constitution specifically recognizes the Islamic heritage and nature of Kyrgyzstan.[48]

In all the republics the growth of religion has increased the role of the non-SADUM clerics even more than that of the SADUM clerics. Local clerics now derive real power from their communities, both in the cities and, even more so, in the countryside. The religious authority of most of the formerly 'unofficial' mullahs, most of whom are conservative traditionalists, has been formally recognized by SADUM. Though these clerics often lack the formal religious education which the 'fundamentalists' enjoy, the sort of society they are promoting is no more modern than that of the fundamentalists. This is particularly true in Uzbekistan. Throughout Central Asia local religious élites are emerging as leading figures in local political life, and are likely to wield increasing influence in communal affairs. In Tajikistan the opposition government includes clerics or clerical influence in the management of all spheres of the republic's social life.

Distinct from the newly recognized 'unofficial' mullahs, but often working in parallel, are the madrassa-trained 'fundamentalists', who are opening religious schools and trying to increase public observance of Islamic tenets. They often deal easily with and make common purpose with SADUM-recognized officials. In rural areas local political authorities also tolerate their activities.

However, it is the local clerics actively involved in trying to bring Islam into village schools who are in closest contact with the populace.

This group is influenced by the fundamentalists, with whom they share the goal of returning their people to Islam. The influence of both the fundamentalists and the village clerics is expanding locally as the two groups develop economic bases and build mosques and other structures through contributions and businesses.

There has been considerable speculation in the Western press about foreign Islamic actors in Central Asia's religious revival. There are two groups of Muslim missionaries functioning in Central Asia, one working with the fundamentalists and financed by fundamentalist organizations from Pakistan and Bangladesh, and opposition groups from Egypt and Syria, themselves funded through the United Arab Emirates. The other, much richer, is sent by Saudi Arabia and Kuwait and has been working through SADUM.[49]

With the exception of Tajikistan, the influence of Iran is not great, and even in Tajikistan, religious activists take their spiritual orientation from Sunni (and not Iranian Shi'ite) sources. Since the fall of Najibullah, emissaries from Afghanistan to various republics of Central Asia have been exerting some influence as well, particularly in Tajikistan, but it is hard to evaluate whether they are missionaries or political pragmatists interested in using a neighbouring state to advance their own local interests.

The masses

Obviously, the major reason for everyone's concern about Islam is the fear of the existing élite, partocrats and non-partocrats alike, that Central Asia will become engulfed in a fundamentalist wave. It should be specifically noted that the theme of 'Islamic revolution' is sounded loudest by the Russians and their Russified native dependants, who use their discussions of the need for a 'secular society' to obscure the fact that under the new governments they are losing privileges they once enjoyed. Talk of secularism plays well in the West (its intended audience) because Western societies have grown so accustomed to their own Christian cultural heritages that they no longer perceive the Christian underpinnings of 'secular society'. In fact, to non-Christian eyes, much of 'secular society' is simply Christian culture in which people do not necessarily attend church.

All evidence suggests that the bulk of the Central Asian population, especially the rural majority, lived through the Soviet period in traditional social structures, to a high degree shaped and controlled by traditional Islam, with ethnic and religious identities firmly shaped by events and territorial configurations which could be as much as hundreds of years old. The little that is known of this mass of rural labourers and herders suggests that, while they may not have articulated or even been conscious of a need for sovereignty or independence, they are not now adverse to having it, especially as independence has made it easier to live in openly traditional ways, with no need to pay even lip-service to Soviet-era slogans. This is particularly true in regard to Russians and Russian domination. In the pastures and cotton fields of Central Asia, Soviet Russia was unambiguously a colonizer, and the masses are highly reluctant to permit any arrangement which leaves Russians in any sort of control of their societies. Religion is important too; regardless of oddities of practice, or even lack of practice, the one thing that all Central Asians 'knew' about themselves was that they were Muslim; now that that identity can be openly embraced again, people are hostile to anything which seems a return to the non-denominational society of the past.

Thus the masses present a kind of mute but implacable pressure, defining a vague limit beyond which the élites can not pass in their internecine struggles to retain control. This is not to suggest that an 'Islamic revolution' is inevitably threatening in Central Asia; rather it is to remind that Central Asia is already Islamic, and has been for centuries. What exists now is the potential for elite groups to make use of the widespread sense that Islam has suffered enough indignities and limitations, and that people are prepared to fight to preserve an identity they already have.

Nevertheless, it is also true that there is a growing distaste, even disgust, for the degrees to which present élites are willing to go to preserve their privileges. That distaste is certainly exacerbated by the failure of the governments to provide basic services, and to deliver on other promises that they made when independence was first announced. This combination of disillusion and scorn creates fertile ground for alternative élites, who in their struggle for power may wish to turn this distaste to their own advantage; if they do, their most immediately useful weapon will be the accusation that the existing élites are Russified or, what amounts to virtually the same thing, anti-Muslim.

Notes

The released time from teaching necessary to research and write this paper came from support received from the Defense Academic Research Program (DARSP) during 1992–93.

1. The leader of this party, Muhammad Salih, was defeated when he ran for president of Uzbekistan on this independence platform, most of whose features had already been usurped by Islam Karimov. See *Financial Times*, 31 December 1991.

2. *Izvestiia*, 10 December 1991.

3. For details of the manoeuvring of the Central Asian leaders up to the creation of the CIS, see Martha Brill Olcott, 'Central Asian Independence', *Foreign Affairs*, lxxi/3 (1992), pp 108–30.

4. For background material on the rise to power of all but Akaev, see Martha Brill Olcott, 'Gorbachev, The National Problem and Party Politics in Central Asia', in Dan Nelson and Raj Menon (eds), *Assessing Soviet Power* (Lexington Ky: Lexington Books, 1988), pp 63–84. On Akaev see Bess Brown, 'The fall of Masaliev: Kyrgyzstan's "silk revolution" advances', *RL Report on the USSR* (19 April 1991), pp 12–15.

5. For details on these treaties see Martha Brill Olcott, 'Central Asia and the New Russian–American Rapprochement', in George Ginsburgs, Alvin Rubinstein and Olef M. Smolansky (eds), *Russia and America: From Rivalry to Reconciliation* (Armonk NY: M.E. Sharpe, 1993) pp 127–39.

6. See Martha Brill Olcott, '*Perestroyka* in Kazakhstan', *Problems of Communism* (July–August 1990), pp 55–77.

7. For an account of the formation of this as well as all of the major parties and political movements in all five Central Asian republics, see Aleksandr Verkhovsky, *Srednaia Aziia i Kazakhstana: politicheskaia sprektr* (Moscow: Panorama, 1992).

8. *Nezavisimaia gazeta*, 6 May 1993.

9. *Nezavisimaia gazeta*, 13 February 1993.

10. For details see T. Sasidbaev, *Islam i obshchestv* (Moscow: Nauka, 2/1984).

11. For an account of how the 'battle' proceeded, see *Sovetskaia Kyrgyzia*, 15–31 October 1990.

12. *FBIS Daily Report: Central Eurasia*, FBIS-SOV-92-175, 9 September 1992, p 46.

13. For details about Rahmonov and his political programme see *Izvestiia*, 12 January 1993.

14. *Khorezmskaia pravda*, 20 April 1993.

15. This emerges in the debates over the new constitution, adopted 5 May 1993. See *Slovo Kyrgyzstana*, 10–27 April 1993.

16. For a series of Nazarbaev addresses that relate to this theme, see *Kazakhstanskaia pravda*, 16–20 December 1992.

17. For an article which speculates on the fading quality of Akaev's leader-

ship (and the controversial but rising star of Vice-President Feliks Kulov), see *Svobodnye gory*, 16 March 1993.

18. For a typical example see *Turkmenskaia iskra*, 5 December 1993.

19. I. A. Karimov, *Uzbekistan svoi put' obvnovleniia i progressa* (Tashkent: 'Uzbekiston', 1992).

20. *Literaturnaia gazeta*, 18 November 1992.

21. For a long interview with Muhammad Salih, see *Narod i demokratiia*, nos 7–8 (1992), pp 24–27.

22. *Kommunist Tajikistana*, 14 January 1988.

23. *Komsomolets Tajikistana*, 12 March 1990.

24. *FBIS Daily Report: Central Eurasia*, FBIS-SOV-92-088, 6 May 1992, pp 52–6.

25. *Izvestiia*, 2 October 1992.

26. *Komsomolskaia pravda*, 2 April 1993; *Moscow News*, 9 April 1993.

27. For a concise account of some of the ethnic background and political splits in Tajikistan, see Bess Brown, 'Tajikistan: The Conservatives Triumph', *RFE/RL Research Report*, ii/7 (12 February 1993), pp 9–12.

28. Clan or family background are noted by both Nazarbaev and Kunaev in their autobiographies. See Nursultan Nazarbaev, *Bex pravykh i levykh* (Moscow: Molodaia gvardiia, 1991), Chapter 1; and Dinmukhammed Kunaev, *O Moem vremeni* (Alma Ata: Dauyr, 1992), Chapter 1.

29. *Komsomolskaia pravda*, 3 April 1993.

30. Ostankino television, 16 October 1992.

31. This is a topic upon which no reliable material has been written, and virtually everything contained in this section is conjecture based upon extensive interviewing in the region. It also reflects a lecture given on the topic by Arkady Vaksberg at Meridian House, Washington, DC, on 18 March 1993. See also Sergei Poliakov, *Religion and Tradition in Rural Central Asia* (Armonk NY: M.E. Sharpe, 1992).

32. *Izvestiia*, 22 January 1992.

33. *FBIS Daily Report: Central Eurasia*, FBIS-SOV-93-006, 11 January 1993, p 16.

34. *Kazakhskaia SSR. kratkaia entsiklopediia*, vol. i (Alma Ata: Glavnaia redaktsiia Kazakhskaia entsiklopediia, 1985), pp 225–6.

35. *Rossiskaia gazeta*, 16 April 1993.

36. *Nezavisimaia gazeta*, 6 February 1993.

37. *Rossiskaia gazeta*, 29 April 1993.

38. *FBIS Daily Report: Central Eurasia*, FBIS-SOV-92-139, 20 July 1992, p 64.

39. *Nezavisimaia gazeta*, 7 May 1993.

40. *Rossiskaia gazeta*, 7 May 1993.

41. The supervision of this has fallen to a language committee that was appointed by Nazarbaev in April 1993. See *FBIS Daily Report: Central Eurasia*, FBIS-SOV-93-065, 7 April 1993, p 78.

42. *Vechernyi Bishkek*, 1 October 1993.

43. Interviews conducted by author in Bishkek, 17–23 October 1993.

44. *Izvestiia*, 29 April 1993.

45. *Rossiskaia gazeta*, 8 May 1993.

46. *Rossiskaia gazeta*, 28 April 1993.

47. *Radio Liberty Daily Report*, 30 April 1993.

48. *Slovo Kyrgyzstana*, 28 December 1992.

49. These conclusions are based on trips made to the Ferghana Valley in March, May and October 1992.

3

The Potential for Political Instability and Regional Conflicts

BORIS Z. RUMER

With the breakup of the USSR, its five Central Asian republics – Uzbekistan, Tajikistan, Turkmenistan, Kyrgyzstan and Kazakhstan – have emerged from more than a century of Russian and Soviet domination. These five countries, which in modern times have never enjoyed the status of independent actors in international politics, have started to define their geopolitical orientation. The outcome, indeed the very process, threatens to alter political and military equations from China to the Persian Gulf.

Even for the distant West, it is difficult to overestimate the importance of Central Asia, for the region directly affects countries and causes that are of strategic concern to the United States and its allies. With an area roughly half the size of the United States, Central Asia borders on Russia, China, Afghanistan and Iran; and it is separated from Pakistan only by a thin stretch of land. Its population of 50 million is chiefly Turkic, but some of them also have strong ethnic, linguistic and cultural ties to Iran. The predominant religion is Islam. Economically, the region is poor but possesses extensive and still largely unexplored natural resources, including natural gas, oil, gold and uranium. Unlike many underdeveloped areas, Central Asia has a significant technical and scientific intelligentsia and facilities of potentially considerable military importance. Not least, the region is home to a large contingent of ex-Soviet military units, with large stocks of weapons and military equipment.

None of this has gone unnoticed in capitals from Ankara to Islamabad to Beijing, where the sudden geopolitical vacuum in Central Asia has been viewed with ambivalence – concern about potential instability, but also an awareness of new opportunities. This new 'great game' in the heart of Asia is unfolding not so much among the old colonial powers as among their former minions, many of whom are themselves just emerging from colonial domination and seeking to define their roles in their regions and the world.

Turkey and Iran have been the most active in pursuit of new opportunities in Central Asia, building on ethnic, linguistic and cultural ties to the region. For Turkey, Central Asia offers an irresistible political opportunity to bolster its international standing. Its ambition is fuelled not only by memories of lost empire and a desire to assert Turkish influence among ethnic kin, but also by the hope that leadership in Central Asia would enhance Ankara's standing in Europe.

Iran's interest, based initially on its ties to the Persian-speaking Tajiks, can also be explained by its desire to break out of international isolation. Tehran plainly seeks to establish a sphere of influence in a region of great importance to its neighbours and competitors. Its ambitions are further fuelled by a desire to export its own brand of politically active Islam. Although Central Asia has no tradition of such Shi'ite Islamic fundamentalism, the Iranian creed might well exert strong appeal in a time and place of socio-economic deprivation.

Saudi Arabia's growing involvement in Central Asia – as a source of economic assistance and as a sponsor of cultural and religious activities – promises to turn the region into the strategic rear of the Persian Gulf. In other words, a struggle for influence between Iran and the Saudi kingdom could entwine Central Asia in the larger rivalry and competition of the Gulf itself.

Such geopolitical domino theories can easily suggest a scenario of explosive instability. The destabilization of Central Asia could come to include China, whose western provinces are still at times called 'East Turkestan'; after all, the latter area is home to a significant Turkic minority of Uighurs, Kazakhs and Kyrgyzes, who have a long history of resistance to Beijing. No less vulnerable is Afghanistan, whose northern regions are populated by millions of Tajiks and Uzbeks, all contesting the dominance of Afghanistan by the Pashtuns. The Pashtun population of Pakistan, in turn, would hardly remain indifferent to a Tajik–Pashtun conflict in Afghanistan. India, given its fragile relations with both Pakistan and China, could also become embroiled. And of course destabilization in Central Asia would inevitably involve Russia, given its long-standing involvement in the region, its economic interests, and the presence there of ten million ethnic Russians.

These prospects for destabilization are very real indeed, given the unstable nature of the core Central Asian region. Although often lumped together by outsiders as a single entity, the five Central Asian states are anything but homogeneous. Central Asian boundaries are the product of Russia's nineteenth-century military drive towards the south-east and of the arbitrary territorial divisions of the Soviet era. Borders cut across ethnic enclaves, making Central Asia a patchwork quilt rent by ethnic, regional and tribal disputes over land and natural resources. Other volatile and widespread elements are poverty and territorial grievances, which threaten to undermine both the existing regimes and the equilibrium in the region. The consequence of such an unfortunate but likely turn of events would be felt throughout Asia and would inevitably have a significant impact even on the remote powers of the North Atlantic.

Moscow's attitude

For more than a year after the breakup of the USSR, Moscow had no coherent policy towards its former colonies in Central Asia. The foreign-policy strategists of the new Russia were too preoccupied with reconfiguring a relationship with the West. Central Asia remained on the periphery of Moscow's attention.

In the summer of 1992, however, Moscow suddenly exhibited keen interest in Central Asia, becoming deeply concerned about developments in the area. Moscow's passivity had created a geopolitical vacuum that invited intervention by the neighbouring states of the Islamic East. Nationalistic circles in Tashkent, Dushanbe and Ashkhabad began to dream of resurrecting a 'Greater Turkestan', dismembering Afghanistan, creating various confederations (with the participation of Iran, Afghanistan and Pakistan) and forming regional economic unions. Moscow finally recognized the mounting danger of an Islamic political union on its southern borders and reacted by unleashing a flurry of activity to restore its ties with the regimes in Central Asia.

Partly as a result, the predominant forces within the Commonwealth of Independent States (CIS) became no longer centrifugal, but centripetal. Previous expectations that the CIS would break up gave way to a new consciousness about the need for its survival. By the summer of 1992, there had clearly emerged from the 11 members of the CIS a group of states deeply interested in collaboration, especially in the military and political spheres.

Moscow's efforts to define its policy towards ex-Soviet republics have been impeded by the rising conflict within Russia – between 'Westernizers' (who renounce an imperial policy) and 'national patriots' (who retain imperial ambitions and continue to see Russia as a super-power). This conflict has shifted from the ideological sphere to the political arena, where the Westernizers are represented by the Ministry of Foreign Affairs (MFA) and the national patriots by the parliament. The two camps are uncompromising and openly display their enmity. Staff from the MFA label the parliamentary opposition as 'dreaming troglodytes', while the latter derisively scorn the Westernizers as 'Moscow fops'.[2]

Moreover, a clash of personal ambitions within Russia's new political establishment is unfolding against this background of polemics about Russia's 'national interests'. One powerful player is Evgenii Ambartsumov, a Moscow intellectual and political scientist who now serves as chairman of the parliamentary committee on international relations. Espousing the need to rebuild 'a great, but democratic state', Ambartsumov summarizes his position as follows:

> As far as I am concerned, it is incontrovertible that Russia is something larger than the Russian Federation in its present borders. Therefore one must see its geopolitical interests more broadly than what is currently defined by the maps. That is our starting premise as we develop our conception of mutual relations with 'our own foreign countries' [the former components of the Soviet Union].[3]

Many Russian parliamentarians share Ambartsumov's view, including influential politicians like Sergei Stankevich and Oleg Rumantsev.

On the other side, the first deputy minister of foreign affairs, Fedor Shelov-Kovediaev, admonished the national patriots not to forget 'that [our] fatherland is surrounded by independent states and subjects of international law, just like Russia, and correct relations with them can only be built on the basis of commonly accepted principles and norms; that coercion and pressure can only bring serious complications and nothing else.'[4] Expressing deep concern about nationalistic tendencies, he added: 'There is gradually consolidating a group of representatives of different parts of the political spectrum that confuse two conceptions: "powerful policy" [that is, effective policy] and "power politics" [that is, policy based on force].'[5]

The Russian foreign ministry evidently reflects the position of President Boris Yeltsin, and follows his policy with respect to the Central Asian states. So far, Yeltsin himself cannot be accused of exhibiting superiority or condescension in his relations with colleagues in Central Asia. He constantly underlines the equality of all members in the Commonwealth and denies any imperial ambitions on Russia's part. Nevertheless, the intensifying campaign by the national patriots inevitably disturbs leading circles in Central Asia and provokes a corresponding reaction among the nationalistic segments of the population.

Central Asia's attitude towards Moscow

The disintegration of the Soviet Union, in its initial phase, led to a deterioration in relations between Moscow and the Central Asian republics. Although Central Asians, especially President Nursultan Nazarbaev of Kazakhstan, were convinced exponents of the need to preserve the Union, the Great Russian attitude among the democrats who came to power in Moscow after the August putsch provoked intense irritation in Central Asia. Nazarbaev, ordinarily a model of equanimity, made the following blunt observation:

> August is now behind us. And now, strangely enough, riding the waves of victory, the democrats have gone too far. Chauvinistic refrain is to be heard in their speeches. What is the result? Centrifugal processes have again been unleashed in the republics.[6]

Demonstrating the supercilious attitude traditionally prevailing among the USSR's 'Slavic brothers' was their failure to invite the leaders of Central Asia to the summit at Belovezhskaia Pushcha, where President Boris Yeltsin of Russia, President Leonid Kravchuk of Ukraine and Stanislav Shushkevich, chairman of the Belorussian parliament, agreed to liquidate the Soviet Union and to establish the CIS. This flagrant expression of superiority aroused deep enmity in Central Asia. The semi-official Turkmenistan newspaper, *Turkmenskaia iskra*, wrote: 'Such a separation (if not confrontation) has nothing in common with the civilized norms of international relations.'[7]

But when the heads of the Central Asian republics gathered in Ashkhabad, the capital of Turkmenistan, they nevertheless suppressed their vexation and proposed that the organizers of Belovezhskaia Pushcha convene jointly with them to liquidate the USSR and to establish the CIS. That proposal, however, was rejected. As Nazarbaev has observed of this period:

> The Slavs met alone. And now the Muslims will also meet separately. The danger of confrontation at this time was very great; we were indeed very close to it. We had a plan to create an Asiatic confederation. It is difficult to say what this global confrontation could have led to – especially when one considers that there are also Turkish-speaking republics inside Russia.[8]

As the political establishment of Central Asia discussed the idea of creating a common political and economic region, the phrase of Askar Akaev, 'the new philosophy of the states of Central Asia', became exceedingly popular and widespread.

By the spring of 1992, however, the situation had begun to change. At a Central Asian summit in late April, the idea of a Central Asian confederation was decisively laid to rest. It was undermined by the president of Turkmenistan, Sapurmurad Niazov, who refused to sign the protocol to create a single investment fund and investment bank for the states of Central Asia, to adopt a common price policy, and to coordinate the programmes for economic development in the region.

Thus was buried the myth of solidarity among the Muslim republics in the southern part of the former USSR. This schism in the Islamic family is explained largely by the differences in wealth among its members. Kazakhstan (which possesses vast natural resources and which has well-developed industrial and agricultural sectors), Uzbekistan (the main supplier of cotton to the former Soviet Union) and Turkmenistan (which has rich stores of natural gas) do not wish to support their poorer brethren in Kyrgyzstan and Tajikistan; having obtained independence, the three richer states showed their determination to find useful partners and markets outside the ruble zone.

However, it soon became apparent how myopic was the policy of the newly minted Central Asian presidents – four of whom had, as recently as 1991, been party bosses in their republics. (The exception is Akaev, president of Kyrgyzstan, who was a scientist.) By May 1992, when the group met in Ashkhabad, their attitude towards CIS – and hence Moscow – had changed radically. The presidents of the two 'regional superpowers' (Kazakhstan and Uzbekistan) abjured any scepticism about the viability and significance of CIS, emphasizing instead that their policy assigned the highest priority to close ties with Russia – this at a meeting which included the heads of state from Iran, Pakistan and Turkey.

What impelled Nazarbaev and Karimov to disregard the humiliation of the Belovezh'e summit and seek new ties with Moscow? Cold fear. They had good reason to fear the threat of bloody inter-ethnic conflict, which could easily lead to the toppling of their own regimes. They also feared the surge of Islamic fundamentalism, which had started to sweep through the region and threatened to destroy their regimes. It was perfectly clear that Moscow was in no position to provide credits, food or equipment. But no one could or can replace Moscow as the region's 'policeman'; only Moscow can maintain some semblance of order – and, by extension, the existing regimes in Central Asia. In May 1992, therefore, the president of Uzbekistan, Islam Karimov, candidly declared that 'Russia must become the guarantee for security in the region.'[9] What specifically inspired Nazarbaev, and especially Karimov, to perceive the impending danger was the situation in Tajikistan, which threatened to shatter the fragile peace in the region and to turn it into a second Lebanon.

Greater Tajikistan

The internecine war in Tajikistan is driven by a host of forces. Dominant among them are: old tribal animosities; the poverty of the rural population (70 per cent of the total population), compounded by its profound attachment to Islamic tradition; high rates of unemployment and fertility (the highest in the CIS, in both categories); attempts by the former party élite (headed by former President Nabiev) to restore the Communist Party; an awareness by the rulers of Tajikistan of the Tajiks' common ties with neighbouring Afghanistan, of their linguistic and cultural links with Iran, and of the intensification of both the Islamic factor and anti-Western and anti-Russian attitudes under the influence of the Tajiks' foreign kinsmen.

These are only the primary factors, which are combining to produce the explosion in Tajikistan. Other factors, less visible on the surface, are nonetheless important. Because Tajiks are from Persian-speaking Iranian stock, Tajikistan is the key beachhead for Iran, which seeks to extend its influence across Central Asia. Political circles in Uzbekistan are firmly convinced that Iran is the source for both the idea of creating a Greater Tajikistan (an Islamic state uniting the people of Tajikistan with their fellow Tajiks in northern Afghanistan), and the weapons to realize that goal. The scenario of a Greater Tajikistan, presumably inspired by Iranian fundamentalists, puts Akhmed Shah Masud – a truly popular leader of Afghan Tajiks – at the forefront of the movement; he is widely perceived to be someone capable of uniting all Tajiks because of his military skills and well-armed troops. All this must be a nightmare for Karimov, but such prospects ought to disturb Yeltsin as well. Indeed, such prospects ought to be unsettling for Western states.

Uzbekistan and Tajikistan

Consider the ethnic composition of Uzbekistan and Tajikistan. In Uzbekistan, Uzbeks comprise 71 per cent of a population of 21 million; Tajiks represent 5 per cent according to official statistics (but actually 10 to 15 per cent, according to Tajiks and even Uzbek specialists). In Tajikistan (which has a total population of 5.5 million), Tajiks account for 62 per cent of the population and Uzbeks for 24 per cent.

The Tajik enclave in Uzbekistan is close to the border with Tajikistan and numbers two to three million people. Moreover, they are concentrated in Samarkand and Bukhara – the two largest cultural and economic centres of Central Asia and two of the oldest as well. Similarly, the Uzbek enclave in Tajikistan is close to the Uzbekistan border; it numbers approximately 1.3 million Uzbeks and is located in the most economically advanced segment of the Tajik republic.

The Tajik minority in Uzbekistan has felt victimized by overt discrimination from the very outset of Soviet rule. Before 1917, Tajiks made up the majority of the population in Samarkand and Bukhara, but according to the 1926 census (which many Tajiks consider to be falsified) the numbers changed dramatically during the interim. This census thus aroused deep indignation among the Tajiks and provided the impulse for a separate Tajik republic in 1929. Because of the manner in which the territory was divided, however, 90 per cent of Tajikistan consisted of mountainous areas, while the Zerafshan Valley and other fertile areas were consigned to Uzbekistan.

The Uzbek minority in Tajikistan also regards itself as the victim of discrimination. The status of Uzbeks in northern Tajikistan has so deteriorated that they have begun to demand that their enclave be united with Uzbekistan.

Afghanistan

In addition, the Tajik people are divided by the border established in 1895 (by an Anglo-Russian treaty) that runs along the Piandzh River and leaves at least four million of their number in Afghanistan (about as many as are in Tajikistan itself). In the event of conflict between Tajikistan and Uzbekistan, the Tajiks in Afghanistan are almost certain to become involved.

Turkey

In considering the implications of a 'Greater Tajikistan', one must also reckon with Turkey's interests in Central Asia, and especially with the close ties it established with Uzbekistan in 1992. President Karimov has repeatedly declared his devotion to the 'Turkish model'. Because Turkey and Iran are now struggling to exert their influence over the region of Central Asia, a conflict involving Uzbekistan and Persian-speaking Tajikistan would have the potential for drawing in Turkey and Iran.

Russia

In any event, the Tajik–Uzbek conflict will inescapably affect the interests of Russia. At the most basic level, Uzbekistan and Moscow belong to a military-political bloc, the CIS. But beyond that, 400,000 Russians reside in Tajikistan. Moscow (and especially the Russian parliament, where the most nationalistic wing of the Russian political establishment reigns) will not remain indifferent to the fate of these Russians, who believe that a pro-Iranian Islamic regime would threaten them with physical destruction. On the other hand, the 'Afghan syndrome' is still so powerful in Russia that one can hardly imagine Moscow's leadership would dare risk an armed conflict with the Afghan *mudzhakhedy*.

Kyrgyzstan

Tensions in Tajikistan are mounting not only with respect to the Uzbeks, but also with another neighbour – Kyrgyzstan. The conflict, which has repeatedly erupted, centres on claims to contiguous stretches of arable land, which is a precious commodity in this mountainous area. Predictably, revanchist sentiments have mounted steadily since Moscow's hegemony over the region collapsed. When Tajiks were asked at the Bishkek conference in April 1992 whether Tajikistan renounced its territorial claims *vis-à-vis* Kyrgyzstan and other neighbours, the question itself provoked intense indignation among the Tajik representatives.[10]

The refusal to alter borders

Tribal wars over land and water have been fought in this arid region of the world from the most ancient times; the situation, however, has been made even more explosive by two contemporary factors. First is the decline of water resources and the exhaustion of soil fertility as the result of half a century of Moscow's economic policy in the region. Second is Moscow's arbitrary division of the former Bukhara and Kokand khanates into 'republics' of the Soviet Union – entities that have now become independent states in fact. These troubles are still further compounded by the threat that Kazakhstan will break up, if the majority in its northern areas (where the main ethnic group is Russian) opts for unification with the Russian Federation. All this makes clear why Central Asian heads of state issued a declaration on the inviolability of existing borders, and why they pushed so urgently to conclude treaties guaranteeing the status quo.

But the danger does not lie only in territorial conflict between states. No less ominous is the conflict within republics, between nationalities and between clans. Sometimes this conflict is provoked and fanned by political, religious and organized-crime groups that operate anonymously and behind the scenes. At the same time, however, conflict between nationalities includes much that is spontaneous, based on the impulsive behaviour of large masses of people who are guided by some common ideas and sentiments. The bloody excesses in Sumgait, Ferghana, Osh and elsewhere reveal a common feature: in each case the aggressive violence first emanated from an enraged crowd. Analysing the social-psychological dynamics of the massacre in Ferghana, the Uzbek writer Timur Pulatov provided this typical description:

> The crowd includes many diverse attitudes, which might seem mutually exclusive, but which nonetheless move in a single stream of energy – from the legal to the criminal. Judging from the massiveness and scale of the disorders, several moving forces were at work here. If at first separate, they gradually came together and fused. For all their fusion, ... to

some degree the interests of each are still visible. An openly brutal criminality, which led to murders, arson and plundering, was combined with demonstrations and meetings, where participants advanced economic and ecological demands. And all this received a kind of 'spiritual' coloration through the speeches of a small segment of the local intelligentsia, whose minds were filled with a potpourri of ideas from Lenin, newest slogans of perestroika and Islamic dogma that proved more powerful than common sense.[11]

These tragic events exposed the inability of local authorities and republic leaders to avert conflict or to control the situation once it developed.

The Russian out-migration

During the decades of Soviet rule, two very different societies developed within the Central Asian republics; now each lives according to its own economic laws and has its own life-style, culture and mentality. The only elements that they hold in common are the territory in which they reside and the regime that rules over them.

Uzbekistan is an example of these bifurcated societies. The aboriginal Uzbek population works primarily in the agrarian sector of the economy: 53 per cent of all working-age Uzbeks till the soil, compared with just 2.5 per cent of the Russian population. In the industrial sector the reverse obtains: only 11 per cent of Uzbeks work in industrial enterprises, compared with 33 per cent of the Russian labour force. Uzbeks constitute a minority among professionals, but dominate the positions in trade and government. Significantly, even though Uzbeks comprise a minority of the industrial labour force, they represent about 70 per cent of heads of industrial enterprises.

Following the collapse of the Soviet Union, out-migration by nonnative nationalities has created a vacuum in many key sectors of the economy, not only in Uzbekistan but in all the Central Asian members of the CIS. This is especially true in such important areas as industry, science, education and medicine. According to rough assessments by specialists in Tashkent and Ashkhabad (interviewed by this author during a visit to the region in October 1992), approximately 10 per cent of the non-native population is now leaving the region each year. The republics' leaders seek to do everything within their power to stem this outflow – official policy and propaganda attempt to persuade potential emigrés that they are not threatened by the native population. But daily experience teaches otherwise: non-natives encounter growing antagonism and menacing threats on public transport and in public places such as the market; they also feel that they suffer discrimination in promotions and salaries.

In these circumstances, assurances by republic leaders do little to assuage the fears and anxieties of the non-native population, which is seized with alarm and anticipates new conflicts. This is how Viktor Zapol'skii, an ethnic Russian and deputy to the Kyrgyzstan parliament, describes the situation:

> Anxiety fills the air. Distrust. The moral and psychological condition of Russians is in a state of extreme flux. Not only Russians, but also Kyrgyz have a sense of insecurity. So too the Dungan and the Koreans. By nine o'clock in the evening no one dares to venture onto the streets. Everyone has his guard up; everybody is ready to strike back.[12]

The reasons for concern are not hard to find. There are presently 3.2 million Russians in Central Asia (excluding the special case of Kazakhstan, where another 6.3 million live). These Russians are concentrated mainly in urban areas; indeed, in Kazakhstan and Kyrgyzstan they comprise over half the urban population. But Russians now find their jobs significantly more difficult as the language of the local nationality becomes the official tongue. In Tashkent, for example, less than 6 per cent of the Russians speak Uzbek fluently; 69 per cent cannot speak Uzbek at all.[13]

The economic factor

Nowhere are the paradoxes of the post-Soviet economy so starkly ingrained in the social fabric as in Central Asia. In the not-so-remote Soviet past, this region was the most backward of the empire, both economically and socially. Indeed, in terms of 'backwardness', Central Asia seemed to constitute a separate, definable unit.

Today, when analysts have ceased to regard the former Soviet Union as a unified whole, they should do the same with respect to Central Asia. Each of the new independent states is waging a fight for its survival; they have little desire to attend to larger, common interests. The so-called 'unifying factor' of Islam is of little consequence in the face of hard economic realities. Nor do the republics exhibit solidarity in defending their interests with Moscow, and the gulf separating the resource-rich (Uzbekistan and Turkmenistan) from the resource-poor (Kyrgyzstan and Tajikistan) has significantly widened.

The role of Turkmenistan

In April 1992 the Central Asian presidents met to formulate a unified policy and to establish a common market, steps that were to ensure a coordinated approach before the CIS summit in Tashkent the following month. The presidents certainly had an ambitious set of good intentions with regard to economic integration, including a joint investment fund, a regional bank, and a united front *vis-à-vis* the CIS.

All these plans quickly evaporated, however, when President Niazov of Turkmenistan openly refused to accept a common policy. At the meeting of eight Asian states – including Iran, Pakistan, Turkey and the five Central Asian countries – held in Ashkhabad on 9–10 May 1992, Niazov again took the same anti-integrationist position.

In Niazov's view, the region should not establish an inter-state regulatory structure along the lines of the European Commission; rather, the states should rely upon bilateral agreements, which in fact have already begun to appear. In the case of large regional projects involving all the Central Asian states (for example, transnational pipelines for natural gas and oil, or development of the industrial and transport infrastructure), the scale of construction and usage by each individual state will determine its share of financing and participation. In short, there should be no philanthropy: a state should not expect to live off the resources of its neighbours.

Turkmenistan has indeed acquired a strong voice in the region, selling gas to its Central Asian neighbours for hard currency and at high prices. Its fellow republics now owe substantial debts to Turkmenistan, which has begun to demand that its 'brothers of the faith' pay off their debts or see their gas deliveries cut off.

Thus, Turkmenistan (in an outlook shared by Uzbekistan) believes its survival depends upon foreign investments, not joint efforts within the framework of a Central Asian bloc, which, both countries believe, are more likely to work contrary to their own interests. As a result, these Central Asian states are hoping to establish ties with the Muslim world. According to newspaper reports in Moscow, Saudi Arabia has promised to grant Turkmenistan $10 billion in credits and investments for its oil and gas industries.[14] The exploration and development of new reserves will, in turn, expand the country's potential for export and hard-currency earnings.

In short, Turkmenistan – once the poorest of the republics – is well on its way to becoming the wealthiest state in the CIS, on a per capita basis. People in Turkmenistan proudly refer to their country as a 'second Kuwait'.

In a desire to imitate Turkmenistan, two other republics of Central Asia, Uzbekistan and Tajikistan, have sharply stepped up explorations for oil and gas. Some natural gas has been extracted in Uzbekistan since the early 1960s, and oil for a century. But the volume is relatively small, for Moscow attached little significance to the oil resources in Uzbekistan. Now liberated from the directives of Moscow, the Uzbek government has focussed its attention and resources on expanding oil exploration and has even invited in JEBCO Seismic (one of the most experienced and best-equipped foreign firms) for this purpose. The results were quickly evident, as deep drilling revealed the presence of oil reserves. Indeed, a powerful flow of oil has already begun to gush from a well in the Ferghana Valley. The government of Tajikistan, which hitherto has had no known oil or gas reserves, also intends to begin exploratory work. Representatives of the American business community visited Tajikistan in early 1992 in order to make plans for oil and gas exploration.

But all this lies in the future (perhaps the near future) and requires foreign capital. The present economic situation is exceedingly difficult throughout Central Asia, including Turkmenistan. These difficulties result from a host of factors, but especially from the collapse of the Soviet Union, which sundered traditional economic ties and left Russia itself in economic chaos. The industries that Moscow had moved to Central Asia were able to exist only by the grace of financial subsidies from the centre. In short it was Moscow, not Tashkent, that controlled expenditures for investment and individual consumption. With the collapse of the Soviet Union, as one Central Asian economist has remarked, the republics of Central Asia 'found themselves in the position of a baby who has lost its parents'.

The leaders of the Central Asian republics recognize the need to develop their own strategy for economic reform, but their mentality, education and practical experience are all rooted in the Soviet system. They have not yet succeeded in cutting the umbilical cord that links them to Moscow and they still look in that direction to see what measures are being propounded by economic strategists in the Russian Federation.

In addition, of course, all the Central Asian states share one problem: they are bound to Moscow in the sense that all still function within a single 'ruble zone'. Their financial and credit policies inevitably depend on Moscow, which, however, tends to act without heed to the situation in Central Asia. The Uzbek president, uncharacteristically, complained of this tendency:

> Moscow is not taking us into consideration in formulating its next measures. This is a cause of great concern for us. What will the reforms produce tomorrow? What will the Russian government reconsider next? And in what kind of situation will these developments put us?[15]

Not surprisingly, Central Asian states are now preoccupied with plans to create their own financial and monetary system.

Moscow as a defence shield

The economic concerns felt by Islam Karimov and his colleagues are probably heightened by a further factor: the awareness that their own political positions are anything but secure. Each of them is walking a tightrope amid complex social forces; none has the support of a cohesive, fully fledged party or a reliable social base; none can effectively implement whatever policies he might design. Central Asia has not yet generated coherent interest groups that can offer viable political support. People who voted for the presidents of the Central Asian republics do not feel any true allegiance to them and are easily mobilized, in moments of crisis and conflict, to join protests and movements against them. As a result, the leaders of Central Asia feel obliged to seek support wherever it can be found, even among former political adversaries. Hence they are the hostages of the clans, which offer conditional assistance and manipulate situations to serve their own narrow interests.

To be sure, the degree of instability is variable. Niazov of Turkmenistan, whose regime is essentially a dictatorship, has perhaps the most secure hold on power. The position of Uzbek President Karimov is relatively stable at present, but he is showing signs of nervousness, not only because of events in Tajikistan, but because of an intensifying dissident movement, the spectre of politically active Islam and dissatisfaction among the country's intellectual élite. The Kazakh president, Nazarbaev, who has a reputation as a skilful and sophisticated politician, has for the moment succeeded in restraining Kazakh nationalists and established a balance between the various ethnic groups – essential for peace in a republic where non-natives comprise 60 per cent of the population. However, Nazarbaev will find it difficult to maintain this fragile coalition. President Akaev of Kyrgyzstan has the closest ties with Moscow, which is both his greatest strength and greatest weakness.

Given their already unstable situations, the Central Asian presidents – even if willing to flirt with Islamic forces – recognize that only Russia can help defend their regimes against the menace of Islamic revival. This is not a figment of their imaginations; the ominous threat from Afghanistan looms on the horizon.

Thus, the decision to maintain the collective armed forces of the CIS is a critical factor in ensuring stability in the Central Asian region. This vital issue underpinned the various summit meetings convened in Central Asia during 1992. The Tashkent conference in May, for example, dealt with the creation of a regional security system, or a military-political bloc with Russia. At present, the Central Asian presidents are seeking to reach a compromise that would enable them to keep the troops of the former military districts on Central Asian territory, but would also satisfy nationalist sentiments by giving the troops a 'national' status. The Kazakh and Uzbek presidents have explicitly endorsed the model of NATO, and the other presidents have indicated their agreement as well. The plan is that each republic should have its own armed forces, but on a relatively small scale. The Uzbek military, for instance, is to number no more than 25,000 to 30,000 troops; the Turkmenistan army will have a mere 2000. In principle, these troops are to defend their state's fundamental laws and government institutions. In addition to these national military units, the CIS will then station a considerably larger number of forces in Central Asia.

Discussion of these military arrangements is being conducted under conditions of extreme secrecy. It seems likely, however, that the negotiations will probably deal with three key issues: first, the status and subordination of any military units on Central Asian soil; secondly, the quantity and nature of military hardware and facilities in Central Asia; and thirdly, the apportionment of costs to individual states. These difficult issues have not been resolved and the discussions are at this writing still under way.

Moscow and Muslims

The leaders of the Central Asian states are seeking to obtain as much economic aid from the Middle East as they can, while at the same time professing their desire to maintain their ties with Russia. The reason is clear: the Central Asian leaders need Moscow for defence, but Muslim capital for development; consequently, to use a Russian peasant saying, they are trying to milk two cows at once.

These leaders are certainly aware of the tensions and contradictions inherent in this two-edged policy. At the May 1992 meeting in Ashkhabad, attended by the Central Asian presidents and the heads of state from Iran, Turkey and Pakistan, the participants were careful to emphasize that their agreements were not directed against Russia. Nazarbaev of Kazakhstan declared, 'we are strengthening our relations with other countries, but our first priority is exclusive relations with Russia, with whom we foresee a continuation of close ties in our life and politics.' He added, with particular emphasis, 'I am approaching this meeting, and economic cooperation in general, without any religious bias whatsoever.'[16]

Nevertheless, the Islamic powers – Iran, Saudi Arabia and Turkey – have actively competed for influence in the area. Recently, for example, Iran has taken several steps to solidify its economic ties with Central Asia. Currently, it is developing plans to lay pipelines and railway tracks from Turkmenistan, thereby connecting Central Asia with Tehran. The Saudis have also been actively courting the leaders of Central Asia. The Saudi foreign minister visited Uzbekistan, Tajikistan and Turkmenistan in February 1992, and is reported to have discussed the possibilities of forming a single 'Organization for Economic Cooperation'. Obviously Riyadh is by no means indifferent to Iran's active involvement in the area and therefore has good grounds to give high priority to its relations with the states of Central Asia. Significantly, the member states of the Union for Cooperation – Saudi Arabia, Kuwait, the United Arab Emirates, Qatar, Bahrain and Oman – immediately recognized the independence of the Central Asian republics. These Gulf states represent a potent force in counterbalancing Iranian influence in the area.

Turkey's plans and activities have been still more ambitious. At the symbolic level, it has received the presidents of Central Asia with great pomp and fanfare during their visits to Ankara. The Turkish leadership, by all accounts, finds the idea of economic cooperation with Central Asian states extremely alluring. Concretely, Ankara is making plans to introduce a common identification document for Central Asia, which would confer the right of free travel and, more important, that of free business activity. In short, it is contemplating something like a 'Turkish Common Market' to enhance its ties to Central Asia. Moreover, Turkey has launched a host of other projects – including offers of financial assistance and the participation of Turkish firms in large-scale projects – to strengthen its hand in the area. Uzbekistan, for example, will receive $500 million in credits; the Turkish Bank, Eksim, will invest $75 million in the Kyrgyz economy.

In addition to bilateral contacts, Turkey has further proposed a new international consortium: a development bank for Central Asia, with headquarters in Ankara, which would raise and allocate capital for economic reform and development in Central Asia. Turkey's initiatives have elicited a positive response from the leaders in Central Asia. And this is not only because of the promise of financial aid: they see secular Turkey as a valuable counterweight to the influence of Iran and the intrusion of Islamic fundamentalism. As is evident in the following statement by President Karimov of Uzbekistan, the present leaders in Central Asia strongly prefer Turkey to Iran:

> When Uzbekistan, as an independent state, is faced with the dilemma of which course of development to choose and one that accords with our own interests, I can definitely say that the Turkish path of development is more acceptable for us [than the Iranian one], first and foremost because it leads to the development of a secular, civilized society. Of course, we must work out our own path of development, using Turkey as a model.[17]

In case any ambiguity remained, he added bluntly, 'the Iranian model will not work for us.'

But the question of Islam in Central Asia is not of interest only to the immediate area. The Atlantic Community and the United States are both increasingly fearful that Islamic fundamentalism is on the rise in Central Asia and will destabilize the whole region, with serious consequences for European and world security. Now that Moscow has lost control over its former colonies, it would be extremely short-sighted for Washington to leave unsupervised a region seething with passions, not to mention one possessing a military arsenal of considerable proportions. Such factors as the visit by US Secretary of State James Baker to the new states of Central Asia in early 1992 (followed by the visits of other Western officials), the inclusion of these states in the Conference on European Security and Cooperation, and the economic aid granted by the European Commission all testify to the

West's interest in the region and its refusal to cede Central Asia to the Muslim East.

But not only Islamic and Western powers are interested in Central Asia: during the spring and summer of 1992 China also undertook a flurry of diplomatic activity in the area. Leaders from four of the five Central Asian republics (Tajikistan being the exception) travelled to Beijing, where they were accorded an exceedingly warm reception. Although China granted only a modest amount of credits, its stock rose sharply in Central Asia. The visitors from Central Asia drew the conclusion that the Chinese model has much to commend it; its authoritarian power, with a firmly regulated market, seems far more appropriate for Central Asia than Moscow's 'shock therapy'. President Karimov declared in Beijing that he 'intends to study the Chinese experience in the most careful manner'.[18]

Implications for the West

It is all too easy to script a scenario for Central Asia that would make the tragedy of Yugoslavia pale in terms of human suffering and political repercussions; far more difficult is sketching out a policy by which Western states can help ensure stability in an area highly susceptible to acute social stress, Islamic fundamentalism and economic dislocation.

First and foremost, however, Western policy-makers must recognize the limits to their potential influence. In Central Asia, much of the traditional culture is preserved intact and is fundamentally different from that of the West. As a result, policies that work well in the West could erode rather than enhance stability in Central Asia, if those policies presuppose values and concepts utterly alien to traditional societies in the region.

Fortunately, this does not mean that the West must remain aloof from Central Asia. The countries there are manifestly in need of economic help. Of course, foreign investment will be particularly attracted to such projects as exploring for oil and gas resources; but it is no less important that water management be targeted. Indeed, investment in the latter could produce disproportionately generous pay-offs, as well as making a significant contribution to social and political stability, which are in turn preconditions for economic and political liberalization.

Thus, in approaching Central Asia, there is no need for the West to abandon democratic and free-market ideals, but there is a need for the West to take a gradualist and multi-faceted approach. Specifically, it will be important for Westerners to match their free-market assistance with the support of intellectual and cultural programmes, and these should involve both private and public organizations. Such a long-term 'propaganda-by-example' campaign will be the West's best hope for strengthening its bonds with Central Asia.

Notes

1. A version of this article was published in *Orbis*, xxxvii/1 (Winter 1993).
2. *Nezavisimaia gazeta*, 25 July 1992.
3. *Megapolis-Express*, 6 May 1992.
4. *Nezavisimaia gazeta*, 3 August 1992.
5. Ibid.
6. *Nezavisimaia gazeta*, 6 May 1992.
7. *Turkmenskaia iskra*, 25 August 1991.
8. *Nezavisimaia gazeta*, 6 May 1992.
9. *Nezavisimaia gazeta*, 15 May 1992.
10. *Nezavisimaia gazeta*, 25 April 1992.
11. T. Pulatov, 'Ferganskaya tragediya', *Druzhba narodov*, November 1990, p 233.
12. *Izvestiia*, 24 June 1992.
13. Iu. Arutiunian and L. Drobizheva, 'Russkie v raspadaiushchemsia Soiuze', *Otechestvennaia istoriia*, 1992, no. 3, p 14.
14. *Nezavisimaia gazeta*, 6 May 1992.
15. *Nezavisimaia gazeta*, 15 May 1992.
16. *Nezavisimaia gazeta*, 29 May 1992.
17. *Nezavisimaia gazeta*, 15 May 1992.
18. *Komsomol'skaia pravda*, 26 June 1992.

PART II

Forging New Relations with Russia and the Southern Tier

4

Tajikistan's Relations with Iran and Afghanistan

MURIEL ATKIN

Tajikistan and Iran have shown increased interest in each other since the last years of the Soviet Union's existence. However, that does not mean that the reasons for this interest are the same in both countries or that either sees the other as the linchpin of its foreign policy. Culture, economics, religion and politics all play a role in relations between these two countries. Tajikistan's interest in Iran has broad support but is tempered by wariness of subordination to Iran. Iranian interest in Tajikistan has a narrower base of support, being largely a function of government ambitions, but ranges more broadly in its objectives.

Some of the same factors which link Tajikistan to Iran link it to Afghanistan as well. However, this relationship is complicated by the fact that one virtually has to speak of 'Afghanistans' rather than a single entity, since the country is divided on many lines, including the political gulf between the supporters of the now-defunct Communist government in Kabul and the opposition to it, which is itself divided along ideological, religious and ethnic lines. Ethnicity divides not only the mujahedin but also the population as a whole between the traditionally dominant Pashtuns and all others, who are divided among themselves and include Tajiks as well as other Persian speakers.

The Tajiks of the former Soviet Union and the dominant nationality in Iran, the Persians, as well as the various Persian speakers in Afghanistan, are similar – though not identical – in language and other aspects of culture. That fact has been important to educated Tajiks in Central Asia as they manoeuvred for advantage in the context of Soviet nationality relations and began the process of building a viable independent state in the post-Soviet period.

Tajik national identity

Although the term 'Tajik' has a venerable tradition of use, not only in Central Asia, to differentiate Persian speakers from Turkic peoples, the use of that name to designate a nationality in a political sense is a twentieth-century creation of the Soviet regime. The subdivision of Soviet Central Asia during the 1920s and 1930s into republics defined in terms of nationality gave ethnicity greater weight in the politics as well as the social, cultural and economic concerns of the region than it had had in the past.

Elites of all the major Central Asian nationalities had to deal with the way the Soviets defined their national identity for them. This included categorizing all of them as 'formerly backward peoples', who owed their progress not only to Communist rule but also to the guidance of the more advanced Russians. In addition, the Soviet way of defining nationalities in Central Asia could be more inclusive in some cases than what had existed traditionally, as in the subsuming of tribal, local or even ethnic identities into larger national categories, but divisive in others, emphasizing the separateness of officially defined nationalities from kindred peoples inside or outside the Soviet Union. At the same time that Central Asian nationalities had to deal with the Kremlin's policy towards them, they also competed among themselves on many points, including political power, access to natural resources and educational opportunities. This competition has persisted and in many ways intensified in the post-Soviet era. In coping with nationality relations on both Union-wide and regional levels, educated Tajiks have made significant political use of their kinship to other Persian speakers for nearly half a century.

Tajiks and Persian culture

One of the most important ways in which many Tajiks in general as well as Tajikistan's Communist officials have sought to counter denigrating interpretations of their identity by either Moscow's officials or their Turkic neighbours has been to stress their links to the Persian past and present.[1] As a practical matter, before the political reforms of the closing years of the Soviet era, they often had to classify as Tajik anything Persian from beyond Central Asia to avoid provoking Moscow's wrath.[2] Less important than the accuracy of this designation is the way in which it has enabled Tajiks to evade, at least to some extent, Moscow's efforts to regulate the content of their culture. The crux of this interpretation is that Tajik–Persian culture is not 'formerly backward' or a mere addendum to the Turkic character of Central Asia but is highly developed and ancient in origin. In 1989 Tajikistan openly recognized the importance of Persian culture to its own when it enacted a law making Tajik the state language; the wording of the law treated Tajik and Persian as one language.[3] Non-Communist Tajik organizations have taken the same view of the kinship between the two.[4] In Tajikistan's first year of independence, it became commonplace to use both names for the language simultaneously and to use only the name 'Persian' where 'Tajik' would have been used in the past. Even in pushing for 'Persian and Tajik' to supplant Russian as the primary state language, advocates have looked to other formerly Soviet republics, not just Iran, for justification. For example, Latvia has been held forth as an example of a state with a language policy worth emulating.[5]

During the late Soviet and early post-Soviet periods, in Tajikistan as in many republics, nationalism has gained strength while simultaneously people see a need to develop new foreign contacts to supplement or replace the old centre–periphery relationship with Moscow. Thus, it is logical for Tajikistanis to pay particular attention to Iran since they hope that Iran will be useful to them in a variety of ways.

Much of the interest is cultural. Tajik nationalists perceived their people as having been deprived of much of their heritage by the Soviet decision in 1929, to abandon the modified Arabic alphabet in which Persian is written. The result has been, as Moscow intended and contemporary Tajik nationalists regret, to impede communication between Tajiks and fellow Persian speakers outside the Soviet Union. The only Persian-language writings to which Tajiks have subsequently had access are the few that the Soviets chose to publish in the new alphabet (briefly Latin, subsequently modified Cyrillic). This has been blamed for what is said to be the decline in the state of the Tajik language and culture.[6] The solution proposed to end this artificial isolation is a return to the use of the Arabic alphabet, as called for by the 1989 language law and endorsed by non-Communist nationalists.[7]

Iran has tried to play a major role in this change by providing teachers, printing materials and publications.

The ultimate effects of the new language policy remain to be seen but it will not necessarily provide the solution its proponents seek. Whatever the wisdom of the alphabet change in 1929, it occurred at a time when most Tajik speakers were illiterate; the current attempt to revive the use of the Arabic alphabet is directed at a population that is almost entirely literate – in the Cyrillic alphabet. Three years after the enactment of the new language law, a proponent of the use of the Arabic alphabet estimated that only 1 per cent of Tajikistan's population was literate in it.[8] The vast majority of Tajik-language publications are still in the Cyrillic alphabet. In the current alphabet reform efforts, Tajiks are trying to avoid exclusive dependence on Iran. For example, Tajikistan has sought Arabic-alphabet printing materials from Pakistan.[9]

Moreover, the change of alphabet and reliance on aid from Iran in accomplishing it poses particular problems for Tajik speakers. Vocabulary change has become a point of controversy as a consequence of the increased emulation of Iranian usage. Tajik nationalists look forward to dropping Russian loanwords and replacing them with words drawn from Persian speakers in Iran and Afghanistan.[10] However, the choice of replacements is not clear cut. Some of the vocabulary differences between Tajik and the Persian spoken elsewhere are not the consequence of borrowings from Russian but the survival of older Persian terminology and the incorporation of words from eastern Iranian or other regional languages. It remains to be seen whether Tajiks will be willing to discard these under the influence of Iranian Persian. There has been some controversy over this in the early independence period.[11]

In addition to Iranian–Tajikistani relations in language matters, the two countries have cooperated in various other cultural spheres since 1989. An agreement made in 1990 paved the way for Iran to send books and magazines of diverse content to Tajikistan.[12] Such materials have indeed begun to reach Tajikistan, accompanied by special exhibits of publications and a festival of Iranian films. Iranian officials visited Tajikistan in connection with such occasions. There have been visits in both directions by cultural and media figures as well as athletes. A few Tajikistanis have been sent to Iran for specialized education. Iranian programmes were broadcast on Tajikistan's state television network.[13]

Although Iran's religious ideology is reflected in its publications, not all of those sent to Tajikistan are primarily about Islam. For example, two of the magazines sent to Dushanbe for a press exhibit in August 1992 were *Symbols and Meaning in Cinema* (*Nishanehha va ma'na dar sinema*) and *Photographers and Photography* ('*Akasan va 'akasi*). Iran has launched a monthly magazine, *Oshno* (*Acquaintance*), aimed at Persian speakers in Central Asia. The first issue opened with a discussion of how much Iran has in common with the republics of Central Asia, including language, literature, the arts and history, as well as religion. That issue and the next contained articles on ancient (and therefore pre-Islamic) and medieval Persian and Arabic literature and on the writings of Ali Shariati (1933–77),[14] whose views were echoed in the ideology of Iran's Mojahedin-e Khalq, which was defeated in a violent power struggle with the Islamic Republican Party in the early 1980s.

Economic interests

Relations between Tajikistan and Iran involve economic as well as cultural matters. The two countries have considered the establishment of joint ventures, including to process cotton, the dominant element in Tajikistan's economy.[15] This is especially significant for Tajikistan because for decades almost all of its cotton crop was turned into finished goods by other republics of the former Soviet Union. With the passage of time and Tajikistan's emergence as an independent state, Iran has shown a willingness to increase the scale of its economic involvement in Tajikistan. It has offered the Dushanbe government $50 million in credits to buy Iranian-made equipment for use in light industry. Officials of the two countries also signed agreements on banking and commercial cooperation.[16]

As newly independent Tajikistan seeks solutions to its mammoth economic problems, some nationalists look to Iran for inspiration on the grounds that it is a country which, according to its own propaganda, had progressed from economic subordination to independence and strength.[17] However, that is not the sole or even dominant orientation in Tajikistan. There are also advocates of economic dealings with many countries, which differ on religious and cultural matters and on the kind of economic system they follow. These include Pakistan, Turkey, Saudi Arabia, the United States, Germany, Israel and China, as well as former Soviet republics.[18]

Diplomatic relations

The governments in both Dushanbe and Tehran have encouraged increased political and diplomatic contacts. The turning-point came in June 1990, when Tajikistan's vice-chairman of the Council of Ministers, Otakhon Latifi, headed a delegation from his country to Tehran for ceremonies marking the first anniversary of Ayatollah Ruhollah Khomeini's death. Two years later, Tajikistan participated more emphatically in similar observances by sending a delegation of 150 to Tehran. The occasion was not only ceremonial but was also used for negotiations with Iranian officials on the expansion of relations between the two countries. Iran signalled its desire to capitalize on the opportunity by paying the travel expenses of the entire delegation.[19]

A summit meeting between the two countries had to be cancelled because its start, scheduled for 25 August 1991, was overtaken by the attempted overthrow of Gorbachev a few days earlier and the ouster of Qahhor Mahkamov, simultaneously president of the republic and First Secretary of its Communist Party, in the post-coup backlash. Undeterred by the missed opportunity, Iran's foreign minister stopped briefly in Dushanbe in December 1991 while visiting several Soviet republics. He held talks with Tajikistan's new president, Rakhmon Nabiev, and other officials.[20]

The summit meeting finally occurred when Nabiev visited Iran on 28–30 June 1992. Religious solidarity was not the issue for this representative of the old, Brezhnevite politics. Both governments revealed the pragmatic uses each had for the other when they concluded agreements on cooperation in the spheres of economics, culture, and scholarship; they also planned to establish a governmental commission to promote further cooperation. An important part of the lesson Nabiev wanted Tajiks to draw from the visit, as he explained after his return, was how much they and the Iranians have in common. 'We and the Iranians,' he said, 'have a single language, a single faith, we have a single science and culture. Moreover, right up to the 15th century we and they lived in a single state.'[21]

Despite the enthusiasm for the Iranian connection, Tajikistan has maintained its practice of trying to maximize its options. Thus, the Nabiev delegation proceeded directly from Iran to Pakistan and there signed similar agreements.

After the demise of the Soviet Union, Iran became the first country to establish an embassy in Dushanbe, on 9 January 1992. On that occasion, the two countries declared their intention to establish aeroplane links between Dushanbe and Tehran, Mashhad and Tabriz.[22] In recognition of Iran's timeliness in opening its embassy, the street in Dushanbe on which it is located, formerly named for Maxim Gorky, was renamed Tehran Street. (In a sense, the new name has comparatively neutral connotations, associated with Iran in a generic sense rather than the Islamic Republic in particular. In contrast, the street on which the Soviet embassy in Tehran was located was long known as Stalin Street.) Remarks by members of the Iranian delegation sent to Tajikistan for the occasion reflected some of the Tehran regime's thoughts on the significance of relations between the two countries. Among the points highlighted by the Iranians were economic benefits and cultural cooperation. The latter included joint research projects on what an official described as their shared language, literature and history as well as Iran's provision of teaching materials to Tajikistan for instruction in the Arabic alphabet. A member of the Iranian delegation also stated that his country planned to open a bookstore, to be called al-Hoda (the path to salvation), to sell Iranian works on literature, history and culture.[23]

The second country to establish an embassy in Dushanbe was the United States. Although many countries recognized Tajikistan's independence soon after the breakup of the Soviet Union, few sent their own diplomatic representatives to Dushanbe in the first year of its independence.

For all Tajikistan's attention to developing its relations with Iran, neither its government nor its intelligentsia want the republic simply to fall into Iran's orbit. It is one thing for Tajiks to try to use contacts with Iran to strengthen their own position and quite another for them, at a time when nationalism is strong, to accept subordination to anyone else.

Tajiks' own version of the Iranian heritage

One of the ways educated Tajiks deal with this is by treating their heritage as deriving not only from the western Iranian Persians but also from the eastern Iranians indigenous to Central Asia. Initially, this owed much to the Kremlin's objective of maximizing the differences between peoples living within the Soviet Union and without. However, Tajik nationalists have taken up the point for their own reasons. This gives them another type of Iranian heritage in which to

take pride, especially in its Soghdian form.[24] (The Soghdians of ancient
Central Asia were active in commerce along the silk route and had a
highly developed culture.) One reflection of this symbolism is that a
group of Tajik reformers formed an organization in 1989 and named
it Sughdiana. Tajik nationalists' use of the eastern Iranian heritage
serves three political aims: to counter the Soviet line about their
former backwardness; to refute the arguments of some of their Turkic
neighbours that the Turkic peoples are the original Central Asians
while the Tajiks arrived only after the Arab conquest; and to counter
the tendency of many Persian speakers in Iran to regard Tajiks (to the
extent that they notice them at all) as mere provincials on the periphery of the Perso-Iranian world. This exploitation of the Tajiks' eastern Iranian links extends to recent gestures by the government in
Dushanbe to allow speakers of eastern Iranian languages living in
contemporary Tajikistan greater latitude to use their own languages.[25]
(For decades these peoples were allowed access to education and the
mass media only in Russian or Tajik.)

The Tajiks' concern not to be relegated to the margins also appears
in the way they look at the Persian component of their heritage. The
accepted Tajik view of the revival of Persian as a literary language
after the disruption caused by the Arab conquest is that it took place
not in what inhabitants of the contemporary Iranian state think of as
the Persian heartland – the Iranian plateau – but was focussed in
Central Asia and adjoining parts of Iran and Afghanistan; only after
this revival was well under way did literary Persian spread south-west
across the Iranian plateau.[26]

Some of the ways Tajiks now look at their Persian heritage do not
coincide with the views of the more militant Islamicizers in Iran. One
aspect of this is the interest in pre-Islamic Persian civilization. For
example, Tajik nationalists praise the Zoroastrian religion as a Tajik
contribution to world civilization and praise Zoroastrian texts, among
other reasons, as an embodiment of Tajik civilization and an ethical
guide.[27] The Tajiks' attention to their Persian heritage certainly includes ample discussion of cultural figures who lived in Islamic times,
but not all of them represent views of which the Tehran government
would approve. Among these figures is Ahmad Kasravi, a historian
noted for his criticism of religion in general and Shi'ism in particular,
who was assassinated by a Shi'ite militant in 1946. (Ayatollah
Khomeini also disapproved of Kasravi.) A particularly striking example
of this Tajik enthusiasm for dissident Persian voices is the attention

paid to Nasiri Khusrow (1004–c. 1072), a Central Asian who was important as both a Persian literary figure and a proselytizer for Isma'ili Islam, which is quite different from the Imami Shi'ism which predominates in the Islamic Republic of Iran. In addition to the increased and positive public discussion of his intellectual contributions, the pedagogical institute in the city of Qurghonteppe was renamed in his honour in 1992.[28]

The Islamic connection

Even though the majority of Tajikistan's population is Muslim and aware of its Iranian heritage, that does not guarantee that it will emulate the Islamic politics of Iran. In addition to the fact that the Tajiks distinguish between Persian cultural pride and Iranian hegemony, the Tajiks' *de facto* reclamation of Persian culture and history began roughly half a century ago, long before politically militant Islam came to power in Iran. There is no reliable evidence about the views of the vast majority of ordinary inhabitants of Tajikistan about Islamic politics, whether along Iranian, Afghanistani, Saudi, Pakistani or other lines. In the absence of truly free elections or reliable public opinion surveys, or even a successful coup with broad-based support, there can be only speculation based on selected anecdotes and rumours. Many Tajiks and other indigenous inhabitants of the republic consider Islam valuable in a cultural or religious sense or both. However, the tendency of some Western observers to equate being a Muslim with being an Islamic 'fundamentalist' demonstrates only the observers' confusion. Similarly, the stories in the Soviet and post-Soviet media about Islamic conspiracies to establish an Islamic state are, by themselves, proof mainly of the fears and propaganda methods of their authors.

Some Tajiks think that the fact that Iran's Islamic regime is Shi'ite while most Tajiks are Sunni minimizes their susceptibility to Iranian religious influence. At least some Tajiks admire Iran in a general sense, as a country where Islam is practised freely (in contrast to conditions in Tajikistan until the Soviet collapse) without wanting to emulate the specific Islamicizing politics of the Iranian government. One vocal Tajik nationalist who is also something of an Islamicizer has used an Iranian precedent to legitimate the form of government he advocates for a post-communist Tajikistan – but draws his example from pre-revolutionary Iran. He wants the country to be governed by an executive and a *majlis* (legislature) but with a president rather than a shah filling the role of the executive.[29] Tajikistan's most powerful religious figure, its *qadi*, Akbar Turajonzoda, stated repeatedly that most inhabitants of the republic do not want to emulate Iran's Islamic republic. For example, in an interview with a German newspaper, he contended that Iran could not possibly be a paradigm for Tajikistan:

> The conditions are completely different. In Iran there was never a Communist Party in power. The 70-year predominance of atheism has had an effect on our country.... Today the people are afraid of an Islamic regime, and why should one make the people afraid?... The people understand religion in their way: they do not want the women to wear the chador [veil] again and to sit at the hearth, they reject polygamy, and they are afraid that human rights will be restricted if Islam comes to power. This at least is what they have been taught. Psychologically, they are not ready to support an Islamic state.[30]

He made this point not only for foreign consumption but also to a domestic audience of opponents of the Nabiev regime, as in his remarks to demonstrators in Dushanbe during the political crisis there in spring 1992.[31]

Similarly, one of the leaders of Tajikistan's Islamic Revival Party asserted that the republic would find its own gradual path to an Islamic state rather than follow the Iranian example.[32] Although the concern of the United States about the destabilizing threat of Islamic 'fundamentalism' is known in Tajikistan, one of the founders of the Islamic Revival Party there, Davlat Usmon, deputy prime minister in the republic's short-lived coalition government of 1992, publicly expressed good wishes towards the United States and advocated the growth of mutually beneficial relations between the two countries.[33]

While Islamicizers in Tajikistan have often, though not always, talked moderation, the first president of the newly independent republic, Rakhmon Nabiev, who had no intention of letting an Islamic state supplant communist rule, played on religious links to Iran for reasons of his own. In the face of growing opposition to him among his predominantly Muslim fellow countrymen, Nabiev tried to associate himself with Iran's Islamic republic. For example, he sought to impress Tajikistanis with the fact that Iran was the first foreign country he visited as president, that he was received by high-ranking Iranian officials, that he visited the 'blessed grave of Imam Khomeini', and that he recognized the existence of an Islamic bond between the two countries.[34] Significantly, when he made that trip he had intended to include Qadi Turajonzoda and the head of the Islamic Revival Party, Muhammad Sharif Himmatzoda, in his delegation. However, neither man chose to accompany him.[35] On 10 May 1992, when demonstrators in Dushanbe seemed on the verge of toppling his government, Nabiev was the first of the republic's political figures to ask Iran's President Ali Akbar Hashemi Rafsanjani for help.[36]

Iran's interest in Tajikistan

In contrast, when officials in Iran look towards Central Asia, including Tajikistan, they see a region which they think should not only be orientated towards Iran but should also defer to its leadership. This is not an issue of particular concern to large sections of the Iranian public but is the policy of the regime. Such an approach reflects both ideological ambitions and the more conventional diplomatic and economic interests of the Iranian state. On one level, the Islamic Republic of Iran has broadcast its message by radio to Central Asia since the early years of the republic's existence; on another level, the Tehran regime has also increased its efforts to develop relations through state-to-state channels since the late 1980s.

Underlying Tehran's activity in this area is the presumption of a right to lead expressed in both religious and cultural terms. The foremost example of the religious justification found expression in Khomeini's letter (1 January 1989) to Gorbachev. Khomeini praised Gorbachev for making reforms and urged him to carry the process much further. The Ayatollah's fundamental message was that Islam held the solution to the Soviet Union's problems. Now that the bankruptcy of Marxism had been demonstrated, he argued, Gorbachev ought not turn to the West for answers for it could provide none. Instead, he ought to learn about Islam because its 'sublime and world-encompassing values...can be a means for the well-being and salvation of all nations'.[37] Khomeini counselled the Soviet Union to look to Iran for guidance because Iran, 'as the greatest and most powerful base of the Islamic world, can easily help fill-up [sic] the ideological vacuum of your system'.[38] As regards those citizens of the Soviet Union who are already Muslims, Khomeini praised Gorbachev for allowing them religious freedom and depicted Iran as the fitting advocate of their interests, for 'We regard the Muslims of the world as the Muslims of our own country, and we always regard ourselves as partners in their fate.'[39] Thus, Khomeini's message was not only about the primacy of Islamic values in worldly affairs but also Iran's role as the arbiter of what Islam is and as the leader of Muslims everywhere. Obviously, this view of Iran's importance is not shared by all Muslims in all countries, including those of the former Soviet Union.

The Iranian leadership has continued to voice similar opinions since Khomeini's death in June 1989. For example, President Rafsanjani, when meeting with the Tajikistani delegation to the June 1990 memorial for Khomeini, highlighted Iran's interest in dealings with Tajikistan and other Soviet republics with Muslim populations.[40] He spoke again of the importance of the Islamic link between such former Soviet republics and Iran in February 1992, when representatives of the five Central Asian republics and Azerbaijan met in Tehran with officials from Iran, Turkey and Pakistan to discuss economic cooperation.[41] Rafsanjani and Iran's foreign minister, Ali Akbar Velayati, have also emphasized the cultural similarities between Iran and the republics to the north as grounds for closer relations.[42]

Iran has openly involved itself in Tajikistan's religious affairs. For example, it funded mosque construction there and supported Tajikistanis travelling via Iran to Saudi Arabia to make the *hajj* in 1992. Its perennial rival, Saudi Arabia, has provided similar aid.[43] Iran's ambassador in Dushanbe, Ali Ashraf Mujtahidi Shabistari, declared that the Tajiks' Iranian culture was only perfected under the influence of Islam and that Tajiks and Iranians are linked by the 'single title of Muslim Iranian', having the 'same race, same culture, same history, same language and same religion'.[44] The foreword to the first issue of a magazine Iran began publishing for Tajiks in formerly Soviet Central Asia ranked Islam prominently among the things Iran had in common with that region.[45]

For all Iran's use of religious rhetoric, much of its interest in Tajikistan and other republics to the north concerns worldly matters such as diplomacy and trade. For example, Iran's objectives at the meeting in Tehran in February 1992 were to obtain the support from other Muslim countries, including the former Soviet republics, for Iran's stance on various diplomatic issues and to promote economic relations with the Central Asian republics, with an eye to direct competition with Saudi Arabia's activities there.[46] Even when Iranian officials discuss their special interest in the Muslim republics of the former Soviet Union, what they see in them is not only co-religionists but also factories, cheap labour and railway lines.[47]

Despite Iran's cultural and economic undertakings in Tajikistan and the speed with which it established an embassy there, much of Tehran's attention north of the border is directed to other republics. In recent years, Iran has sought a *modus vivendi* with the government in Moscow, whether that of the Soviet Union or the Russian Republic. Iranian concerns are related to such issues as the pursuit of diplomatic support for Iran's foreign policy objectives, especially as regards Iraq and Afghanistan, economic cooperation and the purchase of military hardware. Tehran has also concluded agreements with some of the successor republics that are not predominantly Muslim. For example, it has made agreements with Ukraine and Moldova for the sale of oil and natural gas.[48] Moscow has shown a similar interest in relations with Tehran.[49]

Iran looks north

Tajikistan is not Iran's highest priority among the southern-tier republics. Azerbaijan is particularly important to Tehran. Turkmenistan, with its long common border with Iran, is also a special object of Tehran's attentions, especially with regard to cross-border trade and docking rights for Iranian commercial vessels at Turkmenistan's ports. Iran has voiced enthusiasm for an improbably costly and ambitious project in Central Asia: to build additional track to join the Chinese, Russian, Central Asian and Iranian rail networks. The hope is that this will lead to the development of a lucrative cargo route across Iran to world markets, in the spirit of the silk route of antiquity. Turkmenistan and Khazakhstan are crucial to the development of this route; Tajikistan is peripheral to it.[50] (Furthermore, the economic soundness of the entire project is questionable. Iran's railways are not built to withstand a heavy volume of cargo. Its pace of railway construction does not augur well for its 'silk route' project. The railway, intended to link the important south-eastern city of Kerman with the key gulf-coast port of Bandar 'Abbas, had been under construction but unfinished for seven years by the time the new undertaking was proposed in 1992. The highways of Iran, Turkmenistan and Uzbekistan are more promising as routes for hauling cargo.[51] However, Iran has thus far shown less enthusiasm for the development of this more readily achievable alternative.)

The terms in which Iran sees itself as being the natural leader for largely Muslim republics north of the border could limit those republics' willingness to follow. The Tehran view is Iranocentric and risks alienating those who are supposed to heed its appeal. For example, the international coalition of Muslim states which Iran tried to persuade the Central Asian republics and Azerbaijan to join at the meeting in Tehran in February 1992 was predicated on Tehran's assumption that Iran's interests in international affairs were identical with all Muslims' interests.[52] Similarly, Foreign Minister Velayati said, regarding the nationalist upsurge in the Central Asian republics in general, that 'illustrious figures of the history of Islam, Iran, and civilization are the symbols of the revival of the national identity of these republics'.[53] To describe the situation in those particular terms implies that Iran, as the self-designated spokesman for Islam and embodiment of Iranian culture, ought to define the content of other people's nationalist movements.

This is not an isolated slip of the tongue but part of a habitual attitude towards Central Asia. The same assumption has been manifest on other occasions. For example, when Iran's ambassador to Tajikistan said that 40 to 60 per cent of the vocabulary of the Turkic languages of Central Asia was Persian he revealed an impolitic indifference to the strength of national pride among various Turkic peoples of the region.[54] The issue is not what is philologically accurate. After years of being told how much the Turkic peoples of Central Asia were beholden to one outside power, they are not now eager to be instructed in their debt to another.

Tajik attitudes towards Afghanistan

The formerly Soviet Tajiks' attitudes towards Afghanistan are similar in many ways to their attitudes towards Iran but are complicated by the war the Soviet army fought in support of the communist regime in Kabul. During the war years, the proximity of and the cultural similarities between Tajikistan and Afghanistan made the former useful to Moscow as it strove to solidify communist rule in the latter. Moscow sent Soviet Tajiks (and other Central Asian peoples) to work in Afghanistan's government, educational and scholarly systems. It sent publications from Tajikistan to Afghanistan. It used Tajikistan as an example of the benefits of communist rule to show delegations from Afghanistan and as a place to educate young Afghanistanis. Cultural exchanges between these two republics continued through-out the war years. Tajiks from Tajikistan served in the Soviet military in Afghanistan from the invasion to the Soviet withdrawal (despite repeated stories that Tajiks and other Soviet Central Asians were recalled from Afghanistan soon after the invasion).[55]

This last point is a painful issue for some Tajiks. Criticism of the war began to be heard publicly in Tajikistan when the reaction against the failed hard-liners' coup in Moscow in August 1991 created a more favourable climate for the expression of dissenting opinions in Tajikistan. In that context, a few people asserted that Tajiks ought not to have fought in Afghanistan. Their argument was based on ethnic, not religious, kinship. To them, the war amounted to fratricide.[56] Given the subsequent efforts of the communist old guard to reestablish its monopoly of power in Tajikistan and to squelch dissent there, it is difficult to ascertain how many people regard the Afghanistan war in the same terms as the outspoken few.

Tajik nationalists are interested in Afghanistan for the same kinds of cultural reason that attract them to Iran, especially in the areas of language and literature.[57]

In the late Soviet and early independence periods, Tajikistan has begun direct dealings with Afghanistani officials – communist and non-communist, central and regional. The then-communist government of Afghanistan established a consulate in Dushanbe. The two countries have sought to foster trade and joint business ventures.[58] While a communist government remained in power in Kabul, it favoured cooperative undertakings with its Dushanbe counterpart in the areas of education, scholarship and publishing. There was talk of sending young men from Tajikistan to study in madrasas in northern Afghanistan.[59] That idea has considerable practical significance for Tajikistan in the late Soviet and early post-Soviet years. Decades of Soviet policies which drastically restricted access to Islamic instruction have left contemporary Tajikistan and the other Central Asian republics with a wholly inadequate infrastructure for religious education at a time when interest in Islam is more extensive and open than it has been for nearly 70 years.

The Mujahedin and Tajikistan's opposition

The degree of Afghanistan's disruptive influence on Tajikistan, in the form of Islamic 'fundamentalist' propaganda, arms smuggling and ethnic separatism, are controversial subjects on which there is more propaganda than reliable information. Some of the least credible information comes from certain supporters of the old Soviet order who are biassed against Islam and Muslims. A prime example of this obsessive hostility is V.V. Petkel', who was head of the KGB in Tajikistan between 1985 and 1991; he warned that Tajikistan was threatened by hostile foreign forces, above all in Afghanistan.[60] Given that allegations like these come from people who are not disinterested observers, the cunning and extensive subversion they depict ought not to be accepted unquestioningly.

The KGB and other elements of the old Soviet order have been accustomed to deny that there could be any legitimate domestic causes of discontent and to shift the blame to foreign subversion. Some hardliners have even resorted to the much-used Soviet propaganda theme which exploited the trauma of the Second World War in order to warn against an external threat to newly independent Tajikistan.[61] Another recent example of this hoary tradition of stirring up fears of an external threat could be found in a place where Afghanistan and Islamic 'fundamentalism' could not possibly be at issue – Belarus. The head of the KGB there told the press that hundreds of agents of the CIA, various European countries and former Soviet republics have infiltrated Belarus and are trying to recruit its inhabitants by offering them hard currency.[62] Even the Russian-controlled border guards in Tajikistan branded as false a *Pravda* report of a foray into Tajikistan by Afghanistani mujahedin.[63] In fact, according to Tajikistan's Ministry of Foreign Affairs, during the Najibullah era in Afghanistan (1986–92), government forces occasionally dropped bombs on Tajikistani soil when fighting the mujahedin but Tajikistan's government portrayed the incidents as mujahedin attacks.[64]

There are indications that some inhabitants of Tajikistan are impressed in a general sense by the victory of Afghanistan's mujahedin over the Najibullah government. However, it does not necessarily follow that most Tajikistanis draw their ideology from or are members of any particular mujahedin organization. To exaggerate the influence of the mujahedin in Tajikistan is to imply that its inhabitants have no independent perception of their own interests and grievances and are no more than the pawns of outside forces. In any event, the mujahedin organizations are divided among themselves over what the Islamicization of government ought to entail as well as over the struggle for power. They are also associated to a considerable degree (though not exclusively) with different nationalities among Afghanistan's population. Afghanistan's Tajiks are most influential in the

Jami'at-i Islami, which controls much of northern Afghanistan, including part of the area across the border from Tajikistan. Its bitter rival in ideological, political and personal terms is the Hizb-i Islami, in which Pashtuns predominate and which has its power base in more southerly parts of Afghanistan. The Hizb-i Islami has continued its fight against the Jami'at-i Islami in the era of post-communist coalition government in Kabul.

During 1992, when the political power struggle in Tajikistan escalated into civil war, the Najibullah regime in Kabul fell, and the groups arrayed against it fought among themselves for power, rumours increased of Afghanistani involvement in Tajikistan's upheaval. When word reached Tajikistan of the fall of Afghanistan's communist government in April 1992, demonstrators in Dushanbe who opposed their own communist government welcomed this news and found it encouraging in a general sense. However, opposition spokesmen expressly denied that there was any specific link between the developments in Afghanistan and the anti-government demonstrations underway in Dushanbe in April and May 1992.[65]

One particularly common rumour about connections between the Tajikistani opposition and the Afghanistani mujahedin is that the Hizb-i Islami, the most worrisome of the Afghanistani groups, with its radical Islamicizing policies and its readiness to use violence against fellow Afghanistanis, whether civilians or members of rival organizations, is the principal meddler in Tajikistan's affairs. The Hizb was alleged to be arming Islamic militants in Tajikistan during the power struggle in 1992, especially members of the Islamic Revival Party. This is the version of events that the Nabiev regime certainly wanted people to believe.[66] The allegation is part of the propaganda the communist old guard used for months in the face of mounting opposition. The message was that the old guard offered the only alternative to rule by Islamic extremists; that line also tried to obscure the extent to which Nabiev's heavy-handed rule intensified the opposition to him.

The emphasis on the Hizb-i Islami's role was denied by the head of Tajikistan's legislature (and briefly acting president), Akbarshoh Iskandarov, one of the younger generation of communist politicians who was more willing to cooperate with opposition groups. The presence in Tajikistan of Afghanistani mujahedin of any party was also denied by Lieutenant-Colonel A. Jalilov of the border guards.[67]

There is one way in which the Tajikistani opposition has undeniably looked to Afghanistan for help, for they have done so openly.

However, this involves no cross-border subversion. In May 1992, as the confrontation between pro- and anti-Nabiev forces in Dushanbe threatened to turn into a bloodbath, spokesmen for two opposition parties held a press conference to call for outside assistance to halt the violence. They asked for such help not only from Afghanistan but also from Iran and the United Nations. The parties involved were the Islamic Revival Party and the Democratic Party of Tajikistan. The latter advocates full religious freedom for Muslims and others but does not endorse the creation of an Islamic state.[68]

Cross-border Tajik links

One kind of speculation about the political implications of the presence of Tajiks on both sides of the border focuses on whether a new state might be created to unite them. At the time of the crisis in Dushanbe in May 1992, that prospect was discounted by political figures there. The perception in Dushanbe was that Akhmed Shah Masud, the guerrilla leader of the Jami'at-i Islami, who became a hero during the war in Afghanistan and Minister of Defence in its first post-communist government, is not interested because the power struggle within Afghanistan is a far higher priority for him.[69] In the opinion of Qadi Turajonzoda, who has opposed the communist old guard since the republic's crisis of spring 1992, Masud's reputation was not widespread in Tajikistan by the time the mujahedin coalition came to power in Afghanistan and few outside the intelligentsia realized that he was a fellow Tajik.[70] (Reportedly he is better known in Samarkand, Uzbekistan, from which his forebears moved to Afghanistan.)[71] During the political upheavals of 1992, Turajonzoda did not see the creation of a new state uniting Tajikistan with Afghanistan and Iran as a necessary consequence of the cultural and religious kinship of the inhabitants of those lands.[72]

According to an official Tajikistani source, there were Afghanistanis who crossed into Tajikistan in the spring of 1992, or attempted to do so, not because they are mujahedin intent on fomenting revolt but because they were soldiers who had served the communist regime in Kabul and, after its fall, sought safety for themselves and their families across the border.[73] Similarly, unofficial anecdotes indicate that some people (the total number is unknown), presumably associated in some way with Afghanistan's communist regime, crossed into

Tajikistan to escape the turmoil at home but then went on to settle in Moscow.[74]

Tajik refugees in Afghanistan

The escalation of the civil war and the general breakdown of order in southern Tajikistan in late 1992, followed by the mayhem unleashed on the populace by victorious communist militiamen, caused an estimated half million people to flee their homes. Some sought safety elsewhere in the republic or in other former Soviet republics. According to the United Nations High Commissioner for Refugees, some 50,000 to 60,000 people fled to northern Afghanistan by the beginning of 1993, crossing the Amu Daria by whatever improvised means they could. An unknown number, perhaps 200, drowned in the attempt.[75]

Russian border guards claimed many of those who crossed into Afghanistan did so under compulsion. According to General Vitalii Gritsan, commander of the border guards in Tajikistan, 'Islamic guerrillas' forced refugees to go to Afghanistan at gunpoint and killed a few who refused.[76] However, refugees gave a markedly different account to Western reporters who saw them in Afghanistan. Their stories did not refer to intimidation tactics by 'Islamic guerrillas' but stressed the campaign of terror waged upon civilians by communist militia members. Their version of events was that communists killed men, women and children on the merest suspicion that the victims or their families sympathized with the Islamic Revival Party; the militia members also looted and destroyed homes. The attacks refugees suffered on their way to the border came from the communists. Many people who reached Afghanistan arrived wounded, whether in battle or in the process of trying to cross to Afghanistan.[77]

Conditions for Tajikistani refugees in Afghanistan were arduous. Some were sheltered by local families or tried to survive as best they could on the land near the border, but most crowded into refugee camps set up by international relief agencies in northern Afghanistan (especially near the cities of Mazar-i Sharif and Kunduz). Despite the efforts of those agencies, shelter from the winter's cold was inadequate, the diet was meagre, and infectious diseases spread rapidly in the camps.[78] By early 1994, roughly half the refugees had returned to Tajikistan. A small proportion of the refugees, perhaps between 3000 and 5000, formed armed groups aided by Afghan mujahedin, especially the Hizb-i Islami, and staged cross-border raids.[79]

Border troubles

Even if there was no elaborate conspiracy by elements in Afghanistan to topple the Nabiev regime, without a doubt the border between Afghanistan and Tajikistan was no longer well patrolled by 1992 and had been only slightly more controlled in the immediately preceding years. For the first five months of 1992 an official source put the known number of border violations above 250, roughly twice as many as in the first half of 1991.[80] Border guard units were severely undermanned, especially in positions that required some expertise; they were also undersupplied. Inhabitants of the Tajikistan side of the border were hostile to the guards' efforts.[81] According to official estimates, the border guards were at 28 to 40 per cent of their intended strength by the summer of 1992.[82] (Russia and to a lesser degree Uzbekistan, Khazakhstan and Kyrgyzstan subsequently sent in some reinforcements.)

Not all of the border violations are political; smuggling and raiding for plunder have also increased. The significance of these economically motivated border crossings was reflected in the fact that Tajikistan's Cabinet of Ministers listed smuggling first among the kinds of border violations in its declaration on the troubles in that zone. The cabinet also promised to try to ease the problem by increasing the means for people who live along the border to conduct legal cross-border trade.[83] The contraband travels in both directions and includes, according to Colonel P.I. Kuniakov of the border guards, watches, athletic shoes, drugs, gold dust, firewood, currency and stolen property.[84] Along the eastern part of the border, in the Badakhshan area, Tajikistan negotiated an agreement with local Afghanistani leaders in the summer of 1992 which provided, in part, for the latter to curb the smuggling of drugs and arms into Tajikistan; in return Tajikistan undertook, among other things, to permit inhabitants of the area to enter Tajikistan for medical treatment.[85]

Some of the border violators do indeed carry weapons. Border guards have identified a few of these people as Afghanistanis.[86] However, other reports, including from the border guards, indicate that many of those trying to bring weapons northwards during the turmoil of 1992 were Tajiks from Tajikistan who went to Afghanistan and then tried to return home.[87] It is important to note that not all the weapons that have travelled this route are intended for opposition groups. Supporters of the communist old guard in the southern province of Kulob are also alleged to have obtained arms from Afghanistan, seemingly without interference from the border guards.[88] At least some of the cross-border arms acquisitions are business transactions rather than being based primarily on ideological or ethnic cooperation. For example, in October 1992 a group of people was alleged to have stolen a helicopter in southern Tajikistan for an arms-buying trip to Afghanistan; they brought carpets with them to trade for the weapons.[89] Most of the weapons acquired by factions in Tajikistan's civil war came not from across the border but from Russian military units stationed in the republic.

Cross-border raids became a more serious issue after the communist hard-liners' victory in the civil war at the end of 1992. The most publicized incident occurred on 13 July 1993, when an armed band alleged to number some 400 men attacked an outpost of Russian border guards, killing 25 of them and local civilians before withdrawing to Afghanistan.[90] Not all the cross-border attacks went from south to north. Russian border guards periodically directed rifle and artillery fire at the Afghanistan side of the border, producing an unknown number of civilian casualties.[91]

Not all dealings were acrimonious between Tajikistan, under the fragile coalition government which tried to rule the republic for part of 1992, and Afghanistan, under its uneasy coalition government which came to office in April 1992. In July of that year Akbarshoh Iskandarov (then head of Tajikistan's legislature) made an official visit to Afghanistan's new president, Burhanuddin Rabbani, head of the Jami'at-i Islami. The two agreed to the establishment of diplomatic relations between their countries; Afghanistan undertook to combat the smuggling of drugs and weapons into Tajikistan.[92] The next regime in Tajikistan, one dominated by the communist old guard, devoted most of its attention after coming to power at the end of 1992 to defeating its domestic opposition but it, too, made some tentative gestures towards a *modus vivendi* with the Rabbani government.

Conclusions

Newly independent Tajikistan faces a host of challenges, both domestic and external. Although many advocates of change in the republic wanted it to have much more autonomy within the former Soviet Union, few of the politically active people at any point on the ideological spectrum expected Tajikistan to become a separate state so soon. They hoped, over-optimistically, that Moscow would help them meet a variety of needs in economic, environmental, security and other spheres. With the collapse of the Soviet state, Tajikistan had to look abroad to fill that void. Political and economic groups in Iran, Afghanistan and many other countries have their own ambitions to play a role in Tajikistan. That does not guarantee that the republic's inhabitants will respond positively to all such efforts. The kinds of practical assistance, not rhetoric, offered them by foreign countries will surely affect the Tajikistanis' orientation, as may the perceived support that foreign countries gave one side or another in the bitter power struggle there. Tajikistan's social and economic problems are so serious that whoever rules there will have to seek outside help. However, it is an oversimplification to assume that Tajikistan must necessarily fall into another country's orbit because of the cultural and religious similarities between them.

Notes

Part of the research for this study was done with the generous support of the National Council for Soviet and East European Research.

1. 'Ustav i programma organizatsii' Rastokhez' (Vozrozhdenie) Tadzhikskoi SSR', *Rastokhez*, 1990, no. 5, p 3; 'Az rui aqli solim', *Adabiyot va san"at*, 16 August 1990, p 1; 'Izhoroti ishtirokkunandagoni konferentsiyai ta"sisi sozmoni umumimillii tojikon "Mehr"', *Sogdiana*, 1990, no. 3, p 1; 'Pora obnovleniia', *Sogdiana*, 1990, no. 1 (February) p 1; 'Obshchestvo v 1989 godu', *Sogdiana*, 1990, no. 1, p 1; 'Na ruinakh ambitsii', *Sogdiana*, 1990, no. 1, p 3.

2. M. Atkin, 'Religious, National, and Other Identities in Central Asia', in *Muslims in Central Asia*, ed. J.-A. Gross (Durham, NC: Duke University Press, 1992), pp 55–6.

3. 'Qonuni zaboni Respublikai Sovetii Sotsialistii Tojikiston', *Tojikistoni soveti*, 30 July 1989, p 1.

4. 'Pora obnovleniia'; 'Na ruinakh ambitsii'; 'Izhoroti'; 'Ustav'.

5. 'Porlumoni Latviya qonuni zabonro digar kard', *Jumhuriyat*, 3 April 1992, p 1.

6. G. Faizullozoda, 'Nohamvorihoi roh', *Omuzgor*, 15 August 1989, p 5; S. Halimsho, 'Darakhti jovidonkhirad', *Adabiyot va san"at*, 24 August 1989, p 5; A. Istad, 'Ba ki ta"na mezanem?', *Tojikistoni soveti*, 1 July 1989, p 3; 'Muzokira az rui ma"ruzai Dar borai loihai qonuni zaboni respublikai sovetii sotsialistii Tojikiston', *Tojikistoni soveti*, 26 July 1989, p 1; S. Assadulloev, 'Zarurati alifboi niyogon', *Omuzgor*, 6 May 1992, pp 5–6.

7. 'Qonuni zaboni'; 'Pora obnovleniia'; 'Na ruinakh ambitsii'; 'Izhoroti'; 'Ustav'.

8. Assadulloev, 'Zarurati alifboi niyogon'.

9. Interfax (Moscow), 11 November 1991, Foreign Broadcast Information Service (FBIS) *Daily Report: Soviet Union*, 13 November 1991, p 86.

10. M. Qurbon and S. Ayub, 'Tehron, Kobul, Dushanbe', *Adabiyot va san"at*, 10 August 1989, p 2; 'Muzokira', p 3.

11. L. Sherali, 'Pora kunem yo chora khunem?', *Adabiyot va san"at*, 28 May 1992, p 5.

12. M. Olimpur, 'Tehronu Dushanbe baradarshahr meshavand', *Adabiyot va san"at*, 30 August 1990, p 12; idem, 'Paivand', p 12; K. Nasrullo, 'Muhabbati Eron', ibid., 8 November 1990, p 3; 'Tajikistan, jazirahy-i zaban-i parsi dar miyan-i tork hast', *Kayhan-i hava'i*, 23 January 1991 (Bahman 3, 1369), p 14. The author wishes to thank Dr Patrick Clawson for bringing this article to her attention.

13. 'Jashnovorai filmhoi eroni', *Adabiyot va san"at*, 22 November 1990, p 6; Olimpur, 'Namoishi kitobhoi Eron', ibid., 13 December 1990, p 11; A. Nizom, 'Panj soli purtalosh', *Javononi Tojikiston*, 26 March 1992, p 2; 'Chtoby vozrodit' kul'turu', *Narodnaia gazeta*, 18 April, 1992; Sherali, 'Pora kunem yo chora khunem?', p 4; B. Timurov, 'Iz turne po Iranu', *Narodnaia gazeta*, 9 July 1992, p 4; TIA Khovar, 'Za ukreplenie mezhdunarodnykh pozitsii Tadzhikistana', *Narodnaia gazeta*, 18 July 1992, p 1; 'Namoishi nashriyahoi Eroni', *Jumhuriyat*, 19 August 1992, p 1; 'Tojikiston ba qadom sohil mebaroyad?', *Jumhuriyat*, 19 August 1992, p 1.

14. M. Shakuri, 'Payomi oshnoyon', *Adabiyot va san"at*, 4 June 1992, p 14.

15. Nasrullo, 'Muhabbati Eron'; TadzhikTA, 'Mehmoni eroni dar Tojikiston', *Tojikistoni soveti*, 20 October 1989, p 2; Dushanbe domestic radio, 21 April 1991, FBIS *Daily Report: Soviet Union*, 25 April 1991, p 75; 'Bozargononi Iron dar Tojikiston', *Tojikistoni shuravi*, 27 August 1991, p 3.

16. 'Zavershilsia ofitsial'nyi vizit', *Narodnaia gazeta*, 1 July 1992, p 1.

17. Nasrullo, 'Muhabbati Eron', p 14.

18. U. Soleh, 'Ham tijorat, ham kori khair', *Jumhuriyat*, 3 April 1992, p 2; N. Asadullo, 'Dudi khonaro ravzan dedonad', *Adabiyot va san"at*, 21 June 1990, p 3; 'Oshkhonai chekhi dar Farkhor', *Tojikistoni Shuravi*, 29 August 1991, p 3; Moscow domestic radio, 22 September 1990, FBIS *Daily Report: Soviet Union*, 24 September 1990, p 103; Dushanbe domestic radio, 23 September 1990, FBIS *Daily Report: Soviet Union*, 27 September 1990, p 98; Moscow television, 16 July 1990, FBIS *Daily Report: Soviet Union*, 18 July 1990, p 106.

19. MIT Khovar, 'Ravobit vus"at meboyad', *Jumhuriyat*, 2 June 1992, p 1.

20. Dushanbe domestic radio, 2 December 1991, FBIS *Daily Report: Soviet Union*, 4 December 1991, p 83.

21. TIA Khovar, 'Za ukreplenie mezhdunarodnykh pozitsii Tadzhikistana', *Narodnaia gazeta*, 18 July 1992, p 1.

22. TadzhikTA, 'Iranskaia delegatsiia v Tadzhikistane', *Narodnaia gazeta*, 11 January 1992, p 1.

23. 'Saforati Jumhurii Islomii Eron dar Dushanbe', *Omuzgor*, 15 January 1992, pp 1, 4.

24. Tojikon, *Entsiklopediyai Sovetii Tojik*, vii (Dushanbe: Sarredaktsiyai ilmii Entsiklopediyai Sovetii Tojik, 1987), pp 428–9; S. Aini, 'Ma"noi kalimai tojik', *Sadoi Sharq*, 1986, no. 8, p 85; B.Gh. Ghafurov, *Tojikon*, i (Dushanbe: Irfon, 1983), pp 494–6.

25. T.K. Varki, 'Iazyk–est' ispoved' naroda', *Komsomolets Tadzhikistana*, 30 June 1989, p 2; 'Muzokira', p 1; 'Mas"uliyati buzurg meboyad', *Tojikistoni soveti*, 25 July 1989, p 2.

26. Atkin, 'Religious', pp 56–7.

27. Halimsho, 'Darakhti jovidonkhirad'; E. Subhon, 'Az ajdod chi burda ba avlod chi dodem?', *Omuzgor*, 11 July 1989, p 4; R. Sharofzoda, 'Kitob va farhang', *Adabiyot va san"at*, 14 June 1990, p 11.

28. N. Arabzoda, 'Gumanizmi Nosiri Khusrav', *Adabiyot va san"at*, 14 September 1989, p 6; Kh. Dodkhudoev, *Ismoiliya va ozodandeshii sharq* (Dushanbe: Irfon, 1989); MIT Khovar, 'Dar devoni vazironi jumhurii Tojikiston', *Jumhuriyat*, 3 April 1992, p 1.

29. A. Istad, 'Davlati milli chi guna boyad?', *Adabiyot va san"at*, 4 June 1992, p 6.

30. *Berliner Zeitung*, 22 November 1991, FBIS *Daily Report: Soviet Union*, 27 November 1991, p 74; he made the same point in interviews with a Soviet newspaper and a Western journalist: U. Babakhanov and A. Mursaliev, 'Pust' govoriat ob islamskom Tadzhikistane: A kazi protiv', *Komsomol'skaia pravda*, 4 October 1991, p 1; R. Wright, 'Report from Turkestan', *The New Yorker*, 6 April 1992, p 75.

31. Istad, 'Davlati milli'.

32. S. Erlanger, 'Politics in Central Asia Being Shaped by Islam', *New York Times*, 9 June 1992, p A16.

33. 'Priem v posol'stve', *Narodnaia gazeta*, 7 July 1992, p 1.

34. 'Novyi shag na puti k sotrudnichestvu', *Narodnaia gazeta*, 7 July 1992, p 1.

35. TIA Khovar, 'Za ukreplenie', p 1.

36. S. Shihab, 'Asie centrale: l'Iran se pose en médiateur', *Le Monde*, 12 May 1992, p 3.

37. Tehran domestic radio (in Persian), 8 January 1989, FBIS *Daily Report: Near East and South Asia*, 9 January 1989, pp 57–9.

38. Ibid., p 59.

39. Ibid.

40. 'Eron–ttihodi Shuravi–Tojikiston', *Adabiyot va san"at*, 14 June 1990, p 1.

41. 'Muslim Regional Group Welcomes Ex-Soviet Central Asians', *New York Times*, 17 February 1992, p A9.

42. 'Eron'; Tehran television, 8 December 1991, FBIS *Daily Report: Near East and South Asia*, 9 December 1991, p 76.

43. 'Yordami Eron', *Adabiyot va san"at*, 4 June 1992, p 3; M. Olimi, 'Oghozi

id az namozgoh', ibid., p 12; 'Tojikiston ba qadom sohil mebaroyad?'

44. A. Shabistari, 'Payomi safiri Jumhurii Islomii Eron dar Dushanbe ba munosibati barguzorii kungrai bainalmilalii tojikon va hamzabononi burunmarzi', *Jumhuriyat*, 8 September 1992, p 2.

45. Shakuri, 'Payomi oshnoyon'.

46. 'Muslim Regional Group'.

47. IRNA (Tehran), 24 January 1992, FBIS *Daily Report: Near East and South Asia*, 28 January 1992, p 49.

48. *Izvestiia*, 20 June 1990, FBIS *Daily Report: Soviet Union*, 10 July 1990, p 19; Interfax [Moscow], 11 June 1991, ibid., 13 June 1991, p 12; IRNA [Tehran], 11 July 1991, ibid., 12 July 1991, p 12; Tehran radio, 3 January 1989, FBIS *Daily Report: Near East and South Asia*, 4 January 1989, p 51; IRNA, 7 July 1991, FBIS *Daily Report: Near East and South Asia*, 8 July 1991, p 36; Tehran radio, 28 August 1991, FBIS *Daily Report: Near East and South Asia*, 30 August 1991, p 36; Tehran television, 25 December 1991, FBIS *Daily Report: Near East and South Asia*, 27 December 1991, p 27; IRNA, 22 January 1992, FBIS *Daily Report: Near East and South Asia*, 24 January 1992, p 51; *RFE/RL Daily Report*, no. 82 (30 April 1992), p 2; *RFE/RL Daily Report*, no. 157 (18 August 1992), p 3.

49. Tehran domestic radio, 26 February 1989, FBIS *Daily Report: Near East and South Asia*, 27 February 1989, pp 54–6; Tehran radio, 12 February 1991, ibid., 12 February 1991, p 75; IRNA, 18 September 1991, ibid., 19 September 1991, p 40; Tehran radio, 19 December 1991, ibid., 19 December 1991, p 38.

50. Tehran television, 8 December 1991, ibid., 9 December 1991, p 66.

51. The author is indebted to Dr Patrick Clawson for this information.

52. 'Muslim Regional Group'.

53. Tehran television, 8 December 1991, FBIS *Daily Report: Near East and South Asia*, 9 December 1991, p 76.

54. Shabistari, 'Payomi safirii Jumhurii Islomii Eron'.

55. TadzhikTA, 'Dar safi pesh', *Tojikistoni soveti*, 9 December 1989, p 3; Atkin, 'Religious', p 58.

56. H. Kiromov, A. Ruziev and S. Iskandarov, 'Nadidam mehrubon dilhoi az insof kholiro', *Tojikistoni shuravi*, 14 September 1991, p 4; M. Shukurzoda, 'Haqiqat zahr ham boshad, niyush!', *Tojikistoni shuravi*, 14 September 1991, p 4; J. Said, 'Mevae nest beh zi ozodi', *Javononi Tojikiston*, 12 October 1991, p 2; R. Wright, 'Report from Turkestan', *The New Yorker*, 6 April 1992, p 72.

57. A. Siyarov, 'Sukhane chand be idoma 'Har sukhan…', *Adabiyot va san"at*, 15 January 1987, p 15; Qurbon and Ayub, 'Tehron, Kobul, Dushanbe'; Faizullozoda, 'Nohamvorihoi roh'.

58. Kh. Qodir, 'Mekhohem masdari khidmat ba mardumi du kishvar boshem', *Tojikistoni shuravi*, 27 August 1991, p 4; FBIS *Daily Report: Soviet Union*, 1 November 1990, p 106.

59. Dushanbe domestic radio, 7 May 1991, FBIS *Daily Report: Soviet Union*, 9 May 1991, p 76.

60. *Kommunist Tadzhikistana*, 5 December 1989, FBIS *Daily Report: Soviet Union*, 3 January 1990, p 34; TASS, 11 April 1991, ibid., 12 April 1991, pp 74–5.

61. A. Sekretov, 'A pamiat' sviashchenna', *Narodnaia gazeta*, 27 March 1992, p 2.

62. *RFE/RL Daily Report*, no. 21 (31 January 1992), p 3.

63. Ibid., no. 225 (27 November 1991), p 1.

64. J. Steele, 'The Tajiks next door watch Massoud's Kabul,' *The Guardian*, 5 May 1992, p 9.

65. Ibid.; 'Peregovory na granitse', *Narodnaia gazeta*, 5 May 1992, p 2; *RFE/RL Daily Report*, no. 88 (8 May 1992), p 1.

66. 'Sarvari mujohidon dastahoi islomii Tojikistonro musallah megardonad', *Jumhuriyat*, 19 August 1992, p 1.

67. *RFE/RL Daily Report*, no. 161 (24 August 1992), p 3; G. Kleinman, 'Trevozhnyi budni zastavy', *Narodnaia gazeta*, 3 July 1992, p 1.

68. Shihab, 'Asie centrale'.

69. Shihab, 'Fausse sortie au Tadjikistan', *Le Monde*, 10–11 May 1992, p 3; Steele, 'The Tajiks next door'.

70. Steele, 'The Tajiks next door'.

71. The author is indebted to Dr Boris Rumer for this information.

72. Wright, 'Report', p 75.

73. 'Peregovory na granitse', *Narodnaia gazeta*, 5 May 1992, p 2.

74. The author is indebted to Dr Quadir Amiryar for this information.

75. E.A. Gargan, 'Refugees Fleeing Tajikistan Strife', *New York Times*, 14 January 1993, p 12; M. Moore, 'Tajiks Flee Civil War, Find Misery', *Washington Post*, 19 January 1993, p A18; Agence France Presse, 14 January 1993; Reuters Library Report, 21 January 1993.

76. Reuters Library Report, 9 December 1992; for a similar view, see idem, 26 December 1992.

77. Moore, 'Tajiks Flee'; Gargan, 'Refugees Fleeing'; Agence France Presse, 14 January 1993; Reuter Library Report, 17 and 21 January 1993.

78. Moore, 'Tajiks Flee'; Agence France Presse, 14 January 1993; Reuter Library Report, 17 and 21 January 1993.

79. Reuter Library Report, 26 February 1994; Human Rights Watch/Helsinki Watch and Memorial, *Human Rights in Tajikistan* (Human Rights Watch: n.p., 1993), p xix.

80. G. Kleinman, 'Snova tuchi khodiat khmuro', *Narodnaia gazeta*, 28 May 1992, p 4.

81. 'Ruzhoi purtashvishi sarhad', *Adabiyot va san"at*, 14 May 1992, p 3.

82. Cabinet of Ministers, Tajikistan, 'Obrashchenie', *Narodnaia gazeta*, 4 July 1992, p 1; Kleinman, 'Snova tuchi khodiat khmuro'; 'Ruzhoi purtashvishi sarhad', *Adabiyot va san"at*, 14 May 1992, p 3; TIA Khovar, 'Za ukreplenie', p 2.

83. Cabinet of Ministers, 'Obraschenie'.

84. Kleinman, 'Snova tuchi khodiat khmuro'.

85. 'Peregovory na granitse'; 'Safar anjom yoft', *Jumhuriyat*, 8 September 1992, p 1.

86. MIT Khovar, 'Ruzhoi tashvishovari sarhad', *Jumhuriyat*, 19 August 1992, p 3; idem, 'Vas'i sarhad', ibid., 8 September 1992, p 2.

87. *RFE/RL Daily Report*, no. 151 (10 August 1992), p 3; ibid., no. 156 (17 August 1992), p 3; MIT Khovar, 'Ruzhoi tashvishovari sarhad'; Kleinman, 'Trevozhnyi budni zastavy'; Kleinman, 'Snova tuchi khodiat khmuro.'

88. J. Krauze, 'Démission forcée du président tadjik', *Le Monde*, 9 September 1992, p 5.

89. *RFE/RL Daily Report*, no. 205 (23 October 1992), p 3.

90. Ostankino Television, 15 July 1993, as rebroadcast in English on C-SPAN2, 15 July 1993.

91. Reuters, 1 August 1993; Reuter Library Report, 4 August and 14 September 1993.

92. Ibid., no. 136 (20 July, 1992), p 3.

5

Azerbaijan's Triangular Relationship: The Land Between Russia, Turkey and Iran

TADEUSZ SWIETOCHOWSKI

Early in the nineteenth century Russia became the first European power to establish direct rule over a part of the Middle East, Transcaucasia. By comparison, Britain occupied Egypt only in 1882, and France began its overlordship in Syria and Lebanon as late as 1920. Typically for a colonial conquest, the frontiers of the territories seized from Iran in the peace settlements of Gulistan (1813) and Turkmanchai (1828) were drawn arbitrarily, with the primary view to suit the strategic goals of Russia – to facilitate penetration of Iran and to outflank Turkey. While all Georgians following the Gulistan treaty passed under Russian rule, the Turkmanchai treaty split the Azeri-speaking Muslim population into two parts, the larger remaining with Iran. Historians see this treaty as a turning-point in the history of the Azeri people, inasmuch as the proportion of them inhabiting the territory north of the frontier river of Araxes found themselves under the rule of a European power. This division of one people and land planted the seeds for what would become known as the Azerbaijani question, but during the half century following the conquest, the amount of change was limited mainly to administrative reforms. Here was the case of one pre-industrial society conquering another with little initial impact on the structures of the economy and society. Only with the advent of the industrial age centred on the oil extraction in the Baku region, in the 1870s and 1880s, did Azerbaijan north of the Araxes enter a path of historical development divergent from the south. Even so, the parting of ways was to an extent offset by the forging of new links, and the ties between the two Azerbaijans now grew stronger than before with a mass migration of labourers from Iran to the Baku oil belt, the expansion of trade across the border, and the growth of modern transport. The Baku Muslim entrepreneurs, who were losing their positions at home to their Armenian competitors, concentrated on enmeshing the economies of two Azerbaijans.[1] Their efforts had the blessing of the tsarist regime, whose long-range policy was to turn all of northern Iran into a Russian sphere of influence. A contemporary British observer with a keen sense of geopolitics, Lord Curzon, commented on these ambitions of Russia:

> Russia regards Persia as a power that may be temporarily tolerated, that may even require to be humored or caressed, but that in the long run is irretrievably doomed.... Russia covets the splendid province of Azerbaijan for its 40,000 square miles of rich and varied country, its stalwart Turkish peasantry, the military aptitudes of its population, and its great commercial capital of Tabriz. Contiguous over a long stretch of frontiers with military capital Tiflis, it could be invaded with ease and annexed without difficulty.[2]

The age of revolution which began in 1905 in Russia, to be followed the next year by the constitutional crisis in Iran, produced a new kind of link: cooperation between those who opposed the established order on both sides of the Araxes line. In North Azerbaijan, the feelings of identification with the Iranian revolution unfolding in a more congenial environment were stronger than with that of Russia. In the Iranian south, the Armenian–Muslim violence that raged in Transcaucasia awoke a sense of solidarity with the Russian Azeris, the more so because among the victims of the mutual massacres were immigrants from Tabriz province.

A major centre of the Iranian revolution was Tabriz, a vibrant commercial city with close ties to Russia and Turkey. Its proximity to the revolutionized Transcaucasia accounted in a large measure for this role of Tabriz in the Iranian upheaval. The contacts between the two Azerbaijans were extensive, ranging from the supportive posture of the Baku press, to organizing the immigrants politically, to sending armed volunteers to Tabriz after the collapse of the revolution in Russia. The period of the two revolutions saw the high point in the closeness of the divided Azerbaijan. Symbolic of the political cooperation across the border was the person of Mammad Amin

Rasulzada, one of the founders of the social-democrat association Himmat (Endeavour) in Baku, who subsequently became a prominent figure of the Iranian revolution, ending as the leader of the national Musavat (Equality) party north of the Araxes. The Iranian Azerbaijani statesman, Hasan Taquizadeh, who travelled to Baku at that time, reminisced that the native population felt Iranian. 'The Ottoman influence had not yet spread among the Shi'ites,' he commented.[3]

New dimensions of the Azerbaijani question, together with a stimulus to the growth of Azeri ethnic identity, were introduced with the third revolution in as many years, the Young Turkish military coup of 1908 in Istanbul. Unlike its predecessor, the regime of Sultan Abdulhamid II (1876–1909), the new ruling group on the Bosphorus took a strong interest in the Turkic-speaking peoples across the Ottoman borders. On their part the Azeri intellectuals began to flock to Turkey, now the promised land for their literary and political ambitions. With such interrelated programmes as Turkism – promotion of Turkic identity; pan-Turkism – the call for cooperation and solidarity of Turkic peoples; Turanism – the vision of a union of Turkic peoples; or Oghusianism – a more realistic proposition for the unity of the linguistically closest peoples to the Ottoman Turks, notably the Azeris and Turkomens, there emerged the triple configuration of Azerbaijan between Russia, Turkey and Iran.[4] Its by-product was the rise of the specifically Azerbaijani dilemma: historical and religious bonds to Iran; ethnic, linguistic, intellectual and, increasingly, political links with Turkey.

Similarly, among the Tabriz insurgents there surfaced signs of pro-Ottoman orientation, and foreign diplomats reported their cooperation with the Young Turks. Understandably, Istanbul became the favourite place of refuge for the refugees from Iran after the Russian military intervention of 1911 put a brutal end to the constitutional revolution.

Subsequently, Russian forces remained stationed in northern Iran, and its territory became more than ever enmeshed with Transcaucasia, the process enhanced by the completion of the Baku–Julfa railway line in 1916. The virtual occupation of northern Iran by the Russian forces made the Ottoman state appear to be the potential liberator from foreign domination, and sympathies for Turkey ran strong in Iran, and Azerbaijan in particular, during the First World War.

Only in the summer of 1918, taking advantage of the civil war in Russia, did the Ottoman army enter Azerbaijan, both its northern part, where an independent Democratic Republic had just been proclaimed, and the Iranian province of Tabriz. The Ottomans indicated their preference to see formerly Russian Azerbaijan united eventually with Turkey, and in the Iranian part they tended to encourage those who were inclined towards accepting the status of an Ottoman protectorate. On closer examination, the Ottoman Azerbaijani policy in these last months of the war appears to reflect the mutually exclusive ideas of Turanism and pan-Islamism, a programme of unity of all Islamic peoples. It was not a crystallized policy, yet the Ottoman foray into Tabriz province produced in Iran the fear of Turkism as the major danger to the state's unity, and in the long run stimulated efforts to Persianize the Azeri population.[5]

North of the border, under the period of full independence that followed the withdrawal of the Ottoman forces in 1918, the foreign policy of the Democratic Republic feverishly searched for security from the threat of Russia, White and Red. In this quest, the most promising avenue for the Baku regime seemed to be a rapprochement with Iran. The Iranians 'keep telling us that we should unite with them; they want it strongly and talk about our intelligentsia, which does not exist among them', reported Ali Mardan Topchibashev, the Azerbaijani representative at the Treaty of Versailles.[6] For the Baku regime a special stimulus was the desire to slip under the shield of the protection of the British, at that time the dominant power in Iran. An agreement was concluded on 1 November 1919 which provided for a 'political-economic link in the form of confederation' with Iran, an arrangement with the additional advantage of bringing Baku closer to Tabriz.[7] The scheme failed when the Iranian *majlis* refused to ratify the August 1919 agreement with Britain that would turn Iran into a virtual dependency. This setback did not stop the growth of contacts between the Democratic Republic and its southern neighbour, leading to the Iranian–Azerbaijani treaty of friendship and commerce of March 1920.

By contrast, relations with the Turkish Nationalist movement, whose leader was Mustafa Kemal and whose base was central and eastern Anatolia, were complex and uneasy. The Kemalists, in a reversal of the Young Turks' expansionist policies, were concerned mainly with Anatolian-centred Turkey proper, and regarding Azerbaijan they favoured the replacement of the Democratic Republic with a regime friendly to the Bolsheviks that would turn Azerbaijan into a bridge between Soviet Russia and a Nationalist Turkey struggling against imperialism. Under the new foreign policy set by Kemal, Turkey withdrew largely, though never fully, from an active involvement in the problems of the Turkic peoples outside its own borders.[8]

The Soviet period that followed the Red Army invasion in April 1920 continued the process of national consolidation of North Azerbaijan with such policies as *korenizatsiia* – indigenization of the civil service – the spread of education in the Azeri language, and the growth of native cultural institutions, all of which was in sharp contrast to the Iranian assimilationist policies under the new Pahlavi dynasty, which also curtailed contacts across the Araxes border. The native cultural and educational expansion in Soviet Azerbaijan was enhanced by the 1926 Latinization of the alphabet. This reform, which weakened ties to Iranian Azerbaijan, was in step with the promotion of a Soviet Azerbaijani national identity, distinct from Iran and Turkey. The next decade, in the midst of Stalin's purges, saw the coming of Azerbaijanism, a particularistic, ethnically based and strictly secular nationalism, hostile to any broader vision such as pan-Turkism, pan-Islamism or the closeness of the two Azerbaijans. Characteristically, among the countless victims of the purges, the most outstanding group were the followers of the communist leader Nariman Narimanov of the 1920s, the men who had in the past promoted ties between of Azerbaijan and the revolutionary and national movements in the neighbouring Muslim countries, most notably Iran.

In keeping with the new spirit of the times, the adjective referring to country's language and its inhabitants became the rigorously observed term 'Azerbaijani' rather than 'Turkic' (*Tiurskii*). Stalinist-imposed Azerbaijanism went hand-in-hand with the effort at assimilation of the Russian language, and as the Latin alphabet made reading Turkish easy and Russian difficult, another reform changed the script from Latin to Cyrillic as of 1940.[9]

The isolationist disposition of Soviet Azerbaijani nationalism was interrupted in 1941, when Red Army troops occupied northern Iran. The Soviet military presence led to the resurgence of pan-Azerbaijani sentiments – the desire for unity or closeness of the two parts of the divided country. Under the Soviet occupation, the revival of the native literary language, which had largely been supplanted by Persian, was promoted with the help of writers and journalists brought in from north of the Araxes.[10]

In November 1945 the autonomous government of Azerbaijan was formed in Tabriz under Sayyid Jafar Pishevari, the leader of the Azerbaijani Democratic Party, who had a long record of communist activities. There followed an impressive growth of schools and of publications in the native language, and speculations were rife about the two Azerbaijans drawing together under the Soviet aegis. As it turned out, the issue of Iranian Azerbaijan was one of the opening salvos of the Cold War, and largely under the pressure of the Western powers the Red Army withdrew beyond the Araxes. The central government of Iran had repossessed South Azerbaijan by the end of 1946, and the members of the Democratic Party took refuge in the Soviet Union. Pishevari, never fully trusted by the Soviets, died soon afterwards in mysterious circumstances.[11] Manifestations of pan-Azerbaijani feelings in Soviet Azerbaijan were banned almost entirely with the improvement of relations between Moscow and Tehran in the 1960s, a situation that was one of the hallmarks of the long 'period of stagnation', as the Brezhnev rule would come to be called.

Stagnation, in general, continued under the tenure of Brezhnev's successors Yurii Andropov and Konstantin Chernenko, although in Azerbaijan the tremors of changing times were felt earlier than in other parts of the USSR, through the reverberations of the Iranian revolution. A major centre of the revolutionary ferment in Iran was in Tabriz, traditionally a stronghold of regional identity.

The Soviet view of this clergy-led upheaval was that it would be a transitory phenomenon, a stepping-stone to further crises in Iran, driven by ethnic, no longer puritanic, fervour, and then by social and economic grievances. These expectations failed to materialize, and instead tension began to develop between Iran and the Soviet Union, at the roots of which was Iran's sense of strategic encirclement by the war in Afghanistan and the aggression from Iraq.

If Tabriz was the symbol of Islam triumphant, Baku wished to remain the symbol of Azerbaijani identity, and the Soviet reaction to the growing friction with Iran was to play the nationality card. The signal came from Haidar Aliyev, the head of the Communist Party of Azerbaijan, and a rising star on the horizon of the all-Soviet Union politics. He appealed to Azerbaijani writers for 'strengthening literary links with Southern Azerbaijan, developing broad contacts in all sectors of cultural and intellectual creativity'. He reportedly even told foreign diplomats of the need to help the Southern Azeri brethren by the reunification of Azerbaijan. The two parts of Azerbaijan were now frequently referred to as one fatherland. The frontier dividing one people, an 'open wound', was destined to disappear, even though it was never spelt out through what means. The

Turkmanchai Treaty acquired an ugly connotation as a monument of historical injustice.[12]

While such statements as these were not entirely novel, the emphasis and the scope of their circulation were. The revived Soviet pan-Azerbaijani agitation was still kept out of the daily newspapers, especially those in Russian, an indication that the highest degree of official endorsement was lacking. Moscow played an intricate game against Tehran and was not willing to commit itself to any long-term course of action. In Baku, as if through an unspoken agreement between rulers and the ruled, the 'one Azerbaijan' campaign served as a substitute for dissident movements that were germinating in the next-door republics. On their part, those of an independent public opinion (an emerging phenomenon) welcomed this less than full encouragement for the vision of unity across the border. Whatever the permissible measures for this vision, it was expected to be of benefit to Azeri national self-assertiveness, and even the possibility of talking about unity would be a mutual reinforcement of Azeri identity in the face of both Russianization and Persianization.

With Gorbachev's perestroika, Moscow abruptly called off the 'one Azerbaijan' campaign as an unnecessary irritant in relations with Iran. As in the past, depending on the state of these relations the 'on' or 'off' signals would be flashed with no regard for Azeri sensibilities. Otherwise, the onset of the new era did not bring in an immediate national movement in Azerbaijan. Rather, its birth came with the violent outbreak of the Nagorno-Karabakh dispute in February 1988 after the Armenians raised their demands for the incorporation of this part of Azerbaijan into the Armenian Soviet Republic.[13] Azerbaijan, which had lagged behind other parts of the USSR in developing dissident associations, now experienced a political reawakening comparable to that of 1905. The ethnic strife revealed the weakness of the Communist Party as the spokesman for national interests, and in the spirit of glasnost, independent publications, action committees and political associations began to mushroom. Within less than a year the main opposition group, the People's Front of Azerbaijan (PFA), coalesced into the chief political force in the country.[14] Its programme (adopted in June 1989), though marked by cautious formulations, offered the most comprehensive statement of Azerbaijani aspirations at the time of the downfall of Communism, and it took up the issues of the relationship to Iran, the other Azerbaijan, and the Islamic world in general. While stressing its recognition of the indisputable nature of the borders between the USSR and Iran, the People's Front called for the 'restoration of the ethnic unity of Azerbaijanis living on both sides of the border.... Economic, cultural, and social ties between our divided nation should be restored.... The PFA supports decisive steps toward the development of understanding and cooperation with the world of Islam.'[15]

Although in the autumn of 1989 the PFA seemed to be poised for taking over power in Azerbaijan, it remained an umbrella association beset by divisions, and these reflected deep cleavages within the Azeri community.

In the final analysis, the underlying issue was typical of a Muslim society in transition anywhere – the rift between the modern-orientated and the traditionalist-minded elements. In the case of Azerbaijan, there was the perennial split between the intelligentsia, the urban and the better educated on the one hand, and the bulk of the tradition-bound, mainly rural or small town population, often Shi'ite in background, on the other. The two-nations-within-one syndrome reared its head again at a historical turning-point, and the very suggestion of Azerbaijani unity in some future was an additional factor with divisive potential. While the traditionalist–Islamic elements within the PFA showed themselves favourable to a rapprochement with the south as a part of Iran, most of the secular intelligentsia contemplated with horror the possibility, however remote, of Azerbaijan submerged in an Iran ruled by fanatic mullahs.[16]

Against this background began the January crisis of 1990, with the crowds destroying the border installations along the Araxes. The images of joyful people clipping the barbed wire evoked the recent scenes of razing the Berlin Wall. At once differences surfaced in the perception of what was taking place at the border, and these corresponded with the divisions in the PFA. The radical elements saw the opening of the frontier as an effect of the popular upheaval, a step in the direction of Islamic Azerbaijani unity. Similarly, a group of academicians felt inspired to send an address to the Politburo and the Presidium of the USSR, in which the division of Azerbaijan was compared with that of Korea nowadays and Vietnam in the past. 'Azerbaijan was artificially split into two parts after the Russo-Iranian wars of the early nineteenth century, which resulted in the tragic for our nation Turkmanchai Treaty of 1828.' The address called for the 'essential relaxation of the frontier regime between the two parts of our fatherland'.[17]

There were other strains in the unfolding drama, and their effects were felt promptly. Two weeks after the border demonstrations, on 13 January came the sudden renewal of ethnic violence in Baku when mobs attacked the residences of local Armenians. The circumstances were such as to reinforce suspicions of the government's involvement, which in the light of past experience would have been aroused in any case. Yet it was also a measure of the ineffectiveness of the PFA that it was unable to prevent the violence from taking place. The military intervention ordered by Moscow came after the surviving Armenians had left Baku, but by then the authority of the Soviet regime seemed to have collapsed.[18]

The worldwide echoes of the Baku January Days resounded nowhere more strongly than in Iran and Turkey. There were some striking similarities in both countries' reactions to the Azerbaijani crisis, and also remarkable differences in perceptions of the events. The first instinct of the two governments was to keep their distance from a domestic upheaval of their Soviet neighbour. Turkish President Turgut Ozal, at the time on a visit to the United States, declared offhandedly that the Azeris 'are Shi'ites, we are Sunnis', therefore they were more of a concern for Iran than for Turkey. He would later insist that his remark had been misinterpreted, nonetheless he repeated that 'it is impossible for us to interfere in the internal affairs of the Soviet Union.'[19] Ozal's opposite number in Iran, Hashemi Rafsanjani, in the words of a newspaper commentary, 'has been remarkably silent on the issue', seeing the recent economic agreements with the Soviet Union as 'too important to sacrifice on the altar of ideological purity'.[20] The ideological zealots in Iran refused to toe the government line and were outspoken in their views of the Baku upheaval. Ayatollah Ahmad Jannati announced plans to send Shi'a clerics to proselytize in Soviet Azerbaijan, a task to be combined with translating the works of Khomeini into Azeri, in the Cyrillic script. Another Ayatollah, Ali Khamenei, saw an outburst of Islamic zeal in Azerbaijan, and warned that it would be 'a big blunder to think that ethnic and national motives were behind this move'.[21]

Turkish reactions, by contrast, emphasized what appeared to be anathema to Iranian officials, the ethnic character of the Azerbaijani crisis. The Ankara and Istanbul press proclaimed their sympathy and moral support for the indestructible ties between Azerbaijan and Turkey based on a common race, language and culture, but the same newspapers generally endorsed the cautious position of the government – indeed they elaborated on what its thinking might be on Azerbaijan. 'Turkey should not allow itself to fall into the trap arising from the situation in the Caucasus.'[22]

As developments in the Soviet Union kept gaining momentum amid signs pointing to the disintegration of the old order, Ankara's caution and reserve appeared out of tune with the spirit of the time. By mid-1990, Ozal found it appropriate to send his wife to Baku, with the task of making amends with the Azeri public. Her visit marked the onset of an impressive expansion of economic and cultural exchanges between Azerbaijan and Turkey. The Treaty of Friendship and Cooperation, signed in 1991 and enlarged for its renewal the following year, became the model for similar arrangements with the Central Asian republics of the former Soviet Union.[23] These treaties not only expanded Turkish economic influence through investment credits and joint ventures, but also established close cultural and educational ties. In addition to the influx of Turkish press and books, Azerbaijan began to rebroadcast Turkish television and radio programmes on a scale that began to affect colloquial Azeri. In Turkey the universities opened their doors to students from the former USSR, and with a view to influence the renewed debate on the alphabet, large quantities of Latin-character typewriters were donated to Azerbaijan.

As in the past, alphabet reform was of special relevance to the issue of relationships with the neighbouring countries. There was a general consensus that Cyrillic should be rejected as a symbol of the Stalinist-imposed Russianization and a script that had cut off the Azeris from the world outside the Soviet Union, but the question remained: should Azerbaijan restore the Latin alphabet of the 1920s with the prospect of easier contacts with Turkey and the West, or should it return to the Arabic script, a change that would help it draw closer to the Iranian south in addition to recovering the continuity of historic and literary heritage? The latter option would have had the best chance of acceptance on the condition that a comprehensive primary education system was to be established for the Azeri population in Iran. But the possibilities of using the written Azeri language in Iran remained so limited that 'it was not worth the sacrifice' to bring back the Arabic script with all its drawbacks.[24] The fourth alphabet in less than 70 years, adopted in January 1993, was Latin, in a simpler version than that of the 1920s in order to facilitate computerization.

On 30 August 1991 the Communist regime, headed by Ayaz

Mutalibov (who had only a few days before endorsed the Moscow coup), proclaimed the independence of Azerbaijan, following the example of other Soviet republics. The declaration contained popular references to the 1918–20 Democratic Republic and to human rights. It indicated Azerbaijan's eagerness for international contacts and recognition, but at the same time it upheld attachment to the heritage of the USSR. The meaning of independence was still not entirely clear, as the declaration included no references to secession, and Mutalibov had until the last moment castigated the unnamed separatists. In fact, as soon as the Commonwealth of Independent States (CIS) came into existence, he would bring Azerbaijan into its membership without securing appropriate endorsements at home.

The Declaration of Independence was followed by the dissolution of the Communist Party, but the presidential elections held on 8 September seemed to signify business as usual, with Mutalibov running unopposed and returned to office almost unanimously – with 98.5 per cent of the valid votes.[25] Half a year later, by March 1992, he would be voted out of office by the parliament for mishandling the Nagorno-Karabakh conflict. Here the situation was turned into an 'ethnic cleansing' of the local Azeri minority, with ineffective opposition on the part of the fledgling Azerbaijani army. Mutalibov's successor was Abulfaz Elchbayli, the leader of the PFA, who in June 1992 became the first democratically elected president of Azerbaijan.

Of the foreign powers, Turkey was the first to recognize Azerbaijan's independence; the Tehran government initially considered Ankara overhasty in this respect.[26] Before long, Iran came around to establishing diplomatic relations with Azerbaijan, unwilling to be outdone entirely by Turkey's enthusiasm. The two powers officially denied that they were rivals for influence in the Muslim republics of the former USSR; they were even willing to cooperate on particular issues and projects. The most notable example of this cooperation was the Economic Cooperation Organization (ECO), a group which originally had included Turkey, Iran and Pakistan, and in 1992 invited the six Muslim republics, Azerbaijan, Turkmenistan, Kazakhstan, Kyrgyzstan, Uzbekistan and Tajikistan, to join.

Nonetheless, Iranian–Turkish competition has remained a fact. It is also clear that of the two, Turkey had an edge not only because of its head start, but even more because of the linguistic and sectarian affinities of the Soviet Muslims, among whom the overwhelming majority were Turkic speaking, and by the historic and religious background of the Sunni branch of Islam. Furthermore, the group still ruling in the post-Soviet nations, the former *nomenklatura*, is obviously secular-minded, and the same is true of its chief contender, the intelligentsia. From this standpoint secular Turkey appeared incomparably closer to them than the Islamic Republic of Iran. Historically, Turkey enjoyed among the Muslim countries the image of the most modernized, a bridge between their world and the advanced West, a nation which had succeeded in mastering much of what Europe and America had to offer. In an enthusiastic speech Kyrgyz President Askar Akaev called Turkey a 'North Star', to be looked to for guidance. On the Turkish side, amid the continuous disclaimers that old-fashioned pan-Turkism was being revived, statements were heard on Turkey's readiness to take upon itself the responsibility for the state of affairs in the region stretching from the Adriatic Sea to the borders of China.[27] This sounded like a far cry from the tradition of Kemalist foreign policy.

The Turkish and Iranian jostling for positions and influence has been in evidence throughout all the Muslim regions of the former USSR, for instance through visits by dignitaries from both countries, their business delegations and cultural exchange programmes. But it was also becoming clear that the cost of refloating the economies of these underdeveloped regions would amount to staggering sums of tens of billions of dollars, a tall order which neither Turkey nor Iran, nor even both jointly, would be able to meet. Inevitably, the choice of focus had to be made, and most logically, Turkey and Iran alike singled out Azerbaijan for their special attention.

For Turkey, Azerbaijan was the linguistically closest nation, the linchpin of the old Oghusianism, the stepping-stone in any commercial and cultural expansion in Central Asia, a country with a solidly pro-Turkish following among the politically articulate.

For Iran, formerly Russian/Soviet Azerbaijan is linked by countless ties of history; only a few generations ago did its educated class develop an awareness of not being Iranian. This is also a country with a two-to-one Shi'ite majority, the largest group of cosectarians outside Iran, and it is among them rather than the Azeri Sunni minority that the religious revival is most noticeable. The mass of Shi'ites are apt to look to Iran as their spiritual homeland.

But there is the obverse side of the coin, and this, more than anything else, accounts for Iran's hesitations, and difficulties in the competition with Turkey. There are almost seven million comparatively well-educated Azeris north of the Araxes, most of them with a sense of nationality, even if unevenly developed in various groups of the population, with well-established cultural institutions, an active leadership, highly organized political life and indigenous bureaucracy – all attributes of a distinct nation. A deep involvement of Iran north of the Araxes would run the risk of bringing the two Azerbaijans close to each other, thus endangering the long Persianization effort of various regimes in Tehran.

Abulfaz Elchbayli, an intellectual who soon became a target of criticism that he was naive and ineffectual, all the same articulated more clearly than any other Azerbaijani public figure some historically ingrained concerns of the community: emancipation from the all-pervading grip of Russia, closer relations with Turkey, and the need for ties with their co-ethnics across the Araxes frontier, the best assurance of national survival. Not only did he articulate these goals, he also acted upon them, only to find that they exacted a heavy price, and that they could be mutually exclusive.

He wasted no time in withdrawing Azerbaijan from the CIS, a step which prompted Russian retaliation: import duties on industrial products from Azerbaijan rose by more than half, and many Russian enterprises cancelled their contracts with Azerbaijan. At the same time, the demands that Russia prepare to pull out of Azerbaijan made it easier for Moscow to allow the use of mercenaries and equipment on the Armenian side in the Nagorno-Karabakh conflict, which was turning from bad to disastrous for the Azeris.

The PFA regime was discovering that its friendship with Turkey hindered ties with the other part of Azerbaijan, and relations with Iran developed in a troublesome way. Even before his coming to power Elchbayli was known for declarations such as, 'As an independent state rises in the north of Azerbaijan, it will make it easier for freedom to grow in the south', and the Iranian capital greeted his presidency with barely concealed hostility.[28] By contrast, Elchbayli's most formidable rival, Haidar Aliyev, now the head of the Nakhchevan Autonomous Republic, gained a reputation as a man with whom the Islamic Republic could deal. Aliyev cultivated cordial relations between Nakhchevan and Tehran, and on his visit to Iran he claimed credit for some two hundred mosques recently opened in his province. A seasoned politician, he appreciated the potential of the religious revival, and performed a highly publicized pilgrimage to the tomb of Imam Reza in Mashad.[29]

Tehran's position towards Elchbayli's Baku regime had its motivation primarily in an understanding of national rather than religious–
ideological interests, and both the pragmatic and the clerical factions
took the same stand. For those who wondered why the concern over
Tabriz should be more serious because of the PFA Baku regime than
because of Russia, the explanation was that behind Baku stood Turkey,
and behind Turkey, the USA. On the Nagorno-Karabakh issue, Iran
assumed a neutral position, though Baku perceived in it a tilt towards
Christian and Western-orientated but anti-Turkish Armenia. The
Iranian clerics, meanwhile, went quietly about the task of helping to
restore religious life north of the border, in which they faced no
challenge from secular Turkey. With the help of funds from Iran, the
mosques were built or restored, and future ulama were invited to
study in Tabriz.

The PFA policy of rapprochement with Turkey, meant as a replacement for the long Russian presence, unfolded in the atmosphere of
resuscitated pan-Turkish sentiments, and these sometimes went against
the grain of Azerbaijanism, which had put down substantial roots. An
attempt to redesignate the country's language as Turkish led to protests, the extent of which surprised the People's Front government.
Meanwhile, efforts to limit the use of the Russian language met with
silent opposition in the segment of the intelligentsia whose preferred
language of expression it had become.

On the Turkish side, the realization grew of the burdens that the
involvement in Azerbaijan put on Turkey's limited resources, and the
signals from the USA were discouraging. The Congressional Resolution of 17 February 1993 banning aid to Azerbaijan in retaliation for
the blockade of Armenia was understood as aligning the US government with one side of the conflict. Most importantly, the prospect of
Turkey's collision course with Russia's effort to recover its former
empire was foremost in the minds of Turkish policy-makers. Following the death of Ozal in the spring of 1993 there were indications that
Ankara was ready to disengage from its high level of involvement in
Azerbaijan, especially as Russian declarations, including those by the
high-ranking military, were making it clear that Moscow regarded the
Near Abroad territory of the former USSR as its zone of strategic
interest.

The June 1993 military coup in Azerbaijan that led to the overthrow of Elchbayli and his replacement by Haidar Aliyev reflected the
broad pattern of the former Soviet leaders in most of the republics of

the defunct USSR.[30] Together with the comeback of the ex-communist *nomenklatura*, it spelt the restoration of Russia's dominant influence in the region of Transcaucasia. The Azerbaijani public, dispirited by recent debacles on the Karabakh front, accepted the prospect of a *Pax Russica* as the only solution for the conflict. Among Aliyev's first steps as president was to bring Azerbaijan back into the CIS, without, however, inviting Russian troops.

The overthrow of Elchbayli was considered as much a success for Russia as a blow to Turkey. In the perspective of history, the coup appeared to be another failed test for the pro-Turkish orientation in Azerbaijani politics. Not only did it evoke memories of past disillusionments, but it amounted to a setback for the social forces that stood behind this orientation. In Turkey, the coup provoked a tempest of recrimination in press commentaries and controversies among politicians for letting down their friend Elchbayli, but soon the view prevailed that while Turkey was in no position to challenge Russia, efforts should continue to save as much as possible from the Turkish presence in Azerbaijan.[31]

While the winner of the June coup in terms of political influence was Russia, and the apparent loser Turkey, a second winner appeared to be Iran. Tehran welcomed the change of regime in Baku, not only because it alleviated its concern about Iranian Azerbaijan, but also because it improved the prospects for a greater Iranian presence north of the Araxes. This presence, easily noticeable in the aftermath of the coup, was based on the support of those who are apt to call themselves Muslims first, and then Azeris, Azeri Turks or Azerbaijanis.

In restoring a broken thread of history, Azerbaijan has become the arena for a contest between Iran and Turkey, the powers which until only recently had themselves lived in the overpowering shadow of Russia. It was Russia again that resolved much of their contest by returning to Transcaucasia. By 1993, the power vacuum resulting from the collapse of the USSR had proved to be a temporary phenomenon.

An empire does not die easily, especially when it sits astride the geopolitical centre of the world's largest land mass and its relationship to its neighbours evokes the image of a shark among sardines. Yet, while the pendulum swings back, it does not reach the same point. The conditions that brought the Soviet Union to decolonization still obtain, and the former rulers reappear on the scene in a changed, unfamiliar setting.

The process of imperial restoration from the times of trouble was under way in the years 1917–23; the empire did come back, but at the price of the national consolidation of its subject peoples. While Soviet colonialism was totalitarian, the resurgent Russian neo-imperialism is of a different quality. More than ever, Moscow's concern is to secure its strategic and economic position, notably a share in the profits from extraction and transport of Baku oil, without incurring undue burdens. In practice, this approach amounts to leaving a wide and expanding margin for trade, investment and travel, and an even larger one for cultural and spiritual life. The new Russian imperialism harks back, not to the Soviet model of total control, but to the tsarist model of the period before the 1860s.

Russian lack of interest in and inability to fill the empty spaces on its margins leaves room for both Iran and Turkey in Azerbaijan. In the long run, the Islamic revival, a natural reaction to the Soviet-imposed age of irreligiosity, will probably be an important trait of Azerbaijani life, and support for it will come not from secular Turkey but from Iran. Likewise, the Azeris may one day find that a more promising avenue towards rapprochement with their compatriots across the border is not to act against Iran, but through Iran, assuming an openminded change of Tehran's position. On its part, Iran may one day show the foresight to win over Azeri nationalists before Russia again tries to make use of them.

On the other hand, there will remain the historical task of emancipation from Russian/Soviet cultural domination over a large part of the community, which once had lifted the Azeris from their tradition-bound pattern of existence only to impose on them in the end another kind of stagnation and isolation from the non-Russian world. Here the role of Turkey is likely to be paramount.

Should the Iranian–Turkish contest for cultural and spiritual influence turn into a political rivalry, the beneficiary will again be Moscow, just as it has become the real winner in the Nagorno-Karabakh conflict. With Russia's resurgence in Transcaucasia both Iran and Turkey may revert to the geopolitical rivalry of the last two centuries.

As for Azerbaijan, the leading theme throughout its history has been analogous with that of Siyavush, a legendary hero in whose veins flowed Turkish and Iranian blood. Will the Azeris revive the historical role of their country, the land where Iranian and Turkic civilizations, for all their distinctions, have blended in creative harmony?

Notes

1. On Azerbaijan in the 19th century, see Altstadt, A., *The Azerbaijani Turks: Power and Identity under Russian Rule* (Stanford, 1992), pp 15–50; Suny, R.G., *The Baku Commune, 1917–1918: Class and Nationality in the Russian Revolution* (Princeton, 1972).

2. Curzon, G., *Persia*, (London, 1889), vol. iii, pp 593–4.

3. For a recent discussion of the Iranian Revolution and its links to Transcaucasia, see Bayat, M., *Iran's First Revolution: Shi'ism and the Constitutional Revolution of 1905–1909*, pp 76–106; see also Chaqueiri, C., 'The role and impact of Armenian intellectuals in Iranian politics, 1905–1911', *Armenian Review*, xlii/2 (1988), pp 1–51.

4. On pan-Turkism, see Landau, J.M., *Pan-Turkism in Turkey: A Study of Irredentism* (London, 1981).

5. On the 1918 Ottoman occupation of North Azerbaijan, see Balaev, A., *Azerbaidzhanskoe natsional'noe dvizhenie, 1917–1920 gg.* (Baku, 1990). For a contemporary account of the Ottoman policy in South Azerbaijan, see *Der Neue Orient*, iii (1918), p 378.

6. Raevskii, A., *Musavatskoe pravitel'stvo na versal'skoi konferentsii: Doneseniia predesdatelia azerbaidzhanskoi musavatskoi delegatsii* (Baku, 1930), p 50.

7. For a discussion of the independent Azerbaijani Republic and its foreign policy see Swietochowski, T., *Russian Azerbaijan, 1905–1920: The Shaping of National Identity in a Muslim Community* (Cambridge, 1985), pp 129–94.

8. Jaschke, G., 'Neues zur russisch-turkischen Freundschaft von 1919–1939', *Welt des Islams*, new series 6 (1961), pp 205–6.

9. On the Soviet policies in Azerbaijan in the 1920s and 1930s, see Altstadt, A., op. cit., pp 108–50.

10. For a discussion of Soviet cultural policies in South Azerbaijan, see Nissman, D., *The Soviet Union and Iranian Azerbaijan: The Use of Nationalism for Political Penetration* (Boulder, 1987), pp 28–37.

11. For a monograph on South Azerbaijan during the Second World War, see Homayounpour, P., *L'affaire d'Azerbaidjan* (Lausanne, 1967); see also Abrahamian, E., 'Communism and Communalism in Iran: The Tudah and the Firqah-i Dimuqrat', *International Journal of Middle East Studies*, i (1970), no. 4, pp 96–131.

12. On the 'One Azerbaijan' campaign, see Nissman, op. cit., pp 73–8.

13. On the Nagorno-Karabakh conflict, see 'About the events in Nagorno-Karabagh or the Karabagh adventure of the Armenian nationalists', *Central Asia and Caucasus Chronicle*, vii (1989), pp 3–4. For an Armenian view, see Mouradian, C., 'The mountainous Karabagh question: an inter-ethnic conflict or decolonization crisis?', *Armenian Review*, xliii (1990), no. 2–3, pp 1–34.

14. For the rise of the PFA, see Balaev, A., *Aperçue historique du Front populaire d'Azerbaidjan*, n.d.; on the rise of political associations, see Iunusova, L., 'Pestraia palistra, neformal'nykh dvizhenii v Azerbaidzhane', *Russkaia mysl'*, ix/22 (1989).

15. See 'Program of the People's Front of Azerbaijan', *Central Asian and Caucasus Chronicle*, vii/6 (1989), p 8.

16. Balaev, op. cit., p 12.

17. *Azerbaijan* [Baku], no. 2, 11 January 1990.

18. For an official account of the Baku January Days, see Azerbaidzhaskaia SSR, Verkhovnyi Sovet, *Zaiavleniie Komissii po issledovaniiu sobytii imevshikh mesto v gorode Baku 19–20 ianvaria 1990 goda* (Baku, 1990); see also *Chernyi ianvar': Dokumenty i materialy* (Baku, 1990).

19. FBIS-WEU 90–014, 22 January 1990.

20. *Iran Times*, 2 February 1990.

21. FBIS-NES-90, January–February; see also 'Une frontière glaciale dilue l'identité des Azeris', *Journal de Genève*, 2/3 June (1990).

22. 'Le drame azeri divise la Turquie', *Le Monde diplomatique*, March 1990, p 10.

23. For the full text of the treaty between Azerbaijan and Turkey, see *Bakinskii Rabochii*, 29 January 1992.

24. 'Elifba nece olacak', *Odlu yurt*, 8 August 1990.

25. Fuller, E., 'The Azerbaijani presidential elections: a one horse race', *RFE/RL Research Institute: Report on the USSR*, iii/37 (13 September 1991), pp 12–14. See also *New York Times*, 4 September 1991.

26. Reissner, J., 'Iran: Regionale Grossmacht?', Stiftung Wissenschaft und Politik, *Mittelasien zwischen neuen Fronten*, Ebenhausen, SWP-AP 2745, 1992, p 40.

27. *Bakinskii Rabochii*, 1 April 1992.

28. *Azadliq*, 19 July 1991, p 9.

29. *Iran Times*, 15 June 1993.

30. For a detailed account of the coup, see Iunosov, A., 'Giandzhinskii taifun', *Ekspress-Khronika*, 25 June 1993; see also the same author's analysis of the political condition of Azerbaijan on the eve of the coup in 'Bezmolstvuet li narod? Obshchestvenno-politicheskaia situatsiia v Azerbaidzhane', *Ekspress-Khronika*, no. 19, 13 May 1993.

31. For a comprehensive Turkish evaluation of the coup, see Gun Kut, 'Elcibey' in sounu, Turkiye modelinin sonudur', *Cumhuriyet*, 24 June (1993).

6

Islam, State-building and Uzbekistan Foreign Policy

HENRY HALE

Western observers tend to assume that resurgent Islam in Uzbekistan will inevitably push the former Soviet republic into an alliance with the Muslim states of South Asia and the Middle East, perhaps even sending it into the orbit of fundamentalist Iran. Yet in its first year of independence, Uzbekistan cooperated closely with Israel and entered into a military alliance with its former colonial overlord, historically Christian Russia. Since Uzbek foreign policy clearly transcends any simple notions of nationalism or religion, this chapter sets up a new framework to analyse the 'orientation' of states' foreign policies which I call the 'two-level structural' approach. It should be emphasized that Uzbek–South Asian relations can be understood only against the background of on-going Uzbek ties to the states of the former Soviet Union, notably Russia.

This approach reveals tension between three trends, which can be found in a detailed analysis of Uzbek behaviour in the international arena since it declared independence on 31 August 1991. Initially, Uzbekistan is emerging from the enforced protectionism of its Soviet years, establishing normal ties with almost all of its neighbours. Additionally, a cultural shift away from Russian symbols towards Turkic and Islamic ones is driving Uzbek leaders to single out Turkey and other Central Asian States (not Iran) for particularly close relations while it is making them wary of close ties to Russia. Pure geopolitics, however, is keeping Uzbekistan orientated primarily towards Russia, albeit with looser links than in the past 70 years. All three of these trends are pulling Turkic Central Asian states together, as well. While Uzbek ties with South Asia will grow rapidly and remain important,

Uzbekistan is unlikely to shift primarily towards any South Asian or Middle Eastern state in the foreseeable future. Certain circumstances, however, could lead it to sever its most important links with Russia and to become essentially neutral, strongly orientated only towards other Central Asian states.

A suggested framework

In order to understand Uzbek foreign policy, one must eliminate three broad problems which commonly appear in early Western analyses. First, when describing trends in Central Asian relations with South Asia and the Middle East, writers tend to focus almost exclusively on the Islamic world.[1] One typical piece by Cherif Cordahi, for example, considers whether Uzbekistan and the rest of Central Asia will fall under the sway of Iran, Saudi Arabia or Turkey without examining developments in relations between Uzbekistan and its most important foreign partner, Russia.[2] This tells us little about how important (for example) Uzbek–Iranian ties actually are, since they still may be dwarfed in comparison with Uzbek ties to Russia.

Analysts must also guard against simplistic notions of Islam and ethnicity. Importantly, the general phenomenon that outsiders label 'Islam' is not a unified, unchanging force which inexorably draws its believers together.[3] It is better seen as a set of symbols whose meaning is not constant and can be manipulated for myriad different purposes, especially by powerful groups. For example, Sunni and Shi'ite Muslims offer very different notions of what 'Islam' is, and Muslims themselves tend to view these differences as important. Any attempt to link the rise of Islam in Uzbekistan to a particular foreign policy stance must take this malleability into account. If we do not, we are at a loss to explain why almost all group violence to date in Central Asia has pitted Muslims against Muslims and why Muslim Iraq began its last wars against Muslim Iran and Muslim Kuwait. Nor is ethnicity necessarily a better predictor. In the bloody 1989 Ferghana Valley riots, both parties, the Uzbeks and the Meskhetian Turks, were Turkic peoples as well as Sunni Muslims. Clearly we must move beyond simple assumptions of harmony within religious and ethnic groups.

Conceptual confusion has also plagued initial Western analyses of Uzbek foreign policy. What exactly does it mean to say that Uzbekistan might be 'leaning to Iran' or 'orientated towards Iran'? Such phrases are very vague and must be clarified and understood before a serious

analysis can be undertaken. Stephen Walt solves this problem by looking at 'alliances', which he defines as formal or informal relationships
of security cooperation between two or more sovereign states.[4] When
observers of Central Asia talk about Iranian or Turkish influence,
however, they are interested in more than security arrangements, although these would be part of their concern. This chapter thus seeks
to define the broader term 'foreign policy orientation' and to identify
factors that determine it.

In doing so, several issues are addressed. Whom will Uzbekistan
support in local conflicts even in the absence of alliances? Whose
interests might Uzbekistan actively work to undermine? For the sake
of which countries, if any, will Uzbekistan voluntarily constrain its
own decision-making autonomy?

To compare the different foreign policy orientations of states, we
need a common yardstick, some kind of empirical measure by which
we can judge the direction of a state's foreign policy orientation. This
chapter suggests three such measures. First, we can look at the political pacts that a state chooses to pursue with other states, including
Walt's alliances. Here we are interested in pacts with specific political
obligations, such as mutual defence, as opposed to general proclama-
tions of goodwill. A second set of measures consists of economic
pacts which governments (as opposed to private parties) enter, such
as free-trade or other institution-led agreements. In both of these
specific types of agreement, one state deliberately constrains its own
autonomy for the sake of another state, hence they are good (but not
perfect) indicators that the countries involved will work together
politically.

It is often suggested that economic, social and cultural ties established by non-state parties might be good indicators that the states
involved will be political partners. States with greater levels of mutual
trade would be considered more likely to work together politically.
Yet mutual dependence can also provoke great conflict, as is often
seen in cases of empire, since interdependence is rarely symmetrical.
While we cannot consider economic interdependence itself to be an
indicator of foreign policy orientation, we can look at the kinds of
non-governmental international economic ties that states actively
promote. By encouraging mutually beneficial economic ties with another state, a government is willingly increasing the cost of a significant break with that other state. Hence it is constraining its own
autonomy, albeit in a weaker way. We therefore have a working defi-

nition of 'foreign policy orientation': it is the degree to which a particular state is willing to constrain its own decision-making autonomy through its association with another state or group of states as indicated by political and economic pacts and the mutual economic ties that states actively promote with other states.

This chapter seeks to develop a way to understand Uzbek foreign policy orientation regardless of who is actually in power in Uzbekistan, since this can change suddenly. Clearly, one must know the mind of a leader in order fully to explain why he or she made any given foreign policy decision. Unfortunately, we generally have little information on leaders' personalities, especially in new states like Uzbekistan where information is hard to come by; however, we can observe that most leaders tend to behave similarly in important ways. Almost all enjoy their power and do whatever they can get away with to keep it. We therefore assume for the purposes of our analysis that career security is the primary motivation of state leaders.[5]

Accordingly, this chapter proposes a 'two-level structural' approach which focusses on incentives which face all state leaders. We refer to 'two levels' because any leader must worry about both domestic and international affairs in order to stay in power.[6] In domestic politics, the leader must either satisfy the population's strongest desires or employ enough force to keep them in line. This usually means providing economic growth and political stability, sometimes using a repressive apparatus. Meanwhile, in international politics, the leader's fate is tied up with the fate of the state, and he or she must protect the nation by fending off or counterbalancing potential foreign threats. Importantly, the two levels interact: profitable international trade can help keep a population well fed and content, while popular wrath threatens to topple even authoritarian leaders who fail to guarantee national security; leaders who provide security while failing to feed their populace are similarly at risk.

Given this basic behavioural assumption, we can with reasonable accuracy predict a state's foreign policy orientation by looking at the structure of domestic and international politics which provides incentives to its leaders. Domestic political structure includes those institutions that make a leader more or less responsive to popular opinion, such as democracy. It also includes the political resources available to politicians in that society. These resources might be physical, like money or weapons, or they might be cultural. Cultural resources include nationalist, ethnic or religious symbols with which people strongly identify and which politicians can invoke for their own purposes. A leader in a democratic society must be responsive even to aspects of culture which are not currently important to people, such as inequalities between ethnic groups when people either do not attach significance to the ethnic distinctions or are unaware of the inequalities attached to them. This is because a clever political entrepreneur could succeed in making them important and using them to win power. Even an authoritarian leader cannot completely isolate himself or herself from important potential social cleavages or grievances, and will have to be careful to contain them. For example, Uzbek President Karimov, once a republican communist first secretary, is arguably a smart political entrepreneur who sensed the potential of a nationalist and Islamic tidal wave and, rather than waiting for it to sweep him away, has sought to generate it himself on his own terms. Politicians cannot shift endlessly with the political wind, of course. People tend not to trust leaders who drift too much too often. The important point is that major potential shifts in the political landscape eventually tend to produce shifts in policy, whether by a change in leadership or by a leadership altering its own policies. The task of the theorist is to identify these potential cleavages.

Theorists have identified many things with the structure of the international system. Thus Kenneth Waltz seeks to distil the system to geography and the distribution of military power (and, by extension, economic power) among states: clearly, the power and proximity of a state affect whether other states see it as a threat or a valuable potential ally.[7] This chapter proposes to add to the list of theories international infrastructure, which includes those channels of communication and transport between states that make ties with some countries more costly than with others. Usually, it is taken for granted that such ties exist in roughly equal quantities between neighbouring states, but this is clearly not always the case. International infrastructure is of course created by inter-state cooperation; but once created, it has an independent effect. For the purposes of this chapter, therefore, 'capability', geography and infrastructure provide leaders with the most important incentives in the international arena.

In order to speculate on the likely orientation of Uzbek foreign policy over the next ten to twenty years, this framework suggests that the structure of domestic and international politics which would face any Uzbek leader seeking career security be characterized, first by examining Uzbek domestic political structure. Institutionally, Uzbekistan was at first a partial democracy, but has sunk deeper and deeper into dictatorship since 1992. We should expect an Uzbek leader to be most responsive to potential cleavages in society when democracy is strongest in Uzbekistan. This is especially true since the leadership controls virtually all monetary and coercive resources in the country. A potential opponent has only two important sets of resources to challenge an Uzbek leader: cultural cleavages which would alienate a large portion of the population from the leader; and discontent with the economic situation. In light of President Karimov's increasingly harsh crackdown on political opponents, people's general longing for freedom might be added to this list. Economically, an Uzbek leader must use foreign relations to keep people well enough off for them not to consider it profitable to challenge the government; culturally, the situation is more complex. Uzbekistan is undergoing an important shift from its Russian influences to its Islamic and Turkic symbols. Uzbek is a Turkic language approximately as distant from Turkish as Portuguese is from Spanish. The Uzbeks are also a historically Muslim people, and the cities of Bukhara and Samarkand were important holy sites before 1917. With the collapse of Soviet (seen as Russian) power, prominent Uzbek intellectuals are leading a drive to 'rediscover' the roots of a grand culture that they say was crushed by the Russians beginning in the early nineteenth century. This movement appears to have great resonance among the active Uzbek population. To the extent that they are accountable to popular sentiment, then, rational Uzbek leaders will have to ensure that they are not seen as too distant from this cultural movement for fear that potential opponents could use it to their advantage.

When these domestic pressures on the Uzbek leadership interact with the structure of international relations, they lead us to expect three broad trends in Uzbek foreign policy. First, our hypothetical Uzbek leader would seek profitable economic ties with all possible states in order to minimize popular discontent. Such ties would have to rise dramatically just to reach levels normal for neighbouring countries, since Uzbekistan was enclosed within the Soviet Union's protectionist walls. Geography suggests that Uzbekistan should be increasing its ties most rapidly with its closest neighbours with which ties were restricted in the Soviet period, such as Iran and Pakistan.

Secondly, both international capabilities and infrastructure would lead us to expect an Uzbek leader to favour the states of the former Soviet Union, especially Russia. Russia is by far the dominant military power in the region, making it a potentially costly enemy and a valuable friend to a small state with instability on its borders. Whether an Uzbek leader chooses to portray Russia as a threat would likely depend on the domestic factors examined below, so long as there is no immediate threat of invasion. Despite Russia's current economic turmoil, it is still a mighty source of raw and processed materials; it is also an important buyer of many Uzbek products, especially cotton. Further, Soviet planners designed an infrastructure which makes trade much easier for Uzbekistan with Russia and Central Asia than with other states. Thus all major railway lines link Uzbekistan primarily with Russia and the other ex-republics, and the situation is similar with major highways. The first railway line to link a Central Asian state directly to a non-CIS state was expected to be completed between Turkmenistan and Iran in the mid-1990s. From this perspective, we should expect to see an Uzbek leadership orientating its foreign policy towards Russia, and to a lesser extent towards weaker Central Asia.

So far we have examined how a leader's instrumental desire for his or her state's economic and physical security interacts with international structure. When we consider domestic cultural cleavages, however, we can expect a third trend which somewhat contradicts the second. Uzbekistan's cultural shift from things Russian to things Islamic and Turkic means that the more directly he or she is held accountable to popular opinion, the more an Uzbek leader should lean towards Turkic and Islamic states, since a clever opponent could whip up resentment by convincing people that their leader is not really 'one of us'. Such a strategy can be quite effective in times of social turmoil, when people are struggling to define themselves in a new situation and to find scapegoats for their current difficulties. Indeed, it would not be difficult for a clever political entrepreneur to get people to identify things Russian with Russia's own decline and Uzbekistan's woes, while identifying things Turkic and Islamic with the prosperity of states that are members of NATO and/or OPEC. In case of a conflict between Russia and Turkey, for example, this task would be still easier. Importantly, even if people do not yet share strong pan-Islamic or nationalist sentiments, a smart leader must respond to the *potential* of such sentiments.

Overall, our simple framework for analysing foreign policy orientation would predict tension between three themes in the case of Uzbekistan, which we might label 'de-isolation', 'geopolitical realism' and 'Turkification'. The framework itself cannot predict which of these will be dominant, but it helps to determine the conditions under which one trend will tend to prevail. We can conclude that when an Uzbek leader is more directly accountable to popular opinion and when potential political opponents are freer to mobilize cultural cleavages in society, that leader will be more likely to sever ties with Russia for the sake of ties with Turkey; the reverse is also true. The structure of international politics renders a major turn to Turkey even in the former case unlikely, however, since Turkey is distant and not significantly more powerful than other states in the region, neither economically nor politically. Ties with culturally similar but weaker neighbours, expecially Kazakhstan and Kyrgyzstan, can be expected to flourish. I now examine in depth the foreign policy orientation of Uzbekistan as it has manifested itself since independence was declared, determining whether our predictions have been borne out. I then use the above framework to speculate on possible future changes.

The foreign policy orientation of Uzbekistan

Uzbekistan's current behaviour in the international arena reflects a fairly clear set of priorities, which might be labelled 'economics', 'national security' and 'Uzbekistan first'. These priorities were evident early on despite the fact that Uzbekistan won its independence almost inadvertently when Soviet power collapsed around it in August 1991. In his speech proclaiming Uzbekistan's independence, President Islam Karimov stressed that independence is primarily a way to get out of a 'complex and critical' economic situation. This theme of 'economics first' runs through most of Karimov's speeches and is duly reflected in his actions, as will be demonstrated. Karimov also emphasizes the demands of political stability both within and across borders, since Uzbekistan's Ferghana Valley has been the site of numerous bloody riots and two of its immediate neighbours are embroiled in civil wars. At the same time, Karimov makes clear that he is pursuing what he believes is beneficial for Uzbekistan; he is not fighting for any transnational goal such as international communism, Islam, the CIS or pan-Turkism. These priorities, however, have produced different actual policies as events facing Uzbekistan have changed. This chapter now turns to a country-by-country analysis of actual Uzbek foreign policy orientation.

Russia

Uzbekistan has indeed experienced a rise in anti-Russian sentiment since the August 1991 coup, a phenomenon that intensified after it stopped using the Russian ruble in late 1993. This movement, however, has remained primarily in the cultural realm. For example, one typical article in an Uzbek-language intellectual journal blames Russia for ruining a once-prosperous economy and exploiting its southern neighbour,[8] and another decries what it sees as the contamination of the Uzbek language by Russianisms.[9] In terms of actual foreign policy behaviour, however, Uzbekistan has steered a middle course. President Karimov has pursued close ties with Russia, although he consistently seeks veto powers on Russian control. He has been most comfortable with arrangements surrendering formal decision-making power to 'collective' leadership of many ex-republics, especially the Central Asian ones. Indeed, Uzbekistan would clearly like to see a Central Asian core within the CIS which would help offset Russian influence and promote Uzbek hegemony in Central Asia. Actual Uzbek policy, however, has always depended on Russia's attitude, which has shifted significantly since the Soviet breakup. When Russia is willing to cooperate and share decision-making power, Uzbekistan reciprocates; when Russia either withdraws inwards or lashes outwards, Uzbekistan pulls back, although never too far.

Karimov, as the chief spokesman for Uzbek policy, initially supported economic union with the other ex-republics and was sceptical of any political union. Thus an Uzbek signature decorated all drafts of the Economic Community negotiated in the months after the coup, including the final draft of 18 October 1991 which eight republics signed. The Uzbek Supreme Soviet ratified it in the session that opened on 18 November. It provided for absence of trade barriers, maintenance of existing economic links, a common banking system, a common currency (at least for the next two years) and a coordinated economic policy process.

Karimov's initial attitude towards political union was more hesitant. Even before the coup, Uzbekistan had proven not to be the loyal drone that was often portrayed. It rejected the December 1990 draft New Union Treaty which Gorbachev had hammered out to restructure the Soviet federation, claiming that it did not recognize Uzbekistan as one of equal sovereign republics.[10] While Karimov was ready to sign the 20 August 1991 version, the events of 21 August prompted

Uzbekistan to raise its claims selectively. On 14 November the leaders of seven republics initialled a statement of purpose pledging soon to sign a political union treaty. Such a political union would include a unified military, a union parliament and government for foreign and inter-republican policy, a union supreme court, and a language of inter-state commerce: Russian.[11] Karimov gave three basic reasons for rejecting this draft: it did not stress that members are subjects of international law, that borders are immutable, and that all signatories are to build relations on the basis of equality and non-interference in each other's affairs.[12] Karimov was then instrumental in torpedoing the political union treaty. On 26 November the republic's leaders opted not to sign the treaty but to send it back to their supreme soviets instead, a move which clearly foreshadowed rejection.

This set the stage for 8 December, when the leaders of the Slavic republics, Russia, Ukraine and Belarus, met in Minsk and signed an agreement to create a Commonwealth of Independent States. This posed a critical problem for the Central Asian republics. The Slavs had not invited them to the founding CIS meeting. If Uzbeks had any serious desire for a radical break with the Russian-dominated union, this was a clear-cut opportunity. Likewise, it was an opportune moment for a political entrepreneur to whip up anti-Russian or anti-Slav sentiment, especially since Uzbekistan was in the middle of a presidential election campaign. Yet Karimov and his only official opponent, the moderate reformer Mokhammad Solikh, chose to play neither the ethnic nor the radical separatist card. Karimov explicitly chose not to portray Belarus, Russia and Ukraine as the three Slavic republics, stating 'it would be more correct from the ethnic, moral, and political point of view to refer to its members as the founders of the union', that is, as three republics which signed the initial 1922 USSR treaty and which therefore had a right to initiate its demise.[13] The Central Asian states agreed to join the CIS at a summit in Ashkhabad on 13 December, so long as they had the status of equal co-founders.

The initial CIS agreement was quite vague, more of a statement of intent to cooperate than a treaty or institution. There is no one package of legislation which can be branded the heart of the CIS; each area of cooperation is negotiated more or less separately. Uzbekistan has shifted its position on the CIS a few times in its search for the proper balance between integration and independence, at first continuing to favour economic unity and to oppose political unity.

Thus Karimov supported a unified currency, unified economic policy-making, a central CIS bank and free inter-republican trade. It was the only Central Asian state, however, to oppose a fully unified CIS army.[14] Thus in March 1992 Karimov took control of CIS border troops on its territory by decree.[15]

A set of important events in January 1992 prompted the first significant shift in Uzbek attitudes towards the CIS and especially Russia. Russian officials began making claims to be the sole heir to Soviet assets and organizational memberships. Further, it became clear that Russia was determined to move ahead with its programme of economic liberalization in mid-January regardless of other republics' views, forcing Uzbekistan to follow suit. The resulting steep price hike triggered the student riots in Tashkent on the same day, in which between two and 21 people died.[16] The sudden rise in prices also disrupted sectors of the Uzbek economy, which were counting on Uzbek resistance to such 'premature' moves.

Karimov bitterly complained that Russia was not behaving like an equal partner, as called for in the CIS treaty and the old Economic Community treaty. He also objected to what he saw as Russian attempts to control the army and called on the leaders of 'some republics' to drop their 'imperial ambitions'.[17] In response, Uzbekistan began to reconsider the value of CIS economic structures. Karimov continued to push for joint CIS decision-making on currency and pricing issues, but would not support these if CIS structures were only a cover for Russian dominance. Since Russia showed no willingness to wait for weak CIS institutions to coordinate price liberalization, Uzbekistan also felt compelled to go its own way. Karimov then declared that each republic should conduct its own pricing policy, since increasing prices to the levels already reached in Russia 'could cause the situation to explode' in Uzbekistan.[18]

Similarly, Karimov and Uzbekistan's state bank chairman repeatedly warned that they would opt for their own national currency if the CIS did not represent true joint policy-making.[19] Russia, however, had appropriated union banking structures for its own Russian state bank, controlling all official ruble emissions. Thus by June 1992 Uzbek State Bank Chairman Feyzulla Mullazhanov was already declaring that the new state now had no choice but to introduce its own money, a move it did not make until late 1993.[20]

A second set of important events occurred around April 1992 and triggered another important shift in Uzbek policy towards Russia and the CIS. Chaos suddenly enveloped two states on the Uzbek border. In Afghanistan, the mujahedin rebels finally managed to launch a major assault on the capital, Kabul, ultimately overrunning it after bloody fighting. No sooner had the rebels won when they split into factions, and the Islamic fundamentalist faction led by Gulbuddin Hekmatyar began its own onslaught against the new authorities. Meanwhile, in Tajikistan, demonstrations exploded in the capital, Dushanbe, unleashing a chain of events which led ultimately to the overthrow of the elected president, Rakhmon Nabiev. The situation was complicated by frequent gun-running traffic across the borders of strife-ridden Tajikistan and Afghanistan.

These crises, in Karimov's words, 'sobered' Uzbek leaders to Russia's importance as a guarantor of stability and borders in the region.[21] Karimov began to call for a NATO-style military for the CIS, in which 'each state has its own army and at the same time participates in the pooling of efforts and the creation of a unified operational and strategic leadership within a unified command.'[22] The Uzbek government drew up plans to create a 'nominal' army of 30,000 troops, which Uzbekistan would fund but which, according to Karimov, would form part of the CIS joint armed forces under Commander-in-Chief Yevgeniy Shaposhnikov. At the same time, he said, Uzbekistan would permit CIS strategic forces to supplement Uzbek troops on Uzbek territory.[23]

These declarations set the stage for the most important CIS summit meeting so far that year, which took place in Tashkent on 15 May 1992. Delegates signed a number of agreements, culminating in a mutual defence treaty between Russia, Uzbekistan, Kazakhstan, Turkmenistan, Tajikistan and Armenia.[24] Under it, signatories consider aggression or the threat of aggression against one country to be aggression against all parties.[25] This treaty also creates a peace-keeping force and military observer groups which, with the consent of warring factions, the CIS will send to areas of potential or real conflict. [26] The Uzbek Supreme Soviet ratified the treaty in its tenth session on 3 July 1992,[27] and the Uzbek Foreign and Defence Ministries have already called for more Russian troops to enter Uzbekistan to help protect its border with Afghanistan.[28]

The Mutual Security Treaty once threatened to put Uzbekistan's primary loyalty to the test in the crisis over the Armenian enclave in Azerbaijan known as Nagorno-Karabakh. Armenia and Azerbaijan have been near a state of all-out war over the region; in 1992 and

1993 Armenia was a member of the mutual security pact, while Azerbaijan was not. To complicate matters, Turkish leaders face great popular pressure to come to the defence of their Turkic Azeri brothers, and just before his death in April 1993, Turkish President Turgut Ozal declared that Turkey could not permit Armenian aggression and 'must show teeth'.[29] Russian Foreign Minister Andrei Kozyrev, on the other side, explicitly warned Turkey that in the event of a Turkish attack on Armenia, Russia would come to the latter's rescue.[30]

One would be hard pressed to imagine Uzbeks enthusiastically giving up their lives to defend Russia and Armenia against Turkey and Azerbaijan, but one should not jump to the opposite conclusion either. Uzbekistan quietly warned Turkey to stay out of the conflict and left others guessing as to what it would do in case of a major regional war. Thus Karimov declared to a Turkish newspaper:

> The former Soviet Union's leaders were wrong about Karabakh. The Karabakh problem was in their interest and they fanned its flames. It is up to the two countries there to solve the problem. They must solve it themselves. The deployment of CIS forces helped a little bit. This problem must be solved within the UN framework. Some countries want to intervene to gain prestige, but if a third force interferes it would cause a major tragedy. We as Muslims and Turks are with our Azeri brothers, but for now we must stay out and not get involved while other quarters are not causing any harm.[31]

Pressure was ultimately taken off Karimov when Azerbaijan's parliament voted to join the CIS on 20 September 1993 and signed the Mutual Security Treaty in December 1993.

While Turkmenistan and Ukraine have increasingly cooled to the Commonwealth, Uzbekistan has joined Russia, Kazakhstan, Belarus, Kyrgyzstan and Armenia in trying to create a more tightly integrated core within the CIS. After signing the Mutual Security Treaty in May (without Belarus), this group took its next important step forward at the CIS summit in Bishkek on 9 October 1992. In the days leading up to the summit, Russian President Boris Yeltsin reversed his position and agreed to joint inter-republican control of the ruble. Karimov thus abandoned his threats to create a national currency, signing on to a 'Ruble Commonwealth' which would provide for unfettered use of the ruble throughout the 'ruble zone', true joint control of credit and monetary policies, the removal of any rival forms of currency, and compensation from any state which withdraws from the pact.[32]

Even though an Uzbek national currency had already been printed, Karimov refrained from introducing it, arguing that the experience of Ukraine and the Baltics has shown that such currencies fare much worse than even the ruble.[33] In addition to the Ruble Commonwealth, the leaders of these states agreed to create some central CIS institutions, including an inter-state bank of mutual accounts, an economic court and a 'consultative economic working group', which is really a council for coordinating economic affairs.[34] In late 1992 Uzbekistan and other Central Asian states voted to put some teeth into the Mutual Security Treaty, calling on Russia to provide the core troops for a CIS force to secure order in Tajikistan. Early the next year, at the January 1993 CIS summit in Minsk, Karimov signed on to the Inter-state Bank, which would simplify transactions betwen republics but which also formally hands Russia control over monetary emissions. In Minsk, Karimov also initialled a declaration of intent to sign the long-awaited CIS Charter, although he registered objections to the section regulating human rights.

The next major shift in Uzbek–Russian relations took place in the second half of 1993, when Russia again changed its policy on the ruble zone. The crisis began on 23 July, when the Russian Central Bank unilaterally announced that ruble notes printed before 1993 would no longer be legal tender after a short period during which people could exchange them for new ones. Russia then announced that it would demand a renegotiation of the ruble zone before it would supply other former Soviet republics with new rubles. The decision effectively created a new Russian national currency, destroying the fledgling 'Ruble Commonwealth'. Only a decision at the highest level prevented Uzbekistan from leaving the ruble zone immediately, as it was widely expected to do in response.

Negotiations ensued, and Uzbekistan signed on to an economic union in the framework of the CIS which envisioned gradual policy convergence and coordinating central organs. Once again it appeared that Uzbekistan was willing to stick with the ruble zone, paying a high price to do so. One Karimov economic advisor said in September 1993 that Uzbekistan had actually agreed that the Russian Central Bank would effectively be the central bank of the CIS. Nevertheless, bilateral negotiations continued, with Russia demanding that Uzbekistan pay for the new rubles and transfer 40 tonnes of gold from its gold reserves to Moscow to help back the currency. Uzbek leaders argued that Russia had intentionally forced Uzbekistan from the ruble zone under the influence of prominent Russian politicians like Boris Fedorov, who had long argued that the ruble zone is a source of inflation and economic instability. Others saw the Russian proposals as completely reasonable, the only way for Russia to maintain a ruble zone without it becoming a drain on its economy. Whatever the reasoning, Uzbekistan ultimately decided Russia's price was too high, introducing the 'som' on 15 November 1993.

Uzbekistan's exit from the ruble zone marked a dramatic shift in Russian–Uzbek relations. Tensions between Uzbeks and Russians in Uzbekistan began to rise, as Russians realized they would have to go through a currency exchange process to visit Russia. Many Russians decided to migrate to Russia, bringing with them charges that Uzbekistan was starting to ignore them. Russia also began to pressure Uzbek leaders to allow ethnic Russians to hold dual citizenship. While such events were met with annoyance by Karimov, relations between the two countries began to smooth over by early 1994.[35] As Uzbek leaders stressed, they were still all part of an economic union as well as a mutual security pact despite the breakup of the ruble zone.

Overall, therefore, Uzbek–Russian relations have been among the closest in the CIS, despite occasional rifts. While most core CIS members have left the ruble zone at one time or another, they remain tied to Russia and each other in the economic union and Mutual Security Treaty. Although Uzbekistan has consistently spoken out for close cooperation with Russia, it has had to react to several big shifts in Russian policy. Uzbekistan has been fairly consistent, however, in advocating close ties with Russia so long as decision-making power in any joint institutions is truly shared, a concept with which Russia has not been so comfortable.

Central Asian states[36]

Uzbekistan has also been working to establish a firm alliance of Central Asian states within the CIS. Karimov has repeatedly stressed that the Central Asians want to work within the framework of the CIS, but he has pointedly declared that such a bloc could survive and even thrive should the CIS crumble. This bloc-within-a-bloc would include Uzbekistan, Kyrgyzstan, Kazakhstan and Tajikistan if it regains stability. These states would clearly like to see Turkmenistan participate, but Turkmenistan has recently sought to avoid CIS ties on the strength of its large natural gas reserves and rapidly growing ties with neighbouring Iran. Karimov and Nazarbaev have spearheaded the drive to Central Asian integration, which intensified and began to bear fruit in early 1994.

Uzbekistan's links with the other Central Asian states are special in several ways. To begin with, they are all neighbours with tight infrastructural links. They are quite similar culturally; all but Kazakhstan consider themselves to be predominantly Muslim, and the titular nationalities of all but Tajikistan speak a Turkic tongue. These states are also facing very similar issues such as rural poverty, potential wealth in natural resources, water crises and potential instability in the face of rapid economic reforms.

Thus on 20 December 1991 the Central Asian republics and Kazakhstan officially created a Consultative Council. This was intended eventually to provide social protection against price policy changes; create a regional emissions bank; coordinate republican socio-economic development; regulate ties and enforce compliance; organize joint production of goods in increased demand; create joint ventures; provide joint use of commercial wharves and ports; and build regional infrastructure.[37]

The summit of Central Asian leaders in Bishkek, Kyrgyzstan, on 22–3 April 1992 confirmed many of the initial Consultative Council pledges and added some details. The leaders of Uzbekistan, Kazakhstan and Kyrgyzstan (and later the embattled Tajikistan president) signed documents on the coordination of economic reforms and price policies, the creation of an inter-bank union to coordinate monetary and credit policies, and the protection of all nationalities in the region. They also signed a draft document on the pooling of investments for major international projects such as the Tengiz–Kumkul oil pipeline, renovation of the Rogun hydropower station, and the revival of the Aral Sea.[38] Another important document specifies that regional passenger and freight transport will be free of taxes and state duties throughout the region.[39] These states also joined a Kazakh–Russian agreement on coordination of railway transport.[40] The Central Asian leaders continued these themes at their highly publicized summit in Tashkent on 4 January 1993, where they formally agreed to exchange ambassadors,[41] to use the Tashkent broadcasting centre to transmit radio and television to all of Central Asia, and to launch a newspaper serving the entire region. Thus after the late January 1993 summit of all CIS leaders in Minsk, President Karimov declared that if the CIS as a whole fails to create strong institutions, Central Asia will have to embark on its own,[42] echoing Kyrgyz President Askar Akaev's idea of a 'triple alliance' between Kazakhstan, Kyrgyzstan and Uzbekistan. Karimov, Akaev and Kazakh President Nazarbaev took a major step in this direction on 1 February 1994, removing customs on their states' common borders.[43] This was the first stage of a Central Asian 'economic union' launched by Karimov and Nazarbaev on 10 January 1994. During a summit at Issyk-Kul 29–30 April 1994, Kyrgyzstan officially joined the union, which envisions the creation of a common market by the year 2000.[44] At least one advisor to Karimov was even pushing for a common Uzbek–Kazakh currency in the latter half of 1993, but the two states ultimately decided to deal with the ruble zone separately.

Strong Central Asian cooperation fits into two broader Uzbek foreign policy strategies. Initially, a firm Central Asian bloc could help counterbalance preponderant Russian influence within the CIS. Indeed, Central Asian leaders met as a bloc before deciding to join the CIS in December 1991, and adopted a series of joint demands on the new organization. This pattern has continued, with these presidents using the April 1992 Bishkek summit of Central Asian leaders to hammer out some joint positions for the May 1992 CIS summit in Tashkent.[45] Lower-level Central Asian representatives have similarly held caucuses before meeting with their other CIS counterparts.[46]

Uzbek leaders also believe that they would play the leading role in a Central Asian bloc, since Uzbekistan is by far the most populous state in the region and is centrally located. Thus most talk of a 'unified Turkestan' has emanated from Uzbekistan. One can find Karimov regularly in the press jockeying with Kazakh President Nazarbaev for the role of key regional spokesman.

Karimov has sometimes sent mixed signals regarding his Central Asian strategy; but these are probably meant to reassure Russia that it will not carry Central Asian unity too far.[47] The overall pattern of events clearly suggests that Karimov hopes Uzbekistan will dominate a Central Asian bloc which will be economically beneficial and will help offset Russian hegemony within the CIS.

Karimov knows, however, that a Central Asian bloc will not be enough to offset Russian hegemony in the region. To understand his regime's foreign policy, therefore, the other third of it must be considered: establishing friendly relations and as many economic ties as possible with powerful neighbours.

Iran

Largely because its fundamentalist religious stance is unpopular in the West, Iran has drawn much attention with its activities in Central Asia in the wake of the Soviet collapse. *The Economist*, for example, warns that 'Iran wants to create a shield where its influence is paramount – a shield that must include the Muslim republics of the new Commonwealth of Independent States.'[48] Similarly, the *Toronto Star* reports that 'Iran was first off the mark' in the race for the Central Asian soul after the August 1991 coup.[49] As far as Uzbekistan is concerned, however, the sound has been greater than the substance, although Iran and Uzbekistan have taken significant steps towards economic cooperation.

If Iran is interested in promoting direct ties with Uzbekistan in order somehow to sway its foreign or domestic policy, it appears to have tried hard to thwart itself. Upon arriving in Tashkent on 30 November 1991, some of Iranian Foreign Minister Ali Akbar Velayati's first public words were: 'Iran respects the aspirations of the Soviet republics for self-determination. However, Tehran's relations with the Soviet republics are formulated within the framework of her relations with Moscow.'[50] In Moscow four days earlier, on 26 November, Velayati had declared: 'Islam is an important factor of community with certain republics and we will strengthen contacts with them in every possible way. At the same time, we do see them as an inalienable part of the Soviet Union.'[51] Strikingly, the former statement came four days *after* the final collapse of inter-republican political union negotiations. Even the earlier of Velayati's statements came two weeks after Turkey had recognized the complete independence of the former republic of Azerbaijan.[52] This was hardly any way to woo a potential client state, and this casts doubt on the notion that Iran is zealously pursuing a fundamentalist empire in the whole of post-Soviet Central Asia.

Neither has Uzbekistan shown enthusiasm for any kind of alliance with Tehran. At the same meeting where Velayati declared Uzbekistan an 'inalienable part of the Soviet Union', Uzbek leaders stressed that Iran was only one of many neighbours with whom it wanted to build relations.[53]

Both Iran and Uzbekistan have actively pursued economic ties, however. During the Iranian foreign minister's visit to Tashkent in November 1991, both sides discussed Iran's plan to make Tashkent the hub for a new Iran Air service to the region, and negotiated trade by cargo trains between Uzbekistan and the northern Iranian capital of Mashhad. Iran also proposed setting up direct telephone links between the two states.[54] Later, when Karimov went to Tehran, he and the Iranian president signed various trade and cultural agreements.[55] But while economic relations have grown, political relations betwen the two states have been sour. This stems primarily from President Karimov's open opposition to 'Islamic fundamentalism' in Tajikistan and his willingness to send supplies to what Tehran calls 'bigoted Communist forces' there.[56] Indeed, the sense is that Iran, to the extent that it is actively pursuing links with Central Asia, is focussing on Tajikistan, with whom it shares the Persian language, and Turkmenistan, with whom it shares a border. The ties it is pursuing with Uzbekistan do not appear to be much stronger than those it is pursuing with Armenia.

Observers often speculate that Iran's most serious threat is covert and subtle. Iran, many say, is secretly sending massive aid to Islamic fundamentalists in the region, hoping its efforts will culminate in several brotherly fundamentalist neighbours. As Martha Brill Olcott argues, however, there is little evidence to support such rumours: 'Leaders of Central Asia's Islamic revivalist movement appear far more interested in the teachings of their Sunni Muslim brethren than those of fundamentalist Iranian Shi'ites.'[57] Similarly, James Rupert reports that any such support 'has not yet manifested itself in either the strengthening of such groups or expressions by them of loyalty to Teheran'.[58]

Such a view seems to fit better with Iran's current economic situation. After nearly a decade of devastating war with Iraq, Iran's economy has been wrecked and its political leadership is determined to rebuild. This primarily means a focus on domestic economic reform, but it also means an effort to support development in the whole region. After two wars in the Persian Gulf and another in neighbouring Afghanistan, the whole area threatens to become an economic backwater.[59] In order to push through economic reforms like privatization and foreign investment, Iranian President Ali Akhbar Hashemi Rafsanjani has imposed sweeping political reforms which disqualified about a thousand hard-line fundamentalists out of a total of around three thousand candidates for parliament.[60] In its latest five-year plan Iran has thus given priority to increasing non-oil exports, with hopes that Central Asia will be a good market for its pharmaceuticals, farm machinery and cars.[61] This, combined with the unfertile soil which Sunni Uzbekistan offers for radical Shi'ism, means Iran is likely to spend more effort exporting industrial goods than revolution to Uzbekistan.

Even if Iranian–Uzbek ties are not very extensive, it is politically very much in Karimov's interest to pursue and publicize them. To the extent that other states worry most about the Iranian threat, Karimov can win valuable concessions from the West. Thus fears of Iranian influence prompted the USA to establish diplomatic relations with Uzbekistan without the clear demonstration of democracy and respect for human rights that it originally demanded.[62] Overall, therefore, ties with Iran provide Uzbekistan with economic and political benefits. While these ties may help Uzbekistan become less dependent on Russia, Uzbekistan's foreign policy is certainly not orientated primarily towards Iran, nor is it likely ever to be so.

Turkey

Turkey appears to be much more active than Iran in Uzbekistan, and Uzbekistan seems to be pursuing Turkish ties much more aggressively than Iranian ones. Karimov's primary political aim seems clear: Turkish ties can strongly counterbalance, although not replace, Russian ones. 'We regard Turkey as an elder brother,' he went so far as to declare in late 1991.[63] This initial burst of enthusiasm for Turkish ties has faded, however, as Uzbek leaders have come to recognize that Turkey is much weaker economically and technologically than many West European and South-east Asian countries.

Turkey is attractive to Uzbekistan for several reasons: it is nearer than most Islamic states, it is relatively prosperous, it faces many of the same problems that Uzbekistan does, and the native languages of the two states are quite similar, Uzbek being a Turkic tongue. Further, Turkey represents what most Uzbek political leaders want their state to become. People in Uzbekistan are increasingly aware of the historic ties between the Turks and Uzbeks. Turkey has even established a Turkish Cultural Centre in Tashkent to promote just such an awareness.[64] Imagery of bygone centuries adorns most Uzbek publications and historians regularly unearth and resurrect important Turkic figures; the most significant of these is Amir Timur, also known as Tamerlane, a descendant of Genghis Khan, who built a vast Asian empire during the fourteenth and fifteenth centuries and whom

Uzbeks claim as an ancestor. Uzbeks tend to look to Turkey as to a relative who is obligated to help out. Thus Karimov, the official Muslim establishment and the leading (largely) secular opposition movements, Birlik (Unity) and Erk (Independence), all support the 'Turkish model' for Uzbekistan.[65]

The 'Turkish model' is both dynamic and static. Turkey is currently a relatively prosperous, Western-orientated, traditionally Islamic country with a secular state. Its history is also relevant to Uzbekistan. Under Ataturk, Turkey pursued self-sufficiency through import-substitution and state-run industry. In 1980 President Ozal began to lead the nation back into the world economy, liberalizing the economy, abolishing quotas, and slashing tariffs.[66] Karimov has thus publicly stated his intention to emulate the 'Ozal model'.[67]

Karimov initially played fast and loose with pan-Turkic rhetoric in pushing his cause and drumming up Turkish support. In one interview with a Turkish newspaper in April 1992, he went so far as to declare: 'God willing, the Turkic nation and its single root, language, and religion will soon live united again. The borders inside the Turkic world will be eliminated; we will soon get the means to do this.'[68]

Official ties with Turkey began to blossom in mid-December 1991, when Karimov visited Ankara and Turkey became the first state to recognize Uzbekistan's independence. Leaders of the two countries signed nine separate protocols during the summit, including a treaty on inter-governmental relations and pacts on cooperation in economics, trade, culture, education, science, transport and communication.[69] Specific examples include a joint bank under Turkey's Eximbank, a flight to Istanbul available on Uzbek Airlines (Uzbekiston Havo Yollari) and a 'Turksat' satellite which has already begun to broadcast national television programmes to Turks from Berlin to Almaty.[70]

On 4 March 1992 Turkish Foreign Minister Hikmet Cetin visited Tashkent to lay the groundwork for opening an embassy in Tashkent, as well as to hold talks on trade, defence and education issues.[71] Burgeoning Uzbek–Turkish ties reached a zenith on 27 March 1992, when Turkish Prime Minister Suleyman Demirel arrived in Tashkent to attend the opening ceremony of the new Turkish embassy. There, he promised Uzbekistan $500 million in credits to purchase two million tons of wheat and 250,000 tons of sugar from Turkey.[72] He and Karimov also signed a series of agreements providing, for example, security guarantees for Turkish investments in Uzbekistan, bank cooperation and collaboration in issues concerning transport.[73] Other

Turkish initiatives include training Uzbek diplomats and joining with US banks to initiate Uzbek banks into the world of commercial banking.[74] Turkey also plans to supply books, films, typewriters and printing presses in order to spread use of the Roman alphabet. It also hopes to help Uzbekistan modernize its communication networks, all of which should help bind Uzbekistan more tightly to Turkey.[75] Importantly, Uzbek and Turkish officials are seeking to imbed these budding ties in an institutional framework; indeed, Turkey has created an 'Eastern Department' in its Foreign Ministry for just this purpose. Karimov is even pressing for a Turkic common market.[76]

The biggest media event in Turkic–Uzbek relations so far has been the Ankara summit of leaders of Turkic-speaking states held on 30–31 October 1992. Western observers predicted the resurrection of Greater Turkestan as these leaders signed what became known as the 'Ankara Doctrine'. It has a political and an economic section. The political section declares that ties between the Turkic-speaking states are unbreakable and that their political aims are common, and promises joint action to resolve local conflicts and ensure local stability. The economic section foresees cooperation between the six states in the spheres of technology and communication as well as in the oil and gas industry.[77]

Such a blossoming of Uzbek–Turkish ties fits well with Turkish foreign strategy since the Cold War. During the Cold War, Turkey could always count on aid and favourable treatment from western Europe and North America since it was the only NATO member to share a long border with the USSR. Now, however, it risks being pushed to the periphery of Europe, especially with the renewed significance of the European Common Market and possible steps to European Union.[78] By taking on a new role as model and mentor for Central Asia, it remains strategically important to the West.

It is evident that Turkish inroads into Uzbekistan are much greater than those of Iran. Uzbekistan is much more enthusiastic about ties with Turkey than with Iran, as is reflected, for instance, in the numbers of students that Uzbekistan has sent for a year of study to non-CIS states: 22 to Saudi Arabia, 40 to Pakistan, 2000 to Turkey and none to Iran.[79] Further, cheering crowds in the tens of thousands greeted Turkish Prime Minister Suleyman Demirel on his visit to Tashkent, while no such enthusiasm has reportedly surrounded the visits of top Iranian officials.[80]

It would be a mistake to assume that Uzbekistan is embracing all things Turkish and rejecting all things Russian, however. Despite the cultural affinity between Uzbeks and Turks, Uzbekistan has been decidedly lukewarm on some important Turkish foreign policy issues. Addressing the Cyprus conflict in an interview with a Turkish news-paper, Karimov stated that the Greek and Turkish communities there have the right to live separately and that 'our heart goes out to our Turkish Cypriot brothers', but warned that 'other states should not interfere or support one of the sides.'[81] This position resembles Karimov's stance on the Azeri–Armenian conflict discussed earlier: 'heartfelt sympathy' for the Turkic party coupled with a warning to all third parties (save the UN) not to get involved, even if the non-Turkic side is winning (as was the case at the time of his statements on Nagorno-Karabakh). Notably, the Ankara Doctrine makes no men-tion of the Armenian–Azeri conflict.

In any case, Turks and Uzbeks are finding that many factors limit the extent to which ties between the two nations can develop. Turkey is facing economic troubles and cannot afford to aid Uzbekistan on a massive scale. It suffers from 66 per cent inflation and a large budget deficit, and its growth takes place in bursts (1.6 per cent in 1989, 9.2 per cent in 1990, down again in 1991).[82] The Uzbek side is reeling from the tremendous economic uncertainty and disruption which all states moving from communism to the market have suffered. Until Uzbekistan stabilizes its economy and completes giant steps towards establishing a market economy, a process which Uzbek leaders clearly intend to prolong, a great wave of new trade should not be expected. Turkish companies, like US companies, want to see stability and secure property rights before investing heavily, and this is likely to take many years. This problem is reflected in the comments of frus-trated Turkish businessmen. 'They want everything from chewing gum to blue jeans,' said the head of an Ankara trading company, 'but none of these states have any money. So if you want to trade, you have to barter.' The head of the Sezai Turkes Fevzi Akkaya (STFA) construction company echoes the theme: 'There will be plenty of opportunities, but no money for three, four, five years.'[83] Even then, it will take Uzbekistan years to win international business' confidence that its new laws are stable and enforced. This problem will be com-pounded if serious political turmoil engulfs the nation. Further, as mentioned earlier, transport infrastructure in Central Asia must change before Uzbekistan can begin shipping its goods to new buyers in significantly greater quantities. Meaningful economic agreements between the two states, therefore, have been made difficult and will be unlikely for many years. Perhaps for this reason, Karimov has cooled his pan-Turkic rhetoric, now denying that Uzbekistan has found a 'new big brother' in Turkey and disclaiming any desire to resurrect Greater Turkestan.[84] Significantly, just four days after signing the Ankara Declaration with Turkey, the Turkic Central Asian leaders (minus Turkmenistan's) met with Russian Prime Minister Andrei Kozyrev and called on Russia to bring its troops into Tajikistan.[85] As another Turkish businessman lamented: 'It's a bit like the English saying: all roads lead to Rome. There, all roads lead to Moscow.'[86]

This is not to say that Uzbek–Turkish ties are unimportant. Indeed, Uzbekistan's affections are clearly shifting to Turkey, and ties between the two nations will soon be much stronger than they have been in modern times. Turkey provides Uzbekistan with an important source of investment, personnel, training and technology, which can give Uzbekistan some extremely important economic room to manoeuvre *vis à vis* Russia. Nevertheless, Uzbekistan's ties to Turkey are nowhere near the level of current Uzbek ties to Russia, and immediate plans provide for no great change.

Afghanistan and Tajikistan

Afghanistan and Tajikistan have come to play very important parts in Uzbek foreign policy since 1992 for many reasons other than the fact that they are neighbour states. First and foremost, the anarchy there is a threat to stability in the entire region. Many fear that gun smuggling and drug running from these states threaten to turn Uzbekistan into a second Colombia. Uzbek border guards have already been involved in incidents with parties from Afghanistan, such as that of August 1992, when Uzbek troops killed five border-crossers in a gunfight along the river Amu Darya.[87] Karimov worries that warring Tajiks in Afghanistan and Tajikistan might carry clan-based warfare into Uzbekistan itself, especially in the cities of Samarkand and Bukhara, dominated by ethnic Tajiks. The Uzbek regime also fears a victory by Islamic fundamentalists in either Tajikistan or Afghanistan, since it believes this could inspire rebellion at home. Afghanistan is also a vital link to potentially important southern trading partners like India and Pakistan.

As a result of these fears, Uzbekistan has adopted a tough policy of aiding anti-fundamentalist forces in the area. While it openly aids the self-proclaimed anti-fundamentalist Tajik government under the auspices of the CIS Mutual Security Pact, it denies sending military aid to forces in Afghanistan. Once it became independent, Uzbekistan and other Central Asian states provided fuel and food aid to the formerly Soviet-backed Najibullah regime in Afghanistan, but denied persistent rumours that they were covertly arming it against the rebels. Thus before the rebel victory, Uzbekistan pressured Pakistan to push for a peaceful settlement and worked to prevent a fundamentalist takeover.[88]

Now that the rebels have taken over, rumours continue that Uzbekistan is sending military aid to certain Afghan factions. In particular, a spokesman for Afghanistan's President Burhanuddin Rabbani accused Uzbekistan of aiding the ethnically Uzbek General Abdul Rashid Dostam, who has been fighting Afghan government forces. Uzbek officials have denied any such interference in Afghan affairs.[89] Others have accused Dostam of stirring up fighting between ethnically Uzbek and ethnically Tajik militias in northern Afghanistan.[90]

It is very difficult to authenticate such charges. While many rumours are clearly based on speculation that Uzbeks naturally help other Uzbeks, aiding factions with an anti-fundamentalist reputation is compatible with Karimov's stated goal of preventing the spread of radical Islam. Karimov would also clearly not be adverse to having a friendly force control the northern part of Afghanistan, on the border of Uzbekistan. Given Uzbekistan's own military weakness, however, it is unlikely that such aid would be extensive; extensive aid would have to come from the true regional power, Russia.

Saudi Arabia

Saudi Arabia represents another potential patron for Uzbekistan, and a rich one at that. It has taken an active interest in countering what it sees as Iran's inroads in Central Asia, and has begun to pump great resources into the region. So far it has focussed on religious aid, although it is well situated to be an important future player despite its distance.

In February 1992 Saudi Arabia officially established diplomatic relations with Uzbekistan, declaring that it was ready to discuss all aspects of cooperation.[91] While it has established a bank in Uzbekistan, its primary interest is in cultural and religious ties. Even before the Saudis established diplomatic relations with the traditionally Islamic

ex-republics, they were aiding religious societies and providing religious literature through the Islamic Conference Organization and the
Mecca-based Muslim World League. Thus while Saudi Arabia had
pledged $60 million in aid to Central Asia as of April 1991, most of
it was earmarked for building religious institutions.[92] Accordingly, on
his trip to Tashkent to establish diplomatic relations with Uzbekistan,
the Saudi Foreign Minister, H.R.H. Prince Saud Al-Faisal, granted
one million copies of the Quran to the Islamic republics, and pledged
to host their pilgrims for two pilgrimage seasons at his own expense.[93]

If Saudi Arabia is indeed competing with Iran for spiritual influence in Uzbekistan, it has three distinct advantages: first, it is far
richer than Iran; second, it espouses Sunni Islam as opposed to Iran's
Shi'ism, while Uzbekistan is also traditionally Sunni; and third, Saudi
Arabia contains two of the most holy sites in Islam – Mecca and
Medina. Thus the Uzbek President Karimov made the pilgrimage to
Mecca in late April 1992, but did not visit Tehran until near the end
of that year. The Saudi trip also afforded him the opportunity to
negotiate a planned Uzbekistan Airlines route from Tashkent to
Jidda.[94]

Overall, Saudi Arabia has the potential to be a major force in shaping Uzbek foreign policy, but it has not thus far shown the enthusiasm
of Turkey. Should the mood strike them, the Saudis could be vital
economic allies for Uzbekistan in times of crisis and development.

The Indian subcontinent

The rivalry between Turkey, Saudi Arabia and Iran is not the only
competition taking place in Central Asia; Pakistan is seeking to outflank India in a region it hopes will eventually provide important
markets and raw materials.[95] Even poverty-stricken Bangladesh is
working to establish ties with Uzbekistan. For now, however, an anarchic Afghanistan separates this region from Uzbekistan, giving all of
these states extra incentive to resolve that crisis.

Pakistan has been the most enthusiastic of the states on the Indian
subcontinent to seek economic and political ties with Uzbekistan. It
was one of the first historically Islamic states, along with Turkey and
Iran, to send a high-level delegation to Uzbekistan after its declaration
of independence. Thus in late November 1991 Karimov met with
Pakistani Minister for Economic Affairs Sardar Assef Ahmed Ali in
Tashkent. Karimov stressed, as with Iran, that Pakistan is but one

state with which Uzbekistan hopes to establish close relations. He then called for increased ties with Pakistan, especially business ties, citing the Tabani company as a model. Pakistani banks should also open up filials in Uzbekistan, he declared.[96] The two states signed no major documents and established no major institutions at that meeting, however; that would not be possible until war in Afghanistan subsided, the Central Asian leaders said.

In February the first major events in Pakistani–Uzbek relations took place, while ties with India did not change significantly. Karimov visited Pakistan and the two states agreed to exchange ambassadors.[97] Pressure from Uzbekistan and other Central Asian states persuaded Pakistan to cease arming Hekmatyar's fundamentalist group of Afghan rebels and to seek a peaceful settlement. While events have not become any more stable, Pakistan has nevertheless been promoting joint ventures with Central Asia in tourism, banking, cement, textiles and English-language training.[98] It is still unable to build the railway line it wants from the port of Karachi to Central Asia through Afghanistan, however. In June 1992 Nawaz Sharif, prime minister of Pakistan, visited Uzbekistan to open the Pakistani embassy in Tashkent and to sign bilateral agreements on basic inter-state relations.[99] In return, Karimov visited Pakistan in August 1992 for three days. India, meanwhile, has been content to set up diplomatic relations with Uzbekistan and to develop such economic ties as are possible, but it is ready to take a 'keener interest' should Pakistan or Iran make significant inroads.[100] Uzbekistan has shown nearly as much interest in India as it has in Pakistan, although it harbours little hope for imminent trade breakthroughs because of the continuing Afghan civil war.

Overall, Pakistan and India represent potentially very important markets for Uzbek cotton and other resources, as well as a promising source of technology and industrial goods. Little progress is likely in these ties, however, until Afghanistan sees peace. If the past is any precedent, this may be a long time in coming.

Other states

The Uzbek leadership has pursued bilateral agreements with a host of other countries, notably Western states, South Korea, China and Israel. The West is very important insofar as it is the source of modern technology, its corporations invest there, and it can set the terms for Uzbekistan's participation in key international institutions like the

International Monetary Fund. The USA initially withheld diplomatic ties until Uzbekistan demonstrated adherence to democracy and human rights, but became unnerved by increasing Uzbek–Iranian ties and opened its embassy in Tashkent on 16 March 1992. The USA has also helped its ally Turkey expand its influence in the region. Overall, however, Western ties have been only secondary for the Uzbek leadership, as demonstrated by the fact that Karimov's only significant European visit by the end of 1992 was to Austria, where he signed a series of agreements for joint projects with Austria in agriculture and a programme for Uzbek bankers to train in Austria.[101] Uzbekistan is also pursuing close economic cooperation with Israel, and is particularly interested in its irrigation technology. It has signed agreements with states as diverse as the People's Republic of China, Malaysia, Hungary, Greek Cyprus, South Korea and Egypt.

The Economic Cooperation Organization

Uzbekistan is establishing some of its ties with above-mentioned states in the context of the Economic Cooperation Organization (ECO), whose charter members include Iran, Turkey and Pakistan. Founded in 1963, it began as a loose economic pact between the predominantly Muslim states that had been part of the Central Treaty Organization (CENTO) founded by Britain and the USA in the 1950s to deter the Soviet Union from expanding southward.[102] At its summit on 16–17 February 1992 it voted to admit Uzbekistan, Kazakhstan, Turkmenistan, Azerbaijan, Kyrgyzstan and Tajikistan as full members, and did so officially in late 1992. It is unclear how meaningful the ECO will become. Members clearly hoped the admission of the ex-Soviet states would revitalize the organization, but they disagree in their visions for it. At the February ECO summit, Iranian President Rafsanjani portrayed an activist organization, invoking images of OPEC and the Association of South-east Asian Nations (ASEAN), and suggesting it might get involved in relieving the plight of Palestinians. Turkish President Ozal, however, held up the European Community as his model for ECO. Romania has also applied for membership, calling into question whether ECO will remain a Muslim organization.[103] The ECO members did agree on a few points at the February summit, approving a 10 per cent reduction in trade tariffs, a common market for agricultural products, training of experts and the creation of a common development bank which Turkish businessmen said was to compete with the activities of Saudi-based banks.[104] With such strong personalities involved, however, it seems unlikely that ECO will amount to much more than a forum to negotiate regional trade agreements.

Speculation on the future

While Uzbekistan's most important ties are now primarily with Russia, it would be a mistake to assume that this will continue indefinitely. Since the whims of future national leaders cannot be predicted, possible structural changes in domestic and international politics and how they might affect these leaders must be examined: Uzbekistan will either remain primarily orientated to Russia or it will sever its key Russian ties and become essentially neutral. It is unlikely that Uzbekistan will orientate its foreign policy primarily towards any South Asian or Middle Eastern state, and of these it is even less likely ever to favour Iran. Economic ties will grow rapidly and remain important with all of these states, even if Uzbekistan does not voluntarily constrain its decision-making autonomy for the sake of any of them.

While the geographic location of states is unlikely to change significantly, other aspects of international structure can be expected to shift. Initially, normal market forces and government intervention will build a transactions infrastructure between Uzbekistan and non-CIS states in the region over the next five to ten years, allowing levels of trade that are normal for neighbours. The primary exception concerns Afghanistan; as long as civil war there continues, infrastructural problems will continue to stunt the growth of trade with the Indian subcontinent. Long-run changes in international capabilities are unlikely, since Russia will remain by far the dominant economic and military power, and Iran and Turkey are unlikely to undergo major relative changes absent a war. In the medium term, however, Russian economic power will continue to fall relative to South Asian and Middle Eastern states. Thus in the medium term Uzbekistan (no matter who is leading it) can be expected to increase its economic ties with states like Iran, Turkey and Saudi Arabia relative to ties with Russia; but such ties are limited so long as Uzbekistan delays marketizing reforms and fails to win business' confidence that its investments are secure. Russia will remain the only feasible potential foreign defender of Uzbek sovereignty, however. This will likely be true in the long run as well, when Russia will probably reassert its position as the dominant regional economic power.

Domestic structure can change in two ways: institutional change might make a leader more or less responsive to cleavages in society, and these social cleavages themselves may change. Social cleavages appear unlikely to develop in ways other than those already outlined. That is, Uzbek intellectuals will probably continue their drive to promote traditionally Turkic and Islamic symbols instead of Russian ones, since they have a vested interest in doing so and now have the freedom to act. People will likely continue to respond, since they will be looking for new ways to identify themselves in this time of rapid social change, and since they stand to gain relative to the ethnic Russian élite in the republic. This process is not likely to reverse itself unless Turkey engages in egregious acts against Uzbeks, but this is extremely unlikely. Economic changes could also produce new social cleavages, but these would likely only reinforce cultural cleavages which work against Russian ties. These changes are all moot, however, if leaders are not responsive to popular sentiments.

Domestic institutional change is unlikely in the short term, since no domestic force seems capable of peacefully resisting Karimov's iron grip on power even with the help of pressure from other states. Nevertheless, parliamentary elections are scheduled for December 1994 and the next presidential elections for December 1996. If held, these could provide an opportunity for an opponent to rally popular sentiment against Karimov's Russian-orientated policy. This would force Karimov either to coopt such a movement or to repress it; otherwise, his forces face defeat. If relatively free elections are allowed, a turn away from Russia can be expected around this time. Ties with other Central Asian states would likely remain strong. If Karimov represses the elections (for example, by declaring martial law in response to a renewed Tajikistan crisis), or continues to prevent the rise of real opposition parties, Uzbekistan would probably remain primarily orientated to Russia. Since instability will probably continue to be a threat in both Tajikistan and Afghanistan, and since opposition forces have few resources to resist, it seems most likely that Karimov will somehow thwart competitive elections which he would argue are destabilizing. This would lead to Uzbekistan's remaining primarily orientated towards Russia and other Central Asian states.

Leaderships do not have to change in an orderly manner, of course. A popular uprising could overwhelm the Karimov regime, creating a revolutionary situation where various groups actively struggle to mobilize potential social cleavages to their advantage. This might occur if civil war in Afghanistan or Tajikistan spills over into neighbouring Uzbekistan, if Uzbek dissidents find their anarchic neighbours to be a bountiful source of arms, or if the economy deteriorates sharply. In such a case, political entrepreneurs capitalizing on the ongoing cultural shift to Turkic and Islamic symbols would probably win out, since these symbols are associated with relatively prosperous Saudi Arabia and Turkey and seem to offer a simple solution to national ills, as opposed to symbols binding people in Uzbekistan to Russia, which could easily be portrayed as the avatar of economic ruin. It must be emphasized, however, that a revolutionary shift to Turkic cultural symbols in the capital would likely produce a bloody, drawn-out civil war in other parts of the country. Many ethnic Tajiks, concentrated in the traditionally Tajik cities of Samarkand and Bukhara in Uzbekistan, fear the rise of pan-Turkism and support Karimov's efforts to suppress opposition groups espousing it. Should an opposition seize power that is identified too closely to pan-Turkist ideals, these Tajik cities may well erupt in rebellion. A pan-Islamic movement has more potential to unite Tajik and Turkic oppositions, although so far most such movements have appealed strongly to pan-Turkic sentiments.

Were a revolutionary shift to Turkic and Islamic symbols to take place, it would probably result in a signficant break with Russia, which would likely mean pulling out of the CIS Mutual Security Treaty, withdrawing from other easily breakable CIS arrangements (such as commonwealth-wide media), and curtailing trade despite economic hardship. A significant move to Turkey, however, would still be hindered by distance and Uzbekistan's transitional economic situation, as argued earlier. A major move to Iran in such an event is extremely unlikely, since Uzbekistan's cultural shift is explicitly to things Turkic and since Iran's radical Shi'ism would likely lose out to propagators of the Sunni Islam to which Uzbeks have traditionally adhered. The net result would be a relatively isolated Uzbekistan strongly orientated only towards other Central Asian states.

It is extremely difficult to speculate on the likelihood of revolution. The conditions seem ripe in many ways: economic crisis, anarchy engulfing neighbours, a burgeoning arms market and powerful cultural symbols to unite a movement. For the near future, Karimov's bases of support appear strong enough to keep him in power, and he has managed to coopt many of the opposition's most potent cultural symbols, for example, by making the pilgrimage to Mecca. But economic crises have a way of eroding support from even the strongest of leaders and pure force is often ineffective in the long run, as the Shah of Iran discovered. Much, then, will depend on the success (or the absence of a catastrophic failure) of Karimov's state-led economic reform package. It would thus seem prudent to consider a revolutionary shift away from Russia (but not dramatically closer to Turkey or Iran) to be possible but unlikely within the next ten years.

Overall, this analysis suggests that the future of Uzbek foreign policy hinges primarily on whether revolution engulfs the new state. If revolution occurs, Uzbekistan is likely to sever key Russian ties and refuse voluntarily to constrain its autonomy for the sake of any foreign state save Central Asian ones; if revolution does not occur, Uzbekistan will likely remain primarily orientated towards Russia. Importantly, predictions based on political structure hold regardless of which different parties exist and what they stand for. Nevertheless, these predictions are supported if the major opposition parties tend to espouse views which the theory leads us to expect. Thus while the main opposition group, Birlik, began as a primarily secular democratic movement, it has recently adopted strongly Islamist rhetoric and is cooperating closely now with the Islamic Revival Party. Even the small moderate reform party, Erk, has radicalized in the face of Karimov's recent crackdown, offering to cooperate with Birlik in bringing social discontent out onto the streets. In terms of policy, Birlik's Fifth Congress castigated Karimov for 'betraying the interests of kindred Azerbaijan' by signing the CIS Mutual Security Treaty.[105] The IRP is more mysterious; it has focussed more on grass-roots efforts to promote Islam than on developing policy platforms, perhaps because it is outlawed in Uzbekistan. Thus the major opposition movements in Uzbekistan are converging around a political strategy relying primarily on cultural symbols pulling Uzbekistan away from Russia, and this tends to support the conclusion that revolution in Uzbekistan would mean a break with Russia. Revolution there is possible, but not likely. So long as Uzbekistan remains stable, therefore, it can be expected to remain primarily orientated towards Russia.

Conclusion

This chapter has outlined a 'two-level structural' framework for analysing the foreign policy orientation of states, and has begun to test it by examining in depth the case of Uzbekistan. The particular array of international and domestic structures facing any current Uzbek president may yield three somewhat contradictory trends in Uzbek foreign policy:

(1) De-isolation: Uzbekistan is emerging from a period of severe protectionism; thus it is rapidly establishing ties with all of its neighbours (including Iran and Turkey) which will likely reach the level of ties that most countries have with nearby states.

(2) Turkification: Uzbek culture is undergoing a significant shift from its Russian symbols to its Turkic and Islamic ones, generating greater popular support for economic and political ties with Turkey and other Central Asian states than with Russia or Iran.

(3) Geopolitical Realism: Russian power and proximity mean that Uzbek–Russian ties are costly to break, especially since the two states are tightly interdependent as a result of nearly 70 years of Soviet rule. Thus as soon as civil wars in Tajikistan and Afghanistan became threats to regional stability, Uzbekistan called on Russia, not Turkey or Iran, to send in troops.

The structure of the international system would lead almost any Uzbek leadership seeking career security to orientate its foreign policy towards Russia, whereas the changing cultural structure of domestic politics tends to pull Uzbekistan away from Russia towards Turkey. This means that the more responsive Uzbek leadership is to popular sentiments, the more likely it is that Uzbekistan will move away from Russia, although Uzbek economic chaos and geography still render a major shift to Turkey unlikely. This seems to be borne out by events, since Uzbekistan's first move away from Russia occurred during a contested presidential election campaign in late 1991, while a political crackdown accompanied the reassertion of the primarily Russian orientation of Uzbek foreign policy in mid-1992. In the future, Karimov appears likely to insulate himself well from potential popular pressures for the sake of stability, but he may still be vulnerable to revolution. If revolution does engulf Uzbekistan, the victorious forces will probably be anti-Russian, producing an essentially neutral Uzbekistan. Otherwise, Uzbekistan can be expected to remain primarily orientated towards Russia.

This analysis suggests that the two-level structural approach may be helpful in predicting and explaining trends in foreign policy orientations. The model can be developed in two ways. First, it can be tested by examining events in Uzbekistan as they unfold – do the predictions hold? Second, the other former Soviet republics and even non-CIS states can be examined in depth. Only by rigorously comparing many cases can we achieve greater confidence in our conclusions, thereby advancing our understanding of foreign policy behaviour.

Notes

I would like to give special thanks to Mark Saroyan, who has been extremely supportive and who has provided countless helpful comments and criticisms. I would also like to thank all those who read and commented on earlier drafts of this paper, especially William Fierman, Paul Goble, Pauline Jones and Mark Nagel. I am of course indebted to all those who organized and participated in the Workshop on Post-Soviet Central Asia and South Asia: New Ties and Emerging Relations, at MIT's Center for International Studies, particularly Ali Banuazizi and Myron Wiener. Any errors, of course, are entirely my responsibility and my arguments may not correspond to those of the above-mentioned people.

1. One of few exceptions is Martha Brill Olcott's article 'Central Asia's Catapult to Independence', *Foreign Affairs*, lxxi/3 (Summer 1992), pp 108–30.

2. Cordahi, Cherif J., 'Central Asia emerges into the Muslim world', *MEI*, 3 April 1992, pp 16–17.

3. See the view attributed to US officials in the *New York Times*, 6 February 1992, p 3A.

4. Walt, Stephen M., *The Origins of Alliances* (Ithaca, NY: Cornell University Press), 1987, p 1.

5. This approach renders different results from the realist approach which takes national security as the primary goal of state, assuming away any chance of international political integration. Here, a leader might see his best chance at maintaining power to be federation with another state, especially if he might become head of the new federation.

6. See the literature in international relations on 'two-level games'. The label was invented in an important article by Robert D. Putnam, 'Diplomacy and Domestic Politics: the logic of two-level games', *International Organization* (Summer 1988), pp 427–60; although many of the important concepts were laid out by Thomas C. Schelling, *The Strategy of Conflict* (Cambridge MA: Harvard University Press, 1960).

7. Waltz, Kenneth, *Theory of International Politics* (Reading MA: Addison-Wesley, 1979).

8. Malik, Tahir, 'Yevropasiz yashay olamizmi?', *Uzbekiston Adabiyoti va San'ati*, no. 4, 24 January 1992, p 5.

9. 'Asoratli Suzlar', *Uzbekiston Adabiyoti va San'ati*, no. 16, 17 April 1992, p 2.

10. Critchlow, James, *Nationalism in Uzbekistan* (Boulder CO: Westview Press 1991), p xi.

11. INTERFAX, 1140 GMT, 15 November 1991, FBIS.

12. TASS, 1815 GMT, 19 November 1991, FBIS. Interestingly, the version published by INTERFAX did indeed explicitly declare that members were subjects of international law.

13. INTERFAX, 1725 GMT, 10 December 1991, FBIS.

14. POSTFACTUM, Moscow, 2125 GMT, 31 January 1992, FBIS.

15. Radio Tashkent, 0300 GMT, 25 March 1992, FBIS.

16. For eyewitness accounts of the riots, see *Uzbekiston Adabiyoti va San'ati*, no. 4, 24 January 1992, p 1.

17. TASS, 0951 GMT, 21 January 1992, FBIS.

18. INTERFAX, 1710 GMT, 23 April 1992, FBIS.

19. For example, see the interview Karimov gave in *Nezavisimaia gazeta*, 15 May 1992, p 3.

20. ITAR-TASS, 1107 GMT, 3 June 1992, FBIS.

21. *Nezavisimaia gazeta*, 15 May 1992, pp 1–3.

22. *Krasnaya Zvezda*, 25 April 1992, p 1.

23. TV1, 1904 GMT, 14 May 1992, FBIS.

24. See Radio Mayak, 1413 GMT, 15 May 1992; ITAR-TASS, 1702 GMT, 15 May 1992; TV1, 1700 GMT, 15 May 1992, FBIS.

25. ITAR-TASS, 1701 GMT, 15 May 1992, FBIS.

26. *Uzbekiston Adabiyoti va San'ati*, no. 21, 22 May 1992, p 1; Radio Moscow, 1110 GMT, 18 May 1992, FBIS.

27. Tashkent Radio, 0300 GMT, 3 July 1992, FBIS.

28. TV1 Ostankino, 1700 GMT, 16 July 1992, FBIS.

29. *Izvestiia*, 6 April 1993, p 2.

30. One such warning was made at a Lisbon news conference; see Lisbon RDP Commercial Radio Network, 2100 GMT, 22 May 1992, FBIS.

31. *Turkiye*, Istanbul, 9 April 1992, p 13, FBIS.

32. *Izvestiia*, 9 October 1992, p 1; *Nezavisimaia gazeta*, 10 October 1992, p 1.

33. *Nezavisimaia gazeta*, 10 December 1992, p 3.

34. *Izvestiia*, 12 October 1992, p 2.

35. Brown, Bess. Radio Free Europe/Radio Liberty Daily Reports, no. 27, 9 February 1994.

36. The term 'Central Asia' is here used loosely to include Kazakhstan as well as the states normally considered part of Central Asia: Kyrgyzstan, Tajikistan, Turkmenistan, and Uzbekistan.

37. *Izvestiia*, 19 December 1991, p 1.

38. TV1, 1400 GMT, 22 April 1992; INTERFAX, 1718 GMT, 22 April 1992, FBIS.

39. Radio Mayak, 1440 GMT, 23 April 1992, FBIS.

40. INTERFAX, 1710 GMT, 23 April 1992, FBIS.

41. INTERFAX, 4 January, in Radio Liberty Daily Report, no. 2, 1993.

42. *Nezavisimaia gazeta*, 26 January 1993, p 3.

43. Brown, Bess. Radio Free Europe/Radio Liberty Daily Reports, no. 22, 2 February 1994.

44. Brown, Bess. Radio Free Europe/Radio Liberty Daily Reports, no. 7, 12 January 1994 and no. 85, 4 May 1994.

45. Radio Moscow, 0700 GMT, 13 April 1992, FBIS.

46. For example, see Moscow Radio One, 1600 GMT, 5 February 1992, FBIS.

47. See for example, *Nezavisimaia gazeta*, 29 May 1992, pp 1, 3.

48. *The Economist* [international], 29 February 1992, p 44.

49. The *Toronto Star*, reprinted in *World Press Review*, July 1992, p 10.

50. Tehran IRNA [in English] 0740 GMT, 30 November 1991, FBIS.

51. TVi, 1900 GMT, 26 November 1991, FBIS.

52. Turkey recognized Azerbaijan on 13 November 1991; see *Izvestiia* of that date, p 5, FBIS.

53. *Pravda Vostoka*, 30 November 1991, p 2.

54. Ibid.

55. *Nezavisimaia gazeta*, 2 December 1992, p 3.

56. Izvestiia, 4 February 1993, p 3.

57. Olcott, Martha Brill, 'Central Asia's Catapult to Independence', pp 125–6.

58. Rupert, James, 'Dateline Tashkent: post-Soviet Central Asia', *Foreign Policy*, no. 87 (Summer 1992), pp 180–81.

59. Wright, Robin, 'Islam, democracy, and the West', *Foreign Affairs*, lxxi/3, Summer 1992, p 143.

60. Figures from Wright, ibid., pp 143–44.

61. *The Economist* [international], 29 February 1992, p.44.

62. *New York Times*, 6 February 1992, p 3A.

63. *Cumhuriyet* [Istanbul], 20 December 1991, p 7, FBIS.

64. *Uzbekiston Adabiyoti va San'ati*, no. 5, 31 January 1992, p 7.

65. See *Izvestiia*, 9 January 1992, p 7; TVi, 1300 GMT, 16 November 1991, FBIS.

66. *The Economist*, 14 December 1991, p 5.

67. TVi, 1900 GMT, 16 December 1991, FBIS.

68. *Turkiye* [Istanbul], 9 April 1992, p.13, FBIS.

69. *Pravda Vostoka*, 21 December 1991, p 1.

70. *Los Angeles Times*, 17 December 1991, p 4A.

71. INTERFAX, 1609 GMT, 4 March 1992; 1358 GMT, 5 March 1992, FBIS.

72. INTERFAX, 1502 GMT, 10 May 1992, FBIS.

73. *Izvestiia*, 28 April 1992, p 5.

74. *New York Times*, 4 August 1992, p C2.

75. *Neue Zürcher Zeitung*, reprinted in *World Press Review*, July 1992, p 13.

76. *Cumhuriyet* [Istanbul], 20 December 1991, p 7, FBIS.

77. *Nezavisimaia gazeta*, 3 November 1992, p 1.

78. *Neue Zürcher Zeitung*, reprinted in *World Press Review*, July 1992, p 12.

79. The figures are from an interview with Uzbekistan's First Deputy Minister of Higher Education, Ergash Fazilov, and a talk which he gave at the University of Washington in Seattle, 30 June 1992.

80. *Izvestiia*, 28 April 1992, p 5.

81. *Turkiye* [Istanbul], 9 April 1992, p 13, FBIS.

82. *The Economist*, 14 December 1991, p 3.

83. *New York Times*, 4 August 1992, p C2.

84. INTERFAX, 1824 GMT, 31 July 1992, FBIS; *Nezavisimaia gazeta*, 2 December 1992, p 3.

85. *Nezavisimaia gazeta*, 6 November 1992, pp 1-2.

86. Ibid.

87. INTERFAX, 1820 GMT, 6 August 1992, FBIS.

88. See *The Economist*, 11 January 1992, p 32; *Literaturnaya Gazeta*, no. 11, 11 March 1992, p 9; Radio Rossiya, 1300 GMT, 10 February 1992, FBIS.

89. Bess Brown, Radio Free Europe/Radio Liberty Reports, no. 25, 7 February 1994.

90. Keith Martin, Radio Free Europe/Radio Liberty Reports, no. 97, 24 May 1994.

91. Olcott, Martha Brill, Op-ed, *New York Times*, 30 December 1991, p 15A.

92. Cordahi, 'Central Asia', p 16.

93. SPA, Riyadh, English, 1231 GMT, 21 February 1992, FBIS.

94. Uvatov, Ubaydulla,'Muqaddas Diyor', *Uzbekistan Adabiyoti va San'ati*, no. 17, 24 April 1992, p 1.

95. *New York Times*, 16 February 1992, p.1.

96. *Narodnoe Slovo*, 29 November 1991.

97. Cordahi, 'Central Asia', p 16.

98. *Toronto Star*, reprinted in *World Press Review*, July 1992, p 10.

99. TV1, 1700 GMT, 27 June 1992, FBIS.

100. Cordahi, 'Central Asia', p 17.

101. *Nezavisimaia gazeta*, 2 December 1992, p 3.

102. *New York Times*, 16 February 1992, p 16; 17 February 1992, p 9.

103. *New York Times*, 17 February 1992, p 9.

104. Ibid.

105. *Nezavisimaia gazeta*, 26 May 1992, p 3.

PART III

South-west Asia Looking North

7

Turkey, the Caucasus and Central Asia

SABRI SAYARI

The disintegration of the Soviet Union and the rise of newly independent republics in the vast territory extending from the Baltics to Central Asia had far-reaching consequences for the international system and its regional subsystems. The political earthquake that transformed the landscape of eastern Europe and the USSR ended the bipolar division of the international system, radically changed European security relations and expanded the regional boundaries of the Middle East to include the former Soviet Muslim republics. Turkey has been strongly affected by these historic changes in its regional foreign policy environment. For more than 40 years since the end of the Second World War, the perceived Soviet threat was the principal guiding factor in Turkish foreign and national security policies. Embedded in the historical enmities between the Ottoman empire and tsarist Russia, this perception was buttressed by Stalin's territorial demands from Turkey at the end of the Second World War and Moscow's political pressures on Ankara, particularly during the earlier phase of the Cold War. The perceived Soviet threat led the Turks to forge close military and political ties with the USA, and to serve – in the classic formulation derived from the rhetoric of Cold War politics – as 'NATO's bulwark against communism in the Middle East'.

The end of East–West polarization in world politics, the collapse of communist regimes in eastern Europe and the demise of the USSR were greeted with mixed feelings by Turkey's political leaders. They welcomed the disappearance of the military threat posed by the former Soviet Union and its Warsaw Pact allies, but were apprehensive that Turkey might lose its strategic importance for the West in the post-

Cold War era. Their concern was compounded by the strains between Turkey and its west European NATO allies over its desire to gain full membership in the European Community and the Western European Union.[1] Despite these problems, Turkish policy-makers continued to view the maintenance of close political and economic ties with the West as essential for Turkey's national security, economic progress and democratic political development. Consequently, a major objective of Turkey's foreign policy since the end of the Cold War has been to find new strategies to guard against its possible isolation from the emerging economic and political institutions of Europe and to reassert its importance as a regional power.

These concerns have brought a new activism to the conduct of Turkish foreign policy in 1991–92.[2] For example, Turkey departed from its traditional policy of non-involvement in Middle Eastern conflicts and became a key participant in the allied coalition against Iraq during the Gulf crisis. The late Turkish President Turgut Ozal, the chief architect of Turkey's new foreign policy initiatives, frequently spoke of finding a new regional role for Turkey in the aftermath of the Gulf War. Ankara's leadership in the establishment of the Black Sea Economic Cooperation Organization was another example of Turkey's search for new strategies to reassert its regional importance. By establishing trade, banking and transport links among its member states – Turkey, Bulgaria, Romania, Russia, Moldova, Ukraine, Georgia, Armenia and Azerbaijan – the Black Sea cooperation scheme was intended to create a new regional economic bloc that would also facilitate closer political ties. Turkey has also pursued an activist role since the eruption of the civil war in former Yugoslavia. Due to its special historic ties with the Muslims of Bosnia-Herzegovina, Turkey has lobbied hard in the United Nations, the North Atlantic Treaty Organization, and the Conference of Islamic States to stop the ethnic cleansing policy directed against the Muslims by the Serbs.

Turkey and the reemergence of the Turkic world

The disintegration of the USSR and the rise of independent states in the former Soviet Muslim republics offered Turkey the opportunity to find new sources of political and economic influence. When President Gorbachev launched his radical reforms in 1985 that eventually led to the demise of the Soviet state, few Turkish observers expected that this would drastically alter the political conditions in Central

Asia and the Caucasus and pave the way for Turkey's emergence as a potential key player in a region extending from the Caucasus to China's Central Asian borders. Yet, five years after Gorbachev's historic policies, the unexpected happened, and Turkey found itself in an entirely new set of circumstances that held the promise of fulfilling the Turkish policy-makers' goal of reasserting Turkey's importance for the West in the post-Cold War era.

Turkey's potential as an important player in Central Asia and the Caucasus stemmed mainly from the common ethnic, linguistic and religious ties between the Turks in Turkey and the nearly 50 million Turkic peoples who lived in Azerbaijan, Turkmenistan, Uzbekistan, Kazakhstan and Kyrgyzstan and constituted 85 per cent of the former Soviet Union's Muslim population.[3] The main Turkic groups in Central Asia, the Caucasus and Crimea – Uzbeks, Kazakhs, Tatars, Azeris, Turkomans, Kyrgyz, Chivash, Bashkirs, Karakalpaks, Kumyks, Uighurs, Karachias, Turks, Balkars and Nogais – speak various dialects of the Turkish language with varying degrees of similarity to the Turkish spoken in Turkey.[4] The Turkic peoples, like Turkey's population, are predominantly Sunni, and nearly all follow the Hanafi school of Islam.[5]

Despite these similarities in ethnic, linguistic and cultural characteristics, there was during the past 70 years little contact between Turks in Turkey and their ethnic kinsmen in Central Asia, Transcaucasia and northern Caucasus, Crimea and elsewhere in the Turkic enclaves of the Soviet empire. This was largely due to the policies adopted by Moscow and Ankara following the establishment of the Soviet Union in 1917 and the Turkish republic in 1923. After the artificial division of historic Turkestan into separate republics in 1924, the Soviet leadership employed a variety of administrative, educational and cultural policies to prevent the development of a broad-based Turkic ethnic identity in Central Asia.[6] Moscow's exaggerated fear of pan-Turkism – the ideology that aspired to the establishment of a common homeland for all the Turks – played an important role in its divide-and-rule tactics towards the Turkic peoples and in its endeavour to minimize contacts between Turkey and the Turco-Muslim republics.[7]

The newly founded Turkish republic's policy towards the ethnic Turks who lived outside Turkey in the Soviet Union, the Balkans or the Middle East made Moscow's task easier. The founder of the modern Turkish republic, Kemal Ataturk, defined Turkish national identity exclusively with reference to the Turks living within the country's boundaries. This strategy was designed to strengthen Turkish nationalism at home and to preclude possible irredentist activities on behalf of the so-called 'outside Turks' in neighbouring states. The Cold War and the rise of Soviet military power reinforced the Turkish belief in the wisdom of strict adherence to Ataturk's policy. As a result, with the exception of the extremist nationalist organizations and émigré groups from Central Asia, the Turks displayed little interest in developing close contacts with the Soviet Union's Turkic peoples.[8]

The collapse of communism and the disintegration of the USSR marked a major shift in Turkey's outlook on the former Soviet Muslim republics. As Moscow's authority declined and the Soviet state headed towards a breakup, Turkey departed from its traditional policy and began to establish contacts with the Turkic republics. For example, when he went to Moscow in March 1991 to sign a Treaty of Friendship and Cooperation with Gorbachev, Turkish President Turgut Ozal visited Azerbaijan, Kazakhstan and Ukraine.[9] Within a year these contacts had increased considerably amidst a flurry of diplomatic visits accompanied by the signing of economic, commercial and cultural agreements between Turkey and the five Turkic republics.

Turkey's changing stand on the Turkic peoples and its efforts to expand its relations with the former Soviet Muslim republics were even more clearly highlighted by Ankara's decision to become the first state to recognize Azerbaijan's independence in November 1991. Of the five Turkic republics, Turkey had the closest historic, cultural and linguistic ties with Azerbaijan. By extending diplomatic recognition to Baku, Turkey reaffirmed the special relationship between the Turks and the Azeris. In addition to its symbolic importance, Turkey's quick recognition of Azerbaijan underlined the emerging competition between Turkey and Iran for regional influence since Turkish officials believed that Tehran might get the better of Ankara through an earlier recognition of Azerbaijan. By the end of 1991 the Turkish government had voted to recognize all the former Soviet republics that had declared their independence.

The establishment of official diplomatic ties between Ankara and the newly independent republics gave additional momentum to the expansion of political and economic contacts. Between late 1991 and early 1992 the leaders of Kazakhstan, Turkmenistan, Azerbaijan, Uzbekistan and Kyrgyzstan visited Turkey, and high-ranking Turkish delegations travelled to the capitals of the Central Asian republics and Azerbaijan. These initial diplomatic interactions between the leaders of Turkey and the Turkic states were marked by emotional speeches and declarations attesting to the strength of ethnic and cultural ties among all Turks.[10] While the leaders of the Turkic republics emphasized Turkey's leadership role in the Turkic world and its potential to serve as a role model for the former Soviet Muslim republics, Turkish officials declared their willingness to assist the social and economic development of Central Asia and Azerbaijan.

The reemergence of the Central Asian Turkic world and the establishment of political, economic and cultural relations between Turkey and the newly independent Turkic republics generated an emotional and enthusiastic public response in Turkey that bordered on euphoria. Public opinion polls as well as the more impressionistic coverage by the mass media showed that there was overwhelming public support for the government's efforts to cultivate close ties with the new republics. This emotional outburst of sympathy and friendship for the Turkic peoples was partly due to the joy felt by the majority of Turks upon rediscovering their long-lost ethnic cousins, but it also reflected a psychological reaction related to the sense of rejection they felt in their relations with Western Europeans. At a time when Turkey's prospects for gaining membership in the EC appeared dim and public attitudes towards the Turkish migrants in Europe were increasingly intolerant, the warm welcome and respect Turkey received from the leaders of the Turkic republics proved to be an effective morale-building mechanism and a source of national pride.

Shared ethnic, linguistic and cultural characteristics of the Turks in Turkey and the Turkic peoples in the newly independent republics were a major source of Turkey's potential new regional influence and role; the practical objectives of the Turkic republics, Turkey and Western governments underlined this potential. The leaders of the Turkic republics sought Turkey's support in their efforts to become integrated into the international political and economic system, hoping through Ankara's close ties with Washington to receive American backing for their entry into international political and financial organizations. Uncomfortable with the possibility of an Islamic resurgence in the aftermath of the collapse of communism, the secular élites in the Turkic republics were attracted to Turkey's secular state institutions and policies.[11] Central Asian leaders were also impressed by Turkey's market-orientated economic policies and expected to receive technical know-how, managerial expertise and financial aid from Ankara.

Turkish policy-makers welcomed the expansion of political, economic and cultural relations with the Turkic republics for equally pragmatic policy objectives, believing that the emergence of the Turkic world and Turkey's close ties with the new republics would enhance Turkey's regional power and influence. At the same time, the Turkish government viewed the establishment of close relations with the Central Asian states and Azerbaijan as important to maintain regional stability and to prevent Iran from emerging as the dominant force of the new Middle East. In the immediate aftermath of the disintegration of the former Soviet Union, the Turkish leadership had a very optimistic view of economic and business opportunities in Central Asia and anticipated that Turkey's export-orientated economic growth strategy would benefit extensively from the growth of Turkey's regional ties and influence.

Practical policy concerns were also paramount in Western, particularly American, support for Turkey to become a key player in the region and possibly to serve as a role model for Azerbaijan, Kazakhstan, Uzbekistan, Turkmenistan and Kyrgyzstan. Washington's strategy of promoting the 'Turkish model' for the new republics was based largely on its fear that Islamic fundamentalism, supported by Iran, would make major inroads into Central Asia at a time when there was growing interest in Islam in the Turkic republics and Tajikistan. Turkey, with its pro-Western orientation in world politics, secular state institutions, democratic political processes and market-based economic policies, was clearly preferred to the 'Iranian model' by the USA and European governments.

Turkey's policies towards the new Turkic republics

The former Soviet Muslim republics gained their independence quickly and without much preparation. Their sudden emergence as independent states created serious problems in their search for national identity, political stability and economic recovery. Regional states such as Turkey and Iran were also unprepared to deal with the rise of independent republics in Central Asia and the Caucasus. In the case of Turkey, this problem was compounded by an acute shortage of expertise and knowledge regarding the political, economic and social conditions in Azerbaijan, Turkmenistan, Uzbekistan, Kazakhstan and Kyrgyzstan. Generations of Turks had been educated without any significant knowledge of the historical development or the current political, economic and social conditions in these republics. Since the 1920s successive Turkish governments had refrained from supporting the study of the Turkic peoples of the former USSR, partly because of its possible negative ramifications for Turkish–Soviet relations and partly due to the identification of scholarly interest in the Turkic peoples with extremist nationalist ideologies and activities in Turkey's domestic politics. Consequently, not even the Turkish foreign ministry possessed qualified analysts of Central Asian affairs.

This lack of knowledge about Central Asia was also evident in the prevailing Turkish public perceptions about the Turkic world when the Soviet empire disintegrated. For example, many Turks had a monolithic image of the ethnic and national composition of the Turkic republics and were bewildered when violent conflicts erupted between different Turkic ethnic groups such as the Kyrgyz and Uzbeks in the oblast of Osh in 1990. Unfamiliarity with political and social conditions also played a role in the initial expectations of the Turkish government with respect to Turkey's potential political and economic gains from expanding its ties with the Turkic republics. Buoyed by the laudatory pronouncements of the Turkic leaders about Turkey in the immediate aftermath of the collapse of the Soviet Union, Turkish policy-makers assumed that the Uzbeks, Turkomans, Azeris and others would automatically accept Turkey as an *agabey* or older brother, seek to emulate the Turkish model of political, social and economic development, and provide Turkish businessmen with exclusive lucrative opportunities for trade and investment.[12]

As Turkey's ties with the new republics increased during 1992, the Turkish government and the public have developed a better understanding of Central Asia and the Caucasus, thanks to the extensive coverage of the region in the Turkish news media and visits to the region by numerous businessmen, government officials, academics, journalists and tourists. As a result, the earlier – largely unrealistic and exaggerated – expectations are gradually being replaced by more sober and less ambitious analyses of Turkey's potential regional role and policy objectives. There is now a realization of several factors, for example: that after decades of living under Russian domination, the Turkic peoples of the former Soviet Union are strongly opposed to having a new older brother; that, while attractive, the Turkish model is by no means viewed as the only and best one by all the leaders of the new republics; and that Turkish businessmen can expect to face stiff competition from others – West Europeans, Japanese, South

Koreans, Pakistanis, Indians, etc – in their pursuit of profitable contracts in Central Asia.

To expand its political, economic and cultural ties with the Central Asian republics and Azerbaijan, Turkey launched a number of policy initiatives. When the new republics were in search of membership in Western economic and political institutions following their independence, Turkey provided them with considerable diplomatic support. Ankara's active diplomacy on behalf of the new republics and its close relations with Washington played a significant role in their successful bid for entry into the Conference on Security and Cooperation in Europe (CSCE), the North Atlantic Coordination Council (NACC), the World Bank and the International Monetary Fund (IMF). By pushing for Azerbaijan's membership in the newly formed Black Sea Economic Cooperation Organization, Turkey provided Azerbaijan with an additional resource to develop its commercial, trade and transport links with the countries of the Black Sea lateral. Turkey's support for the participation of the Turkic republics in these international and regional organizations was based on a strategy – drawn up jointly by Turkish and US officials – to end their isolation from the West and to facilitate economic recovery and political stability in Central Asia and the Caucasus.

Ankara's programmes regarding economic and technical aid to the Turkic republics have been largely planned and implemented by a newly established Turkish International Cooperation Agency (TICA), loosely based on the model of the US Agency for International Development. In 1992 Turkey granted the five Turkic republics about $1 billion in aid,[13] mostly allocated to loans, credits and investment guarantees, with some earmarked for technical aid and supplies. Although Turkey's financial aid to Central Asia and Azerbaijan represented a large item in the Turkish national budget, it still fell short of meeting Ankara's initial pledges of economic and technical aid for the region. Turkish officials, in the emotional and euphoric atmosphere of their early contacts with the leaders of the Turkic republics, made promises of economic aid that proved to be impossible to fulfil through Turkey's own limited financial resources. The US government's policies also exacerbated this problem. The expectation of the Turks, based on the signals sent to Ankara from Washington in early 1992, was that Washington would make a substantial contribution to the economic recovery of the new republics, and that it would work jointly with Ankara in this process.[14] However, this did not turn out to be the case and the Turks did not receive the anticipated economic support from Washington for Central Asia.

In addition to loans and investment credits, the Turkish government signed a number of agreements with the Turkic republics regarding large-scale projects in transport and communications, such as commercial airline routes between Central Asia and Turkey through the Turkish airlines and international telephone links for the Turkic republics. As a participant in the newly founded Economic Co-operation Organization (ECO) – whose members include Iran, Pakistan, Turkey, Azerbaijan, Turkmenistan, Kazakhstan, Uzbekistan and Tajikistan – Turkey has been actively involved in a number of schemes designed to promote economic development of the region through intergovernmental cooperation.[15] Despite this activism, however, the Turkish government has so far not succeeded in achieving one of its potentially most profitable commercial objectives, namely to play a leading role in the exploration and transport of oil and natural gas from Kazakhstan, Turkmenistan and Azerbaijan. The Turkish-backed projects for the export of Central Asian and Azerbaijani petroleum through pipelines that would reach the Turkish terminals on the Mediterranean have not materialized for several reasons. These include opposition from Russia and Iran, the problem of providing security for the pipelines in the Caucasus and Eastern Turkey and the availability of shorter and more direct routes between the landlocked Central Asian republics and Russian or Iranian seaports.

While Turkey has had to renege on some of its earlier pledges regarding economic aid, it has achieved greater success in implementing its educational and cultural programmes in Central Asia and Azerbaijan. For example, the Turkish government has given scholarships to about 1000 students from each of the Turkic republics to study in Turkish universities. This project began in 1992 with the administration of the standard Turkish university entrance examination to applicants in their home countries, the successful applicants being invited to Istanbul and other major cities for Turkish-language courses before their freshman year.[16] Turkey also initiated training programmes for the Uzbeks, Turkomans and others for specialization in various governmental institutions such as foreign service and central banking, emerging private-sector enterprises and the military. The educational and cultural activities sponsored by the government during 1992 included visits by Turkish political scientists and constitutional experts to Azerbaijan and Central Asia to discuss issues concerning constitution-writing, electoral laws and the establishment of democratic political institutions. Some private Turkish research groups, such as the Turkish Democracy Foundation in Ankara, have also organized meetings and seminars on these issues in Turkey with the participation of visiting delegations from the Turkic republics.

Turkey's strategy to promote the adoption of the Latin alphabet by the Turkic republics has achieved only mixed results. The Turkish leadership viewed the switch from Cyrillic to Latin as a 'central element of the reform process in these countries that symbolizes the choice between modernism and fundamentalism'.[17] Turkey's advocacy of the Latin script, and its opposition to the replacement of the Cyrillic alphabet with Arabic, stemmed from its desire to increase its cultural influence in the region and to undermine the appeal of fundamentalist Islam. To encourage the Turkic republics to switch to Latin, the Turkish government supplied a large number of Latin-character typewriters to Central Asia and Azerbaijan, but so far only Azerbaijan has adopted the Latin script. While other Turkic republics have not made a decision on this issue, Tajikistan has moved towards replacing Cyrillic with Arabic.

Another major cultural and educational project undertaken by Turkey concerns the establishment of the Eurasia television network system that broadcasts from Ankara to Central Asia via satellite.[18] To reach the new audiences in the Turkic republics, the Turkish government completed this project in record-breaking time and in the spring of 1992 began broadcasting to Central Asia and Azerbaijan over 400 hours weekly of entertainment programmes, news, films (both educational and for entertainment) in simplified Turkish. As in the case of Turkey's initiative in support of the Latin script, the Eurasia television project is intended to contribute to expanding Turkey's cultural influence in the Turkic republics, especially through fostering greater familiarity among the Uzbeks, Turkomans and others with the Turkish spoken in Turkey.

When Turkey began to establish contacts with the Turkic republics in 1991, the absence of information about the economic conditions in Central Asia led many Turkish businessmen to believe that they could quickly form lucrative trade and investment relations in Kazakhstan, Uzbekistan and other republics, as Turkish companies had done with considerable success throughout the Middle East since the early 1980s; they quickly discovered that the economic and political conditions in the Turkic republics present major problems for foreign investors. The limited cash assets available in Central Asia and Azerbaijan, the preference of the governments to conduct trade through barter deals or soft credits, the existence of price controls, and the absence of banking infrastructure have been major obstacles for Turkish companies seeking new business opportunities.[19] Nevertheless, Turkish businessmen have significantly expanded their activities in the Turkic republics since 1990. Construction companies from Turkey have won major contracts in Kazakhstan, Kyrgyzstan and Azerbaijan; several large Turkish trading firms have become prominent players in the newly developing commercial ties between the Turkic republics and the West; and numerous smaller Turkish firms have gained access to Central Asian and Azerbaijani markets through a variety of import-export arrangements.[20]

Turkey and regional security issues

For Turkey's foreign and national security officials, the maintenance of stability and peace in Central Asia and the Caucasus has become a principal policy objective since the disintegration of the USSR. Underlying this objective is Turkey's growing apprehension about the rise of violent conflicts and instability near its southern and western borders in the new international 'disorder' that has replaced the relatively stable and predictable conditions of the Cold War. Currently, Turkey faces a number of crisis points close to its borders. In the south, it is confronted with an unstable situation in Iraq, where Saddam Hussein is still in power and in search of strategies to retaliate against Turkey for Ankara's close cooperation with the allied forces during the Gulf crisis. Moreover, due to the ongoing guerrilla campaign waged by the Kurdish Workers Party (PKK) in south-eastern Turkey, Turkish policy-makers view with considerable apprehension the rise under allied protection of a *de facto* Kurdish political entity in northern Iraq.

The disintegration of the former Yugoslav state and the rise of aggressive Serbian nationalism have seriously undermined stability near Turkey's western borders with the Balkans. Due to the existence of historic ties between Turkey and the Muslims of Bosnia-Herzegovina, and the presence in Turkey of nearly two million immigrants from Bosnia, the Turkish public has become incensed by the 'ethnic cleansing' policy of the Serbs, and has pressured the government to play a more active role in support of the besieged

Bosnian Muslims.[21] If unchecked, Serbia's aggressive nationalism in the Balkans is likely to involve other regional states, including Albania, Bulgaria, Greece and Turkey, in a wider and potentially catastrophic armed confrontation.

The Turks have watched the trend towards increased ethnic nationalism and secessionist movements in the former Soviet Union, Balkans and elsewhere in Eastern Europe with considerable unease, fearing that these might draw Turkey into armed conflicts and exacerbate Turkey's own ethnic problems. Most Turkish policy-makers believe that the intensification of ethnic conflicts in close proximity to Turkey have encouraged the more militant groups among Turkey's large Kurdish minority to use violent methods in their search for political autonomy from Ankara. Turkey's initial opposition to the breakup of Yugoslavia – at a time when Germany and the EC lent their support to the independence of Slovenia and Croatia – and its insistence on maintaining Iraq's territorial integrity reflect Ankara's concern about the destabilizing effects of ethnic and nationalist movements on Turkey and its regional environment.

Viewed in this broader perspective, the eruption of bloody ethnic clashes between the Armenians and the Azeris over the Nagorno-Karabakh dispute has created major security and political dilemmas for Ankara. Turkey shares common borders with both Armenia and Azerbaijan and is in close proximity to Nagorno-Karabakh. The potential for the conflict to spill over into Turkey is increased by Turkey's close historical, linguistic and cultural ties with Azerbaijan, and by the hostility and enmity that have characterized Turkish–Armenian relations since the final days of the Ottoman Empire. Due to Turkey's contrasting relations with the two disputants, there has been an overwhelming public support for the Azeris since the beginning of the four-year conflict. The level of this support has increased with the escalation of the violence, particularly during the massacre of Azerbaijani civilians in Khodzhaly in February 1992. At the same time, Armenian claims and blockade in Nakhchevan have intensified public pressures on the Turkish government to provide military support to the Azeris.

The Nagorno-Karabakh conflict has underlined the policy dilemmas that Turkey might face in its efforts to expand its regional role and influence through close ties with the Turkic republics. Turkey's activist foreign policy carries with it the danger of Ankara's involvement in ethnic and nationalist conflicts in the region. In its approach to the conflict between Armenia and Azerbaijan, the Turkish government faced difficult policy choices between domestic pressures stemming from the sympathy of the Turkish public for the Azeris versus its desire to remain neutral and play a moderating role.[22] In support of the latter, Ankara refrained from providing material support for the Azeris and began a constructive dialogue with Armenian officials to establish new trade and political relations. However, this limited rapprochement in Turkish–Armenian relations came under strong criticism from the Turkish public over the Khodzhaly massacres and the Nakhchevan crisis, and led to demands by some opposition party leaders for a military intervention in support of Azerbaijan.[23] Although Turkey did not depart from its policy of non-intervention in the dispute, the strong official protests from Ankara to Yerevan, accompanied by troop movements in eastern Turkey close to Armenia's border, undermined the credibility of Turkey's claims of strict neutrality in the conflict between Armenia and Azerbaijan.[24]

In addition to the Armenia–Azerbaijan conflict, Turkey's objective of maintaining a stable regional order in the Caucasus has been thwarted by the continuing ethnic strife in the area. Some of this turmoil involves Turkic–Muslim minorities such as the Abkhazians in Georgia, who have appealed to Turkey for help. Apprehensive of involvement in these ethnic conflicts in a volatile region, Ankara has declined to support the Abkhazians or other Turkic groups, believing that ethnic conflicts in the Caucasus and possibly even in Central Asia might prompt the migration of some of these communities to Turkey. If this were to happen, Ankara would face enormous economic and social problems regarding the settlement of thousands of refugees from the Caucasus, especially at a time when there is the likelihood of refugee inflows into Turkey from the Balkans as well.

Turkey's new perspectives on regional security and its efforts to expand its role in the Caucasus and Central Asia have increased the likelihood of tensions with two other regional powers, Russia and Iran. Moscow is uncomfortable with Ankara's new activist foreign policy directed at the Turkic republics, an attitude based not so much on fear of pan-Turkism as on concern over an increase of Turkey's regional influence after a long period of Turkish quiescence in the Caucasus. Although the Turkish policy-makers have carefully avoided involvement in the affairs of the Turkic minorities in Russia, Moscow views the expansion of Ankara's relations with Turkic republics with suspicion. The warning issued by the Russian military command against a possible Turkish intervention in the Nagorno-Karabakh dispute underlines the potential for conflict between Russia and Turkey in the new political environment of the post-Cold War period. Moscow's efforts to reassert Russian dominance over the former Soviet Union's territories in Central Asia and the Caucasus within its 'the near abroad' foreign policy axis have rekindled the traditional Turkish perceptions of the 'threat from the north'. Moreover, Russia's renewed activism in Central Asia and the Caucasus has seriously undermined Turkey's regional goals. In particular, Ankara has received a severe setback in its efforts to forge close political and economic ties with Azerbaijan and turn it into a showcase for the Turkish model. To counter Turkey's influence, Russia first provided training and logistical support for the Armenians to push the Azeris out of Nagorno-Karabakh and occupy nearly a fifth of Azerbaijani territory. The Russians then expediently utilized the ensuing political turmoil in Azerbaijan to oust the country's president Abulfaz Elchbayli, an outspoken supporter of Turkey, and replaced him with a former KGB leader and close ally of Moscow, Haidar Aliyev. Turkey's inability to help Elchbayli and reverse the reassertion of Moscow's influence in Azerbaijan has starkly illustrated the gap between its regional goals and capabilities.

Turkey's relations with Iran – which have experienced intermittent tensions since the downfall of the Shah and the Islamic Republic's efforts to export fundamentalism to Turkey – have also been strained as result of the changing political map of Central Asia and the Caucasus. Each state views the other's efforts to gain political and economic influence in Central Asia and the Caucasus with considerable distrust.[25] The competition between Tehran and Ankara involves ideological elements – often expressed in terms of a dichotomy between the 'Turkish model' and 'fundamentalist Islam' – as well as pragmatic economic and commercial interests.[26] But the most important source of tension in Turkish–Iranian relations relates to the future of Azerbaijan. The Iranian leadership has been apprehensive about the impact on its large Azeri minority of Turkey's emerging close ties with Azerbaijan, and concerned that a union between northern and southern Azerbaijan would lead to the creation of a larger homeland for the Azeris. Iran's covert support for Turkey's Kurdish guerrillas during the Turkish government's offensive against the PKK in October 1992 was clearly planned to send a signal to Ankara regarding Iran's capability to exacerbate Turkey's ethnic problems. The Turks, on the other hand, view Azerbaijan as a test of Iran's ability to spread Islamic fundamentalism in the Turkic republics, and fear that the strengthening of Shi'ite fundamentalism in Azerbaijan through Iran's support could lead to the intensification of religious activism in Turkey, particularly among the Alevis.

The domestic context of Turkey's opening to Central Asia

Domestic political and social factors have played a significant role in shaping Turkey's response to the independence of the former Soviet Turkic republics. Overwhelming public support for the expansion of Turkey's relations with Central Asia and Azerbaijan has created a broad-based domestic policy consensus for Ankara's political, cultural and economic policy initiatives. This domestic consensus has largely remained intact despite the ouster of the Motherland Party from power following the elections in November 1991 and its replacement by a coalition government formed by the True Path Party and the Social Democratic Populist Party. The majority of Turks continue to have a positive view of Turkey's emerging ties with the Turkic republics, although the initial public enthusiasm has dimmed considerably after more than three years of intensive diplomatic, cultural and economic contacts. Responding to this popular support, all Turkey's political parties have endorsed the cultivation of ties with the Turkic peoples. The main source of political opposition to the government's policies has been the Turkish effort to maintain neutrality in the clashes between the Armenians and the Azeris.

Turkey's centre-right and far-right political parties have traditionally stressed nationalism as part of their ideological appeal. They have welcomed the emergence of 50 million Turkic peoples on the world stage, and have sought to capitalize on this unexpected development in their electoral appeals to Turkish voters. This is especially pronounced in the case of Turkey's radical nationalists, organized under the leadership of Alparslan Turkes in the Nationalist Action Party (NAP). For decades, Turkes was the only prominent party leader who spoke out about the rights of the Turkic peoples of the former Soviet Union.[27] Turkes and his followers view the disintegration of the former Soviet Union and the establishment of independent Turkic states as a vindication of their beliefs and a proof of the correctness of their ideological principles; for them the rise of the new Turkic republics represents an opportunity for the dissemination of pan-Turkist and

pan-Turanist ideologies in Central Asia and the Caucasus.[28] Consequently, the NAP has intensified its activities to recruit and organize
followers in the Turkic republics, particularly in Azerbaijan.[29]

Turkey's Islamic fundamentalists too have sought to capitalize on
the rise of the newly independent Central Asian republics. The prin-
cipal political organization of the fundamentalists, the Welfare Party
(WP), has been critical of the government's policy of promoting the
Latin script in the new Turkic republics, and has expressed its support
for the replacement of the Cyrillic alphabet with Arabic. Turkey's
Sunni religious activists have been at odds with the Iranian-backed
Shi'ite fundamentalist movements in the Middle East, and they oppose
Iran's promotion of its brand of fundamentalism in Central Asia. The
WP, with considerable backing from Saudi Arabia, has established
links with the Sunni fundamentalists in Central Asia, especially in
Uzbekistan. The Islamic fundamentalist WP views the disintegration
of the USSR as the defeat of atheism and Moscow's anti-Islamic
policies, and expects this historic change to lead to the victory of
Islam in Central Asia as well as in Turkey.[30]

Turkey's left-wing political forces were traditionally among the
staunchest supporters of the principles laid down by Ataturk regarding Turks living outside Turkey, and had bitterly opposed the views
expressed by the radical nationalists such as Turkes. However, in a
remarkable turnaround following the demise of communist regimes
and the Soviet Union, they have become fully supportive of forging
close ties with the Turkic republics. One of the most notable examples of this attempt by the former leftists to capitalize on ethnicity is
Bulent Ecevit. A former prime minister, ex-leader of the centre-left
Republican People's Party, and the current chairman of the small
Democratic Left Party, Ecevit has emerged as an ardent supporter of
the Turkic peoples, demanding, for example, that Turkey use military
force against the Armenians in the Nagorno-Karabakh conflict.[31]

The emergence of the Turkic republics and Turkey's expanding
regional role have strengthened nationalist sentiments in Turkey, although mainstream Turkish parties and political leaders avoid reference to pan-Turkism as a reason to cultivate close ties with the Turkic
peoples. While most Turks favour these ties, the notion of creating a
larger Turkish entity, or a new Turkestan, does not command popular
support.[32] Prime Minister Demirel and other Turkish officials have
repeatedly stated that Turkey's regional policies are not based on the
ideology and objectives of pan-Turkism.

There is little evidence to support the suggestion that political pan-Turkism, which sanctions irredentism, has been a motivating force in Turkey's relations with Central Asia and the Caucasus; however, this cannot be said about cultural pan-Turkism or the idea of promoting cultural unity among all Turks. Ankara's strategy of promoting Turkish culture and language in Central Asia through the Eurasia satellite television network, its efforts to create a Turkish alphabet based on the Latin script to be used in all the Turkic republics, and its emphasis on developing common educational programmes in Central Asia and Azerbaijan reflect the influence of cultural – as distinct from political – pan-Turkism.[33]

This 'opening to Central Asia' has strengthened nationalist sentiments in Turkey and made ethnicity a key factor in shaping Turkey's foreign policy. Turkey's growing involvement in the Turkic republics may also have significant implications for its own national identity and its relations with the West. Since the founding of the modern Turkish republic, especially in the period following the Second World War, Turkey's leaders have tried to form close political, military and economic relations with the West; Turkey's inclusion in NATO, its bilateral ties with the USA, and its membership in various European institutions were significant indicators of the success of this strategy. But the issue of Turkey's national identity – whether it was a European or a Middle Eastern state – has never been resolved. Recent developments such as the emergence of strains in Turkey's relations with Europe and the growth of Islamic activism in Turkey have further complicated this question. The impact of the Turkic world on Turkey represents yet another complicating factor. Some Turkish commentators have voiced their concern about the possible adverse consequences of Turkey's new regional policy initiatives on its secular state institutions, democratic regime and cultural life. Whether or not their fears are justified remains to be seen. What is certain, however, is that the more the Turks want to expand their influence in the newly independent republics in Central Asia and Azerbaijan, the more they are likely to be influenced in turn by the social and cultural developments in the Turkic world.

Conclusions

The emergence of independent Turkic republics in Central Asia and Azerbaijan represents a turning point in Turkey's regional role and policies. Turkey has become one of the important players in a region where previously it had only marginal influence and no active involvement. The Turks have sought to take advantage of this unique historical opportunity to expand their political, economic and cultural relations with the Turkic republics at a time when their importance to the West was widely questioned in Western capitals because of the radical changes affecting the structure of the international system and regional power balances. Ankara's activist foreign policy orientation has resulted in many programmes aimed at increasing the political, cultural and economic interdependence between Turkey and the five Turkic republics. Encouraged by the West, and initially by the leaders of the Turkic republics, the Turks have readily accepted the challenge of providing leadership for countries in the very early stages of nation-building and economic development. In particular, they have tried to influence the processes of political and social change in Azerbaijan, Turkmenistan, Kazakhstan, Uzbekistan and Kyrgyzstan to conform to Turkey's own model of secular and democratic development.

It is too early to assess the impact of Ankara's strategies on Central Asia and on Turkey's goal of expanding its influence in a stable regional environment. The Turkish model remains attractive for the Central Asian leaders, especially because of its emphasis on creating secular state institutions in a predominantly Muslim society. However, contrary to the initial expectations of many Western and Turkish observers, the former Soviet Muslim republics have begun to examine the relative merits of other models of development, such as China and Indonesia, whose political and economic systems they consider better suited to their goals.[34] Although the Turkish model appeals to influential members of the political and cultural élites in the Turkic republics, many view it as inappropriate for a variety of reasons, ranging from Turkey's experience with democracy to the problems it has faced recently in its efforts to move to a market-based economy.

Turkey's desire to become a leader in Central Asia faces additional difficulties. Except for a tiny part of Azerbaijan – Nakhchevan – Turkey is not physically contiguous with the region. In terms of developing trade and commercial relations, this puts Turkey at a disadvantage *vis-à-vis* other countries such as Iran. Much to their surprise, the Turks have discovered that there are serious differences between the Turkish spoken in Turkey and the various dialects used in the Central Asian republics. With the possible exception of Azerbaijan, where these differences are the least discernible, Turkish officials and businessmen have faced considerable difficulty in communicating with their counterparts in the new republics in the Turkish spoken in Turkey, and have often had to use translators.

Ankara's initial assumption regarding its role as an 'elder brother' to the Turkic peoples of Central Asia and the Caucasus has created additional problems for Turkey. The Turkish government's view was shaped by Turkey's experiences with the Turkish minorities in Bulgaria, Greece, Cyprus or Iraq which – largely as a result of their minority status – are clearly dependent on Turkey and look to Ankara for leadership. This is clearly not the case in Central Asia and Azerbaijan where there is much less reason automatically to accept the role of a dependent of Turkey, especially in the light of the experiences of the Turkic peoples under Soviet control.[35]

The 1990s are likely to be critical in shaping Turkey's relations with Central Asia and the Caucasus. Although economic and political conditions in the region are unlikely to stabilize before the turn of the century, by the year 2000 the newly established republics will have completed their first decade of independent statehood. During this period, Turkish policy-makers are likely to continue their efforts to create new networks of interdependency between Ankara and the capitals of the five Turkic republics. These may include the establishment of new organizations, such as a Turkic regional common market and additional bilateral arrangements concerning economic, political and cultural issues. Although political pan-Turkism is not a viable alternative for the future, Ankara will continue to pursue policies to forge greater cultural unity among the Turks under its leadership. These policies will continue to be challenged by the desire of individual republics to develop their own distinctive national and cultural identities and by Russia and Iran, which will contest Turkey's aspirations to expand its regional influence through greater cultural and economic interdependence between Turkey and the Turkic republics.

Notes

1. For an overview of these issues, see Sabri Sayari, 'Turkey: the changing European security environment and the Gulf crisis', *The Middle East Journal*, xlvi/1 (Winter 1992), pp 9–21.

2. Ibid. See also Kemal Kirisci, *The End of the Cold War and Changes in Turkish Foreign Policy Behavior* (Istanbul: Bogazici University Institute of Social Sciences, Research paper ISS/POLS 92-1, September 1992).

3. Shirin Akiner, *Islamic Peoples of the Soviet Union* (London: Routledge and Kegan Paul, 1986, rev. ed.), p 41.

4. Geoffrey Wheeler, 'The Turkic languages of Soviet Muslim Asia: Russian linguistic policy', *Middle Eastern Studies*, xiii (May 1977), pp 208–17.

5. The main exception to the predominance of Sunni Islam among the Turkic ethnic peoples is Azerbaijan, where nearly 70 per cent of the population are Shi'ite. Estimates of Turkey's Alevis – an offshoot of Shi'ite Islam affiliated with the Alawite sect in Syria – range from 10 to 20 per cent of the country's population of nearly 60 million.

6. See Edward Allworth (ed.), *Central Asia: A Century of Russian Rule* (New York: Columbia University Press, 1967) and Kemal H. Karpat, 'The Turkic nationalities: Turkish-Soviet and Turkish-Chinese relations', in W. A. McCagg Jr. and B. D. Silver (eds), *Soviet Asian Ethnic Frontiers* (New York: Pergamon, 1979), pp 117–44.

7. See Charles Warren Hostler, *Turkism and the Soviets* (London: Allen and Unwin, 1957) and Serge A. Zenkovsky, *Pan-Turkism and Islam in Russia* (Cambridge, Mass.: Harvard University Press, 1960).

8. See Jacob H. Landau, *Pan-Turkism in Turkey: A Study of Irredentism* (Hamden, Connecticut: Archon Books, 1981). Turkey's policy towards the Turkish minorities in the Balkans and Cyprus gradually changed over the years. For example, beginning in the early 1950s and lasting until 1989, the relations between Ankara and Sofia were intermittently strained over Bulgaria's repression of its Turkish minority. Turkey has also taken a strong stand against the treatment of the Turks in Greece, and intervened militarily in Cyprus in 1974 to protect the Cypriot Turkish minority. However, fearing reprisal from Moscow, Turkey's leaders refrained from similar involvement in the affairs of the Soviet Turkic peoples until 1990.

9. Gareth M. Winrow, 'A stabilizing influence in a fragile commonwealth? Turkey and the former USSR', paper presented at the Annual Convention of the International Studies Association, Atlanta, Georgia, March–April 1992, p 1.

10. The coverage in the Turkish press provides considerable insight into the emotional nature of these meetings. See the reports of President Karimov's visit to Turkey (*Sabah*, 18 December 1991) and the visit by Turkey's Minister of Culture to Turkmenistan (*Milliyet*, 30 December 1991).

11. For the views expressed by Central Asian leaders such as Karimov and Akaev regarding the appeal of Turkish secularism, see Bess Brown, 'Central Asia's Diplomatic Debut', *RFE/RL Research Report*, 6 March 1992.

12. The analysis of the Turkic republics in the Turkish press reflected these perceptions. See Bilal Simsir, 'Asya Turk Cumhuriyetleri ve Turkiye' (*Milliyet*, 25-8 December 1991) and Fatih Yilmaz, 'Dagilan SSCB'de Turki Cumhuriyetler' (*Cumhuriyet*, 14–21 December 1991).

13. *The Economist*, 26 December 1992, p 46.

14. 'U.S., Turkey pledge aid to new states', *Washington Post*, 12 February 1992. Ankara's expectations from Washington are delineated in the memoran-

dum presented by Demirel to the Bush administration during his visit to Washington in February 1992. See 'Memorandum on Turkish-US cooperation in favor of the new republics of the Commonwealth of Independent States (CIS)', Embassy of Turkey, Washington, DC, 11 February 1992.

15. To provide international air service for the region, Turkey's state-owned airlines have begun regularly scheduled flights between Turkey and the Turkic republics. The Turkish government has also established branches of Turkey's EximBank, a financial institution that provides credit guarantees for exports, in several Central Asian capitals. Turkish officials have also been negotiating with their Azerbaijani counterparts to expand barter arrangements to provide the Azerbaijanis with consumer goods and machinery in return for a steady flow of oil and gas.

16. 'The boys from Bishkek, Baku, and Samarkand', *The Turkish Times* [Washington, DC], 1 January 1993.

17. 'Memorandum on Turkish–US cooperation in favor of the new republics of the Commonwealth of Independent States (CIS)', Embassy of Turkey, Washington, DC, 11 February 1992.

18. 'Turkey Pushing Eastward – By Satellite', *Washington Post*, 22 March 1992.

19. 'Turkey struggles to make sense of trade with CIS republics', *Financial Times*, 3 March 1992.

20. The total volume of these activities is still considerably smaller than those undertaken by major Turkish firms in Russia and Ukraine. See 'Turkish firms expand in CIS', in *The Turkish Times* [Washington, DC], 1 June 1992.

21. See Sabri Sayari, 'La Turquie et la crise yugoslave', *Politique etrangère*, no.2 (Summer 1992), pp 309–16.

22. Sabri Sayari, 'Turkey: the changing European security environment and the Gulf crisis', *The Middle East Journal*, xlvi/1 (Winter 1992), pp 15–16.

23. Elizabeth Fuller, 'Nagorno-Karabakh: can Turkey remain neutral?' *RFE/RL Research Reports*, i/14 (3 April 1992), pp 36–8, and Kenneth Mackenzie, 'Azerbaijan and the neighbors', *The World Today* (January 1992).

24. Ankara has in fact declared that it could not remain neutral regarding Armenian claims on Nakhchevan. For the text of the strongly worded official statement issued by the government, see 'Turkiye Nahcivan'da Tarafsiz Kalamaz', *Cumhuriyet*, 16 May 1992.

25. See Lauren G. Ross, *The Race for Influence in the Central Asian Muslim Republics*, unpublished paper (Elliott School of International Affairs, George Washington University, Washington, DC, 1992).

26. The Turkic republics have responded to Turkish and Iranian efforts with a similar mix of ideology and pragmatism. For example, while Niazov has often stated his preference for the Turkish model, Turkmenistan has developed the closest trade and cultural relations with Iran. See Bess Brown, 'Turkmenistan Asserts Itself', *RFE/RL Research Report*, i/43 (October 1992), pp 27–31.

27. In his writings and speeches, Turkes often referred to them as the

'enslaved Turks', and called for their 'liberation' by Turkey. Imprisoned because of his pan-Turkist activities in the mid-1940s, Turkes nearly came to power in the military coup of 1960 which he had masterminded with a group of young officers. Outflanked by the military junta's senior commanders, Turkes was exiled abroad in 1963. He returned to Turkey in 1965 and has been active in right-wing nationalist politics since then.

28. Alparslan Turkes, 'Turan Bayragi Yukseliyor', *Yeni Dusunce*, 3 January 1992, and 'Orta Asya'da Ulkucu Agirligi', *Yeni Dusunce*, 15 May 1991.

29. Turkes' electoral support has remained quite limited since the late 1960s. His Nationalist Action Party (the predecessor to the NLP) and the NLP have polled an average of 6 to 8 per cent of the total votes in parliamentary elections.

30. The Islamic fundamentalist vote – represented by the National Salvation Party in the 1970s and the WP since the late 1980s – has averaged about 10 per cent of the total vote in national elections.

31. Ecevit was prime minister in 1974 when Turkey intervened militarily in Cyprus. He has also been one of Turkes' principal critics, and often denounced him for his 'racist' views during the ideologically polarized party politics of the late 1970s.

32. This idea does not seem to carry much weight in the Turkic republics at present, either. See James Critchlow, 'Will there be a Turkestan?', *RFE/RL Research Report*, i/28 (10 July 1992), pp 47–50.

33. See Gareth M. Winrow, 'Turkey and former Soviet Central Asia: national and ethnic identity', *Central Asian Survey*, xi/3 (1992), pp 101–11 for a perceptive argument regarding the cultural pan-Turkist overtones of Turkey's outlook on Central Asia.

34. See Cassandra Cavanaugh, 'Uzbekistan looks south and east for role models', *RFE/RL Research Report*, i/40 (9 October 1992), pp 11-14.

35. The differences between the Turkic peoples and Turks in the Balkans or the Middle East regarding their relations to Turkey are forcefully argued by a Turkish intellectual of Central Asian origin. See Ahat Andican, 'Osmanlidan Gunumuze Turkiye-Turk Dunyasi Iliskileri ve Gelecege Yonelik Dusunceler', *Turkistan* [Istanbul], iv/15 (1991), pp 8–11.

8

Iran, the Caucasus and Central Asia

SEYED KAZEM SAJJADPOUR

From the ascendance of Russia as a major European power in the eighteenth century to the collapse of the Soviet Union, Iran's northern neighbour was a source of continuous security concern. While in some cases Iran was able to outmanoeuvre Russia or the Soviet Union, politically Iran was the weaker side, and it often played the classical games of power-balancing by relying on anti-Russian European states, by inviting third parties to offset some of the effects of the Russo-British domination and rivalry in Iran, and, when all else failed, by granting further concessions to its northern neighbour.[1] Neither the Bolshevik Revolution of 1917 nor the Islamic revolution of 1979 changed the nature of this asymmetry; both revolutions, in fact, complicated this power relationship by adding an ideological dimension to it.

The breakdown of the Soviet Union ushered in a new phase in the relationship between the two neighbours, changing the long-standing asymmetry in Iran's favour. For the first time in its modern history, Iran now enjoys relatively more power than its new neighbours to the north. All three land neighbours of Iran to the north, Armenia, Azerbaijan and Turkmenistan, may be placed behind Iran in terms of such measures of power as land, population, economy, military capability and political cohesiveness.

The aim of the present chapter is to analyse Iran's behaviour towards the post-Soviet republics of Central Asia and the Caucasus in the aftermath of the fall of the Soviet Union in 1991. It is hoped that the analysis offered here would help carry us beyond such simplistic views of the determinants of Iran's foreign policy in this region as the export of Islamic fundamentalism, competition with Turkey and arms purchases (including nuclear technology).

Some determinants of Iran's regional behaviour

Two sets of determinants of Iran's policies towards the post-Soviet republics of Central Asia and the Caucasus may be distinguished. The first has to do with security and political considerations. Since 1991, Iran has had to deal with a volatile security environment to the north. Almost overnight, the number of its neighbours increased from one to three on land and from one to four on the Caspian Sea, a situation experienced by no other country near the former Soviet Union.[2] Furthermore, comparatively speaking, Iran is closer to the trouble spots of the intense ethnic conflicts in the Caucasus than any other country. Only Iran and Georgia, for example, have borders with the republics of Armenia and Azerbaijan.

This security dimension of Iran's relationship with the former Soviet republics is even more significant because of the instability and fluidity of the political situation in Central Asia and the Caucasus. The painstaking process of nation-building, the legitimacy crisis, rapid social and economic transformation, decolonization, ethnic diversity, border disputes, and a catalogue of other issues are sources of instability in the post-Soviet republics. This instability may invite foreign intervention in the region as well as an influx of new refugees into Iran, for which the country is by no means prepared.[3] The military dimension of Iran's security concerns is no less significant: What will happen to the CIS army? Who will finally be in charge of borders in these republics? Will each of these republics have its own independent army? There are as yet no clear answers to these questions.

An additional aspect of Iran's security concerns in the region has to do with what may be called a process of the demonization of Iran. As the West searches for a new enemy after the Cold War, there there has been much talk of Iran as a major threat to regional stability and the need for its containment.[4]

Along with political and security concerns, cultural and economic considerations constitute the second set of influences on Iran's policy towards the ex-Soviet republics. In the cultural sphere, there are deep historical ties between Iran and Central Asia. For centuries, Central Asia, as a part of the greater Khorasan, was one of the two pillars of the Islamic civilization, the other being Baghdad.[5] Such notable

Iranian philosophers and poets as Farabi, Avicenna and Roudaki were born in the areas that are now part of Central Asia. In the Caucasus, too, Iran has long had a cultural presence. And Islam is of course a common cultural denominator between Iran and Central Asia and the Caucasus. The latter region served as a training ground for many Iranian advocates of social democracy during the constitutional revolution of 1905–11.[6]

At the economic level, Iran looks to the region as an important market for Iranian-made consumer goods. Oil and transportation provide additional economic bases for a closer relationship beteween the Central Asian republics and Iran. The landlocked republics look to Iran as a natural linkage and gateway to the high seas. Iran's relatively well-developed oil industry can provide technical assistance to these republics.[7]

Levels of analysis

The dynamics of Iranian policy towards the Muslim republics of Central Asia and the Caucasus may be analysed at domestic and international levels. Domestically, the policy-makers in Tehran have had to deal with 15 different republics in four regions instead of just one centre, i.e. Moscow. The four regions include the Persian Gulf, the eastern parts of the Arab world, the Mediterranean Sea – insofar as Turkey is dependent on Iran for significant land communication with Central Asia – and the Indian subcontinent, at least until Afghanistan achieves greater stability. Iran has had a long history of diplomatic relations with Moscow/St Petersburg, which remained intact during the past two centuries.[8] Dealing with 15 separate capitals after the demise of the Soviet Union has required new expertise, fresh financial resources and the capacity to respond promptly to new developments.

An increasingly significant factor in the development of policy towards this region is the Iranian National Security Council, which was created by a constitutional amendment in 1989 to coordinate the various agencies responsible for both external and internal security. In general and compared to other policy-making bodies in the country, the council has moved with great caution in most foreign policy domains, for example steering the country towards a neutral position in the Iraqi–Kuwait crisis of 1990 in accordance with the resolution of the UN Security Council and playing a leading role in setting Iran's policy agenda with respect to the former Soviet republics.[9] The council's decisions, presided over by Hashemi Rafsanjani, have been much more moderate than, for example, Iran's policies in Lebanon during the 1980s. One of the ripple effects for Iran of the Soviet collapse has been the increasing significance of the country's own northern provinces. The emergence of the three republics of Azerbaijan, Armenia and Turkmenistan has facilitated contacts between peoples on both sides of the borders with Iran, and the increasing level of contact between the officials of these republics and those of the Iranian border provinces has helped elevate the border provinces' status compared with that of other provinces. They are, for example, the only provinces that deal directly with other states.[10]

At the international level, the demise of the Soviet Union deprived Iran of its useful Soviet/Russian card. Over the years since the mid-decades of the nineteenth century, Iran had become quite adept at playing this card to receive Western aid or to solicit support from the Russians or the Soviets.[11] Although that game is over, Iran still remains at the crossroads between Central Asia and the Caucasus and the four neighbouring geographical regions, which assures Iran's status as a major regional power and a crucial partner in any security arrangement in the region.

At the regional level, Iran has played a much more prominent role in the Organization of Islamic Conference (OIC) and the Economic Cooperation Organization (ECO) following the demise of the Soviet Union. In December 1991, for example, Iran was instrumental in having the delegation from the Republic of Azerbaijan attend the OIC summit in Dakar, Senegal,[12] and in February 1992 sponsored the ECO summit meeting in Tehran, where delegations from all the republics of Central Asia and the Republic of Azerbaijan joined the ECO as permanent members or observers.[13] The emergence of several new regional organizations, i.e. those of the Caspian Sea states,[14] the Central Asian states,[15] and the Persian-speaking countries,[16] provides additional economic, political and cultural links between Iran and the post-Soviet republics.

Emerging ties since the collapse of the Soviet Union

Before considering bilateral relations, the general framework within which Iran's policy has taken shape with respect to Central Asia and the Caucasus should be briefly outlined. There are two pillars of Iranian regional policy: security in the Persian Gulf and cooperation with the northern neighbours.[17] Thus a significant diplomatic effort has been made – and continues to be made – by Iran with respect to the ex-Soviet republics. Second, the changing domestic situation in these republics, as well as new international events, have influenced – and will continue to affect – Iran's moves in Central Asia and the Caucasus. A third factor is the centrality of Russia as an important consideration in Iran's policy towards the new republics. Iran is fully aware of Russia's actual and potential power in the CIS, and is careful not to pursue policies that could jeopardize its relationship with Moscow.[18]

Against this background, we may now examine the bilateral relationships between Iran and each of the post-Soviet republics. For ease of analysis, the republics are divided into two regions, the Caucasus and Central Asia.

The Caucasus

Three features of this mountainous region are essential to an understanding of Iran's policy towards it. One is the ethnic and religious composition of the region, with its mixture of Armenians, Azeris and Georgians as dominant ethnic groups among a number of other nationalities. As Shi'ite Muslims, the Azeris are the only post-Soviet people who share identical religious beliefs with Iran. Although due to decades of secularist domination religion is not a dominant factor in the socio-political life of Azerbaijan, Iranians in general, and Iranian Azeris in particular – who hold considerable influence in both the domestic and foreign policies of Iran – take seriously the issue of common religious identity with the people of Azerbaijan. Iran has had good relations with Christians, but the present religious and ethnic conflicts present serious dilemmas for Iran, which has had long-standing historical ties to all three peoples.[19] The second feature of the region is its return, after 70 years of Soviet hegemonic rule, to the geopolitical situation in which three regional powers, Iran, Turkey and Russia, are the main players.

The third significant feature of the Caucasus is the continuing conflict over Nagorno-Karabakh, one of the most complicated conflicts of the post-Soviet era.[20] This conflict, the product of a complex set of variables including ethnicity, national aspirations, self-determination, religion, border disputes, historical claims and the colonial legacies of both Tsarist and Soviet Russia, is very close to Iran's borders.[21]

Furthermore, Iran has a large Azeri population and an Armenian minority. The prolongation of the conflict in Nagorno-Karabakh is very likely to spill over into Iran, although, thus far, its domestic consequences in Iran have been contained.

Full diplomatic relations were established between Tehran and Tblisi in early 1993, with both countries showing interest in expanding their bilateral ties. Several Georgian and Iranian diplomatic and economic delegations have paid visits to each others' capitals and several protocols have been signed.[22] The most important diplomatic exchanges between Iran and Georgia were the official visit of the Georgian leader Edward Shevardnaze to Tehran, during which Iran and Georgia signed a friendship treaty, and that of Iranian Foreign Minister Ali Akbar Velayati to Tbilisi in the spring of 1993. Some Russian papers showed a high degree of sensitivity to the news of Iranian–Georgian cooperation and suggested that Georgia had promised to provide Iran with weapons. This was denied by both Iran and Georgia,[23] although such deals are quite likely; it seems that Georgia looks to Iran as a strategic counterweight to Russia's heavy influence in the region.

Iranian–Azerbaijani relations

Iranian–Azerbaijani relations may be best described as unique among the post-Soviet republics. This uniqueness has its origin in a cultural affinity, the fluidity of power in the Republic of Azerbaijan, and certain anti-Iranian tendencies in Baku's political circles. As mentioned earlier, no other post-Soviet republic is like Azerbaijan in terms of its affinity for Iran, a cultural tie that has both merits and limits. While it can rekindle historical bonds, it also raises mutual expectations which, if not met, could have undesirable consequences. The issue of recognition of the Republic of Azerbaijan is a good example. Azerbaijan expected Iran to grant it early recognition, but Iran could not afford to do so due to its view of the unfolding situation in the former Soviet Union. Iran's slowness in recognizing Azerbaijan has left a negative imprint on subsequent relations between the two countries.

Fluidity of power in Azerbaijan is also a source of fluctuation in its relations with Iran,[24] one of the few countries that had a diplomatic presence in Baku before the demise of the Soviet Union. It is also interesting to note that Hashemi Rafsanjani, then the powerful *majlis* (legislature) speaker, visited Baku in June 1989, after an important meeting with Mikhail Gorbachev and a few weeks after the death of Ayatollah Khomeini. It was in this meeting that Rafsanjani received the approval of the Soviet authorities to expand economic and cultural ties with the Muslim republics.[25] Azerbaijan was at the heart of this new Iranian drive in the southern republics of the former USSR. This process was within the framework of Iranian–Soviet relations; coordination with Moscow and avoiding conflict with Soviet authorities were the guidelines.

Iran was quick to expand its cultural and economic ties with Baku after the Rafsanjani–Gorbachev meeting. An office was established within the Foreign Ministry for the coordination of various activities in the relations between Iran and the Muslim republics.[26] However, the chief aim of this policy was the expansion of official ties with Azerbaijan; the Azerbaijanis, too, desired closer relations with Iran for their own reasons, and almost all the high-ranking officials of Azerbaijan visited Iran before the demise of the Soviet Union in December 1991.[27] This process helped Iran to continue its ties with the Republic of Azerbaijan after its independence because the communist leadership stayed in power, though disguised under new titles. The loss of power by the communists in May 1991, and the victory of the Popular Front led by Abulfaz Elchbayli, marred Iranian–Azerbaijani relations due to Elchbayli's anti-Iranian position both before and after his ascent to power.[28]

Elchbayli was inconsistent in his approach to Iran, showing anti-Iranian sentiments in his early months as president, but later adopting a more cooperative position. The reasons for this shift were his gradual development from idealogue to statesman, the weakening of Azerbaijan's position in its conflict with Armenia, and Iran's move to strengthen its ties with his rival, Haidar Aliyev, the speaker of Nakhchevan, who visited Iran in August 1992 and was well received there.[29] This prompted Elchbayli to moderate his position. It is not suprising that the unexpected departure of Elchbayli in June 1993 and Aliev's rise to power in Baku were welcomed by Iran.

Along with the fluidity of power in Baku, the presence of what might be called anti-Iranian circles in Azerbaijan serves as another source of contention in their relationship. These circles advocate detaching Iranian Azerbaijan, which they refer to as 'Southern Azerbaijan', and uniting it with Northern Azerbaijan. This notion is, of course, not new; it developed in the Soviet era.[30] However, reference to this issue, especially by members of the Popular Front, is an irritant to the Iranian leaders, who are intent on preserving their national integrity.[31]

Regardless of some of the above points of contention, there are areas in which both countries have shown interest in cooperation. Cultural and economic ties cannot be strengthened, of course, without diplomatic ties and initiatives. After the state visit of Rafsanjani, several new diplomatic initiatives facilitated further economic and cultural cooperation. In July 1990 the Iranian deputy foreign minister for legal and consular affairs, during a visit to Baku, concluded an agreement that facilitated trans-border travels – a significant step in opening Iran to the Republic of Azerbaijan.[32] In November 1990, the Iranian Foreign Minister, in a well-publicized visit to Azerbaijan, signed a letter of understanding for cultural and economic cooperation.[33] This trip was a turning-point in bilateral relationships between the two countries, since it was the beginning of new Iranian outlook towards Azerbaijan as a separate entity from the Soviet Union.

After Iran's recognition of the Republic of Azerbaijan and the upgrading of the Iranian Consulate to an Embassy, many high officials of the Republic of Azerbaijan visited Iran, including Mutalibov, then President of Azerbaijan.[34] This diplomatic process reached a climax on 8 May 1992, when Iran concluded a friendship pact with the Republic of Azerbaijan in Tehran, signed by President Rafsanjani and Yagub Mamedov, then the acting President of Azerbaijan. A similar friendship pact was signed with Ter-Petronian, the President of Armenia, on the same day, while he was in Tehran for an Armenian–Azerbaijani–Iranian Summit.[35] This diplomatic cooperation was further enhanced when Iran and the Republic of Azerbaijan abolished visas for diplomats in an agreement signed on 20 April 1992, in Baku.[36]

The effects of these agreements can be seen in the cultural sphere. At the governmental level, the most significant initiative was an agreement signed by Mohammed Khatami, then the Iranian Minister of Culture and Islamic Guidance, and his Azerbaijani counterpart, Bubbul Ogly, on 3 March 1992. Based on this agreement, both countries welcomed the promotion of tourism, the establishment of cultural centres, and the exchange of cultural attachés and delegations.[37] Both countries were quick to implement the agreement. For example, on 4 May the Minister of Information of the Republic of Azerbaijan went to Iran for the 5th Tehran International Book Exhibition, in which Azerbaijani publishers actively participated. The new Iranian Minister of Islamic Guidance, Ali Larijani, paid a visit to

Baku in May 1993, and strengthened the mutual cultural ties between the two countries by signing several new agreements.

At the grass-roots, or people-to-people level, there have been visits, religious pilgrimages by Azeris to the Shi'ite holy shrines in Iran (including Mashhad and Qum), Iranians travelling to Baku on holiday, and Iranians marrying Azeri women – in part at least due to the much higher wedding costs in Iran.[38] These cultural ties have also been effective in reviving mutual interest in literary activities in the Republic of Azerbaijan and the Azeri community in Iran.[39]

In the economic sphere, Iran's interest is shown by the fact that the first Iranian official who visited Baku after the recognition of the Republic of Azerbaijan was Mohsen Noorbakhsh, the Minister of Economic and Financial Affairs. Since this symbolic overture, Iran has engaged in economic cooperation with the Republic of Azerbaijan in three major areas. First is the oil industry, where Iran has agreed to market Azerbaijani oil, to provide technical assistance, and to pump a million cubic metres of natural gas to Azerbaijan in continuation of Iran's deals with the former Soviet Union.[40] Oil officials of both countries frequently exchange visits.[41] One of the major issues in the oil-related cooperation is the transport of Azerbaijani oil via Iran to Turkey. Another is the tripartite gas venture between Iran, Azerbaijan and Ukraine, in which Iranian gas will be pumped to Ukraine via Azerbaijan under an agreement announced during the official visit of the chairman of the Ukrainian parliament to Tehran in May 1993.[42]

The second major economic area is communications, in its broadest sense. One dimension of cooperation in this area is the establishment of the Tehran–Baku air link, which became operational with an Iran-Air flight on 17 March 1992.[43] Iran and Azerbaijan formed a joint shipping company whose first ship travelled between Baku and Anzali, the Iranian port on the Caspian Sea, on 17 February 1993. Another dimension is telecommunications. On 11 February 1992, during the visit to Iran of the Azerbaijani minister of post and telecommunication, it was agreed that Iran would upgrade the telecommunication system of Azerbaijan. The Iranian minister of post, telegraph and telephone paid a follow-up visit to Baku on 3 March 1992, during which Azerbaijan asked Iran to help install a thousand microwave telephone channels between the cities of Lenkaran in Iran and Baku. It was also agreed that Iran would publish postage stamps for the Republic of Azerbaijan.[44]

The third area of economic cooperation is the establishment of an administrative structure for future economic activities. In this regard, two bodies are important. One is the Joint Economic Cooperation Commission, established at the ministerial level, whose major function is to regulate and expedite economic cooperation between the two countries.[45] The second is the Iran–Azerbaijan Chamber of Commerce, established 21 April 1992,[46] which plans to open an office in Baku. Members of Iran's private sector, especially those from the northern provinces, are increasingly active in the Republic of Azerbaijan.

Iran and the Nagorno-Karabakh conflict

The Nagorno-Karabakh crisis is indeed complex and has the potential to develop into a major regional conflict. Being close to this conflict geographically, having both Armenians and Azeris in Iran, enjoying the trust and confidence of both the Republic of Armenia and the Republic of Azerbaijan, and being fearful of the increasing influence of the West in the Caucasus due to a prolonged conflict that may invite foreign intervention, Iran has engaged in an active mediation in Nagorno-Karabakh. In spite of a significant Iranian diplomatic investment and initial successes in bringing the two sides to the negotiating table and getting several periods of truce and ceasefire, Iran has not succeeded in its mediation efforts due to the nature of the conflict and lack of international support for its resolution.

Iran's approach to Nagorno-Karabakh may be seen in three different periods. In the first, before the demise of the Soviet Union in December 1991, Iran viewed the Nagorno-Karabakh conflict as a Soviet domestic issue. The only noticeable Iranian effort during this period was a meeting between Ali Akbar Velayati, the Foreign Minister of Iran, and the President of Armenia in November 1991, in Almaty, at which Iran signalled its readiness to mediate between the two conflicting parties.

The second period of Iranian activist approach began with the Soviet breakup, when Iran became deeply involved, proposing to resolve the conflict through a five-stage plan. In the first stage, Velayati paid a visit to Baku in early March 1992, to explore the situation; in the second, representatives of Armenia and the Republic of Azerbaijan went to Tehran in mid-March. The third stage consisted of more than a month of shuttle diplomacy by Mahmood Vaezi, Iran's Deputy Foreign Minister for European and American affairs, between Moscow, Yerevan and Baku, during which Iran helped establish a ceasefire. In

the fourth stage, a summit meeting between the Republic of Azerbaijan, Armenia and Iran was held in Tehran in May 1992, during
which the 'Tehran Declaration' was issued. In the fifth and final stage,
Vaezi flew to Baku and Yerevan after the summit, but he was unable
to prevent escalation of the conflict. In the final stage Iran emphasized
that it would not accept any border changes, signalling its disapproval
of the way the Armenians were approaching the Karabakh crisis.[47]

The third phase of the Iranian response has become discernible as
the Armenian forces advanced in the territory of Azerbaijan during
the early months of 1993. The Foreign Ministry of Iran issued a
statement on 5 April 1993, expressing its concern about the intensification of military operations. Though it avoided the term 'Armenian
aggression', it was obviously directed against the Armenian forces.
The developments of 1993 have brought a new kind of Iranian response, 'guarded neutrality'. Iran has not been involved in any mediating activity, though it has remained available for such a role. At this
stage Iran has been more assertive on the issue of 'non-violability of
international borders'.[48]

This Iranian policy of sanctity of internationally recognized borders
is also a key to understanding its approach to Nakhchevan, an Azerbaijani enclave between Armenia and Iran. The principle of the sanctity
of borders is contrary to those formulas which prescribe a land
exchange between Armenia and Azerbaijan: giving a corridor from
Armenia to Azerbaijan to connect Nakhchevan with Azerbaijan and a
corridor from Azerbaijan to Armenia to connect Karabakh to Armenia.
Such a formula would deprive Iran of a common border with Armenia.

Iranian–Armenian relations

Iran's relation with Armenia is a long and historical one, going back
to the ancient Persian empire. Iranian–Armenian relations in the post-
Soviet era may be examined in the light of two issues. The first is the
security dimension. As neighbours, the two countries have no specific
problem; nevertheless along with the ripple effects of the Nagorno-
Karabakh crisis, unofficial statements have expressed a concern that
Armenia may become a second Israel, symbolizing a Western presence in a Muslim Middle East.[49] This perception, so far, has not
served as an impediment to the expansion of diplomatic and economic ties between Iran and Armenia.

The second issue concerns economic relations. The first economic-trade protocol between Iran and Armenia was signed on 30 November 1991 at the Sharjah trade fair.[50] Later, on 9 February 1992, the Armenian Foreign Minister, Raffi Hovanmisian, visited Tehran to seek economic cooperation, heading a high-ranking delegation which included the ministers of industry, transport, health, and trade, as well as the mayor of Yerevan. This was a turning-point: the two major letters of understanding which were signed, one dealing exclusively with roads and transport, have become an important foundation for economic relations between the two countries.[51]

Since these accords, Iran and Armenia have had significant diplomatic interactions, relating for the most part to the Iranian mediation in the Nagorno-Karabakh crisis. The speed and magnitude of these interactions, coupled with Iran's sensitivity to Armenian intrusions into Nakhchevan, have placed the Iranian authorities in a difficult position. Some Iranian Azeris have begun to criticize the government's approach, causing a slowdown in diplomatic interactions between Iran and Armenia, and Armenian military activity in April 1993 created some strain in their diplomatic relations. However, economic cooperation between the two countries seems to be proceeding at a steady pace.

Central Asia

Turkoman–Iranian relations

Iran's relation with Turkmenistan has been the best of all those with the post-Soviet republics, due to the absence of any major security problems and the relative political stability of Turkmenistan. Politically, there have been high-level diplomatic visits and discussions between Iran and Turkmenistan. It is the only Central Asian republic which Rafsanjani has visited in his capacity as President of Iran, in April 1992, when he attended a summit meeting of the Central Asian republics. Niazov, President of Turkmenistan, has also visited Iran on several occasions, including a trip on 8 October 1991, when he carried a secret message from Gorbachev to Rafsanjani, and on 16 February 1992, for the ECO summit.[52] Velayati visited Ashkhabad in November 1991; the Turkmenistan vice president, Atta Charyev, paid an official visit to Tehran in January 1992. In March 1992 Alaeddin Borujerdi, the Iranian Deputy Foreign Minister for Asian Affairs, and in April 1992, Mojtaba Mirmehdi, the Iranian Deputy Foreign Minister for Legal and Consular Affairs, visited Ashkhabad. The

Iranian Foreign Minister paid another official visit to Turkmenistan in February 1993,[53] followed by other officials of the foreign ministry, which resulted in new agreements on consular issues, further facilitating diplomatic interactions between the two countries.

At the economic level, there have been numerous contracts and agreements, with the most important area of economic cooperation being oil. Iranian Oil Minister Gholam Reza Aghazadeh reached an agreement on 16 April 1992 in Ashkhabad, according to which Iran will buy natural gas from Turkmenistan for use in the northern part of Iran and will help Turkmenistan transport its oil to Europe.[54]

Transport is another area of economic cooperation. Iran and Turkmenistan discussed the establishment of a joint transport company and the construction of a Mashhad–Ashkhabad railway in December 1991.[55] The two countries reached an agreement on 29 April 1992, for transport by sea between Kranovodsk, Turkmenistan, to the Iranian ports along the Caspian Sea.[56]

Iran showed interest in banking cooperation with Turkmenistan in the visit paid to Ashkhabad by Adeli, the Governor of the Iranian Central Bank, on 5 March 1992. As a result of this trip a joint committee for banking was established two months later, and it was announced that Iran's Export Promotion Bank had granted $50 million to Turkmenistan.[57] Iran also offered to train banking personnel for Turkmenistan. The two countries formed a joint economic commission in April 1993, during the official visit to Ashkhabad of the Iranian minister of heavy industries.[58]

At the cultural level, Iran seems to be less active in Turkmenistan. However, the Turkoman minister of national education and the Iranian minister of culture and higher education signed a letter of understanding for the expansion of cultural and scientific relations on 15 April 1992, in Tehran,[59] ten days after Iran's announcement that it was planning to open an Iranian Cultural Centre in Ashkhabad.[60] A year later, in March 1993, the Iranian Minister of Islamic Guidance signed a cultural agreement with Turkmenistan in Ashkhabad.[61]

Given the pragmatic approach of both Iran and Turkmenistan, relations between the two may be expected to expand even further.

Tajik–Iranian relations

The fact that Tajikistan is the only Persian-speaking republic in Central Asia may help explain not only the Iranian government's approach to Tajikistan, but that of Iranians in general, including those who live outside their country. Persian culture has deep roots in Tajikistan, and the Tajiks view this culture as a means of reasserting their identity. Nevertheless, due to the domestic political circumstances of Tajikistan, any cultural initiative on the part of Iran tends to be interpreted politically. Most of the bilateral agreements between the governments of Iran and Tajikistan are of a cultural nature. For example, Iran provided Persian books for Tajik elementary schools in August 1992; a branch of al-Hoda Book Store, run by the Ministry of Islamic Guidance, has opened in Dushanbe; and Iranian television is broadcast in Tajikistan every night. A second type of cultural activity is by Iranians outside Iran, especially by those residing in the USA. The Foundation for Iranian Studies, in Bethesda, Maryland, has opened an office in Dushanbe.[62] Third, the Iranian intelligentsia has begun to approach Tajikistan as a new cultural frontier. This has included, for example, a great interest in the Tajik cinema.[63]

In the political sphere, in addition to establishing an embassy in Dushanbe, a variety of diplomatic missions have taken place, including the visit to Iran of the Tajik president. In the economic field, the two countries in addition to signing various agreements have decided to establish a joint company called Tajiran,[64] and on 13 March 1992 they signed a civil aviation memorandum.[65] Tajikistan has also invited Iranian investment.[66]

The extremely volatile domestic situation in Tajikistan has had a negative impact on Iranian–Tajik ties. The civil war and the unrest in Tajikistan in late 1992 was reported in the Iranian press with an anti-communist slant. But it did not interrupt diplomatic relations, though the Iranian embassy in Dushanbe had to be closed for security reasons for a short while.

Uzbek–Iranian relations

Comparatively, in spite of its pivotal position among the Central Asian republics, Uzbekistan has not been as attractive to Iran as the other republics. One reason is that Uzbekistan is neither a neighbour nor a Persian-speaking republic, though two of its most important cities, Samarkand and Bukhara, are regarded as the cradles of Persian culture and literature. Tashkent was the last Central Asian capital in which Iran opened an embassy. Foreign Minister Velayati paid a visit to Tashkent in November 1991, and the Uzbek Deputy Commerce

Minister visited Iran on 24 December 1991, to discuss the expansion of economic ties, especially on trade and rail transport.[67] In September 1992 the Foreign Minister of Uzbekistan, Obaidollah Abdolrazaqov, paid a visit to Tehran and met with high-ranking Iranian officials including the president. During this visit, Iran offered to train Uzbek oil industry personnel. On 6 November 1992, Vaezi, Iranian Deputy Foreign Minister, visited Tashkent to inaugurate the opening of the Iranian Embassy. In his talks with Uzbek officials, they agreed to establish a joint economic commission.[68] Islam Karimov, president of Uzbekistan, visited Iran in December 1992, a turning-point in the expansion of bilateral ties. His trip was followed by the Iranian Foreign Minister's official visit to Tashkent in February 1993.[69]

Kazakh–Iranian relations

Kazakhstan and Iran began to expand their bilateral ties when Velayati visited Almaty in November 1991. President Nazarbaev's visit to Iran in early November 1992 might be called the most important diplomatic trip by any Central Asian leader to Iran. This is due to the significance of Kazakhstan in the Central Asian community and in the CIS. The significance of this trip was further underlined by three facts: Nazarbaev went to Iran after participating in the Turkic-Speaking Nations summit in Ankara; he visited the shrine of Imam Reza in Mashhad – a token of the importance of religious ties and a reminder of the centrality of Mashhad in the Greater Khorasan area which once encompassed Central Asia; and a significant statement that he made upon his arrival in Almaty, when, reflecting on his trip to Iran, he said he was able to see the true, liberal face of Iran, an image that contradicts the current view of Iran as 'a country where fundamentalism had been victorious'. He added, 'You can see women behind the wheel of a car more often in Tehran than in [Almaty].'[70]

Nazarbaev's trip was well covered in the Iranian press.[71] In their discussions, Rafsanjani accentuated the common element of Asianness between Iran and the Central Asian nations. Several letters of understanding emphasized the desirability of cooperation between the two countries, especially in the Caspian Sea. In addition to diplomatic relations, a second Kazakhstan–Iran tie is cooperation in the area of transport. In February 1992 the Kazakh Road Minister went to Tehran for mutual cooperation in this field, especially rail transport,[72] and in April the Iranian roads minister attended a session in Almaty of railway representatives from all over Central Asia.[73] A memorandum of understanding on economic cooperation was signed between the Kazakh labour minister and his Iranian counterpart in February 1993.[74]

In the cultural arena, Kazakhstan's minister of culture signed a letter of understanding for the expansion of cultural ties with his Iranian counterpart on 12 April 1992, in Tehran.[75] Later, the chancellor of Kazakhstan's Farabi University paid a visit to Iran.[76]

Kyrgyz–Iranian relations

Kyrgyzstan's relations with Iran are the least developed among the Central Asian republics, probably because of its remoteness from Iran. However, Iran was among the few nations that opened an embassy in Bishkek. Bishkek was also among the places that Velayati visited in November 1991. Several delegations from both sides have visited each others' capitals.

Velayati cancelled his February 1993 visit to Kyrgyzstan, ostensibly due to the extensive relations between Israel and Kyrgyzstan. The resulting strain in bilateral relations, however, was short-lived. Askar Akaev, President of Kyrgyzstan, visited Iran in June 1993, and President Rafsanjani met with his Kyrgyz counterpart in the second summit of the ECO, in Istanbul, in July 1993.[77]

Notes

1. Seyed Kazem Sajjadpour, *Iranian–Soviet Relations in a Security Perspective; 1979–1989*, unpublished PhD dissertation (George Washington University, Washington, DC, 1991), pp 43–60.

2. For Iran's security concerns in Central Asia and the Caucasus see the remarks of Kamal Kharazi, the ambassador and permanent representative of Iran to the United Nations, at the Asia Society, 'Iran and Central Asia', New York, 20 April 1992.

3. For a brief review of refugees in Iran, see Hiram A. Ruiz, 'Assist Refugees in Iran', *Christian Science Monitor*, 14 September 1992, p 18.

4. George Moffett, 'Resurgent Iran Again Challenges Western Interest', *Christian Science Monitor*, 19 November 1992, p 1.

5. Richard Frye, *Bukhara* (Oklahoma City: Oklahoma University Press, 1965), and *The Golden Age of Persia: The Arabs in the East* (London: Weidenfeld and Nicolson, 1975).

6. For the impact of the Caucasus on the Iranian secular intellectuals in the constitutional revolution see Mangol Bayat, *Iran's First Revolution: Shi'ism and the Constitutional Revolution of 1905–1908* (New York: Oxford University Press, 1991).

7. For the economic interests of Iran in the region see *Iran Business Monitor*, September 1992.

8. The Government of the Islamic Republic of Iran, the Foreign Ministry, Institute for Political and International Studies, *Siyasat Gozaran va-Rejal-e Siyassi dar Ravabete Kharejei Iran* [The Policy-Makers and Statemen in Iran's Foreign Policy] (Tehran: The Foreign Ministry of Islamic Republic of Iran, 1986), pp 90–91.

9. For the functions of the National Security Council, see *Constitution of the Islamic Republic of Iran*, published in English by the Islamic Propagation Organization (Tehran, 1989), Chapter XIII.

10. It is interesting to note that the heads of provincial departments in Khorasan and Azerbaijan signed agreements with the ministers of respective bordering neighbours.

11. To cite an example, it was during the Iran–Contra investigation that it was revealed that Iranians and Americans shared a similar view of the Soviet threat; this position was one of the reasons for secret talks between Iran and the USA. See US Congress, 101st Congress, *Report of the Congressional Committees Investigating the Iran–Contra Affair, with Supplement, Minority and Additional Views* (Washington, DC: US Government Printing Office, 1987).

12. It should be mentioned that in the early stage of independence Azerbaijan requested diplomatic help from neighbouring states in becoming connected to the international community.

13. *Kayhan*, 11 February 1992, p 1.

14. This organization represents Iran, Russia, Kazakhstan, Turkmenistan and the Republic of Azerbaijan.

15. Five republics of Central Asia are trying to set up an organizational basis for cooperation. They had their first summit in May 1992, at which the president of Iran and the prime ministers of Pakistan and Turkey also attended as observers.

16. Iran, Tajikistan and a representative of the Afghan resistance organized this group in February 1992, in Tehran.

17. R. K. Ramazani, 'Iran's foreign policy: both north and the south', *Middle East Journal*, xlvi/3 (Summer 1992), pp 393–412.

18. Stephen Blauk, 'Russia and Iran in a new Middle East', *Mediterranean Quarterly*, iii/4 (Fall 1992), pp 108–28.

19. For the historical ties between Iran and this region, see Nina G. Garsoian, 'Iran and Caucasia', *Trans Caucasia: Nationalism and Social Change: Essays in the History of Armenia, Azerbaijan and Georgia*, ed. Ronald G. Syny (Ann Arbor: The University of Michigan, 1983), pp 7–23.

20. For a background on this crisis from the standpoint of conflict thesis, see Nial Frase et al., 'A conflict analysis of the Armenian–Azerbaijani dispute',

Conflict Resolution, xxxiv/2 (December 1990), pp 624–51.

21. Paul A. Goble, 'Coping with the Nagorno Karabakh crisis', *The Fletcher Forum of World Affairs*, xvi/2 (Summer 1992), pp 19–28.

22. Islamic Republic New Agency (IRNA), 30 October 1992.

23. FBIS-SOV, 5 February 1993, p 70, 10 February 1993, p 53 and 17 February 1993, p 78.

24. Elizabeth Fuller, 'Azerbaijan after the Presidential election', *RFE/RL Research Report*, i/26, 26 June 1993, pp 1–7.

25. It should be mentioned that the Soviet officials treated Rafsanjani as a head of state and not simply the speaker of the parliament.

26. This office was established in the winter of 1990.

27. The list of the Azerbaijani officials who visited Iran includes the president, the prime minister and the foreign minister.

28. *Turkish Times*, 1 March 1992, p 3.

29. Reuters, 24 August 1992.

30. David Nissman, *The Soviet Union and Iranian Azerbaijan: The Use of Nationalism for Political Penetration* (Boulder, CO: Westview Press, 1987).

31. It is necessary to mention that even before the demise of the USSR, the issue of unification of Iranian Azerbaijan and Soviet Azerbaijan raised some concern in the Iranian community in the USA. See Sajjadpour, 'Iranian–Soviet Relations', pp 113–17.

32. *Kayhan*, 10 July 1991, p 3.

33. *Kayhan*, 3 December 1991, p 3.

34. *IRNA*, February 16, 1992.

35. *IRNA*, 8 May 1992.

36. *IRNA*, 20 April 1992.

37. *Ettela'at*, 4 March 1992, p 2.

38. For a sample of people-to-people contacts see *Maktab-e-Islam* (December 1991), pp 590–94, *Neda* (the journal of the Society of Women of the Islamic Republic of Iran), ii/2 (Autumn, 1991), pp 30–32.

39. Hassan Javadi, 'Iranian studies of Azerbaijan since the Islamic revolution', paper presented at the 26th Annual Meeting of the Middle Eastern Studies Association of North America, Portland, Oregon, 28–31 October 1992.

40. *IRNA*, 30 April 1992.

41. *IRNA*, 21 October 1992.

42. *IRNA*, 12 May 1993.

43. *IRNA*, 11 February 1992.

44. *Abrar*, 3 March 1992, p 3.

45. For details of its meeting of 17 November 1992, see *Keyhan*, 17 December 1992.

46. *IRNA*, 21 April 1992.

47. Islamic Republic of Iran, Permanent Mission to the United Nations, Press Releases no. 28 (26 February 1992), no. 30 (16 March 1992), no. 31 (23 March 1992), no. 32 (27 March 1992), no. 33 (27 March 1992), no. 35 (7 April 1992), and no. 43 (21 May 1992).

48. Islamic Republic of Iran, Permanent Mission to the United Nations, Press Release no. 72, 7 April 1993.

49. For example see editorial in *Joumhouri-Islami*, 2 March 1992.

50. *IRNA*, 30 November 1991.

51. *IRNA*, 2 March 1992.

52. *IRNA*, 16 March 1992.

53. *IRNA*, 1 February 1993.

54. *IRNA*, 16 April 1992.

55. *Ettela'at*, 20 January 1991.

56. *IRNA*, 29 April 1992.

57. *IRNA*, 5 May 1992.

58. *IRNA*, 14 April 1993.

59. *IRNA*, 15 April 1992.

60. *Keyhan*, 5 May 1991.

61. *IRNA*, 2 March 1993.

62. *Keyhan* [London edition], 20 March 1992.

63. For example see 'Tajikistan cinema' in Kelk, *A Literary Critic's Journal in Tehran* (July 1992), pp 220–28.

64. *IRNA*, 21 October 1992.

65. *IRNA*, 13 March 1992.

66. *IRNA*, 15 October 1992.

67. *Keyhan*, 25 December 1992.

68. *IRNA*, 6 November 1992.

69. *IRNA*, 2 February 1993.

70. FBIS-SOV-92-218, 10 November 1992, p 7.

71. For example see editorial in *Tehran Times*, 1 November 1992.

72. *Keyhan*, 23 March 1992.

73. *IRNA*, 22 April 1992.

74. *IRNA*, 21 February 1993.

75. *Keyhan*, 13 April 1992.

76. *IRNA*, 22 April 1992.

77. *IRNA*, 8 July 1993.

9

Pakistan, Afghanistan and the Central Asian States

TAHIR AMIN

The emergence of six Central Asian republics – Kazakhstan, Kyrgyzstan, Tajikistan, Uzbekistan, Azerbaijan and Turkmenistan – in the wake of the disintegration of the Soviet Union has created a euphoria in Pakistan at both official and unofficial levels. Most Pakistani observers consider it a historic opportunity for Pakistan and are enthusiastic over the prospects of building political and economic relationships with the newly emerged Central Asian states.[1] They visualize the emergence of a common market under the framework of the recently formed Economic Cooperation Organization (ECO) – which consists of the six Central Asian republics and Pakistan, Afghanistan, Iran and Turkey – eventually leading to a broader regional grouping with political and strategic implications. Some observers have even suggested the possible inclusion of China in such a regional grouping. However, other analysts, a minority view, contest this scenario, considering it unrealistic and arguing for a pragmatic, interest-based and limited relationship.[2] They point out some formidable obstacles: the transitional character of the economies and polities of the Central Asian republics and their historical links with the members of the CIS; Russian foreign policy interests, the ongoing problems of Afghanistan; Pakistan's economic limitations; and the greater potential ability of other international actors, Turkey, Iran, the Western powers, India and Israel, to woo the Central Asian states.

The major argument of this chapter is that both the above views are somewhat exaggerated and that the reality lies somewhere in between. Pakistan has embarked upon a series of modest political, economic, communications and cultural moves towards the Central

Asian states, with far-reaching consequences. Pakistan has skilled man-power, consumer and engineering goods, scientific and technical train-ing and could provide significant help in moving the land-locked Central Asian states towards market economies by providing them with the shortest trade route to the outside world. In return, the Central Asian states could provide gas, oil and other mineral resources to energy-starved Pakistan. However, in the absence of an effective communications network, the continuing problems in Afghanistan and the transitional nature of most of the current regimes in Central Asia have continued to inhibit their potentially beneficial relationship. The long-term contours of Pakistan's relationship with the Central Asian states have yet to be crystallized and will largely depend on the nature of the future regimes in Afghanistan and the Central Asian states and the political will of the leadership in these countries. The following is an analysis of the nature of the current relationship between Pakistan and the Central Asian states at bilateral and multilateral levels, and an attempt to identify the impediments to this relationship.

The bilateral level

Political

As the nature of world politics changes in the post-Cold War era, Pakistan finds itself at the receiving end of the New World Order enunciated by the USA. The differences between Pakistan and the USA which had previously been underplayed because of the Afghani-stan crisis, especially the controversy over Pakistan's nuclear pro-gramme, has resurfaced,[3] resulting in a halt to US military and economic aid to Pakistan due to the Pressler Amendment, and strained relations between the two countries. The USA has also reportedly approached Tajikistan and has sought assurances from its leaders that they will not supply enriched uranium to Pakistan or Iran.[4] More recently, the USA has also raised the issue that Pakistan violated the Missile Technology Control Regime (MTCR) when it reportedly received M-11 missiles from China and has also demanded the return of six US ships leased to the Pakistan navy in the 1980s. It has been reported that the Bush administration in its last days was seriously considering putting Pakistan on the list of terrorist states because of its alleged support of the Kashmiris' continuing demands for self-determination.[5] The Clinton administration apparently has not yet

formulated any clear policy towards South Asia, but there are indications that relations between the two countries may continue to worsen
on the issue of Pakistan's nuclear programme and its alleged support
of the Kashmiris.

However, there is an alternative view of relations between Pakistan
and the USA in the post-Cold War era. Some Pakistanis as well as
the US élite consider Pakistan as potentially a major stabilizing factor
in Central Asia. They view Pakistan as contributing to moderate
Islamic tendencies, and are aware of its skilled manpower which could
be instrumental in helping the Central Asian states move towards a
market economy, as well as Pakistan's significance to Afghanistan (a
gateway to Central Asia), because of Pakistan's ten years' involvement
in the Afghan jihad.[6] A recent US Defense Department document
underlines this newly discovered significance of Pakistan for the USA
in relation to Central Asia:

> With regard to Pakistan, a constructive U.S.–Pakistan military relation-
> ship will be an important element in our strategy to promote stable
> security conditions in Southwest and Central Asia. We should, there-
> fore, endeavour to rebuild our military relationship given acceptable
> resolution of our nuclear concern.[7]

The emergence of mass-resistance movements in Kashmir has led
to an escalation of tensions between India and Pakistan. India accuses
Pakistan of supporting the Kashmiri resistance movement and relations
between the two countries have become very tense. The rise of Hindu
chauvinism in India in the wake of the demolition of the Babri mosque
has further aggravated relations between the two countries. Indo-
Pakistan relations took such a downturn that both countries expelled
a number of each other's diplomats and the South Asian Association
for Regional Cooperation (SAARC) summit due to be held at Dhaka
was cancelled.

The troubled relationship with the United States over the issue of
nuclear non-proliferation and the hostile relationship with India over
the long unresolved Kashmir dispute have forced Pakistan to look for
new allies in South-west and Central Asia. Pakistani decision-makers
have begun to attach greater significance to the regional level, especially focussing their attention on the Central Asian states. Besides its
security interest, Pakistan also attaches great importance to regional
economic cooperation. Its leadership considers the opening in Central
Asia as an important opportunity to build an economic community

like ASEAN or the EC. The Pakistani Prime Minister Nawaz Sharif, emphasizing the economic significance of this new regional axis in the global environment, observed:

> We believe that as the East–West confrontation ebbs away and North–South divide widens, regional economic cooperation is a necessity which cannot or could not be ignored. We owe it to the peoples of member countries (EEC) to decide on ways and means of promoting socio-economic growth through expanded technical and scientific interaction and other mutually beneficial arrangements in the fields of economy, industry, agriculture and commerce both in the public and private sectors (*The News* [Islamabad], 29 November 1992).

Pakistan quickly recognized the independence of the Central Asian states and established diplomatic relations with them. Its consulates operate in three republics – Uzbekistan, Kazakhstan and Tajikistan – and the rest will be opened in due course. Nawaz Sharif visited Uzbekistan, Tajikistan and Turkmenistan in mid-1992 and the leaders of all six Central Asian states have visited Islamabad, concluding more than 30 agreements on trade, economic cooperation, communication, infrastructural development and scientific, technical and cultural exchanges.

Although both Pakistan and the Central Asian states emphasize the economic dimension of this relationship, the political and strategic implications of a broader regional grouping are not lost upon Pakistani decision-makers. Pakistan wishes to seek the support of the Central Asian states on such regional issues as Kashmir and Afghanistan. On Nawaz Sharif's visit to Uzbekistan on 28 June 1992, Uzbekistan's leader Islam Karimov recalled that Tashkent had played a historic role in establishing peace between India and Pakistan in 1966 (a reference to the Tashkent Declaration mediated between India and Pakistan by the Soviet Union after the 1965 India–Pakistan war), and called for the peaceful settlement of the Kashmir dispute in accordance with the UN resolutions, an obvious support to the Pakistani position.[8] Similarly, the ECO foreign ministers' conference held at Islamabad on 29 November 1992 strongly endorsed support for the Pakistani position on Kashmir.[9]

On the Afghanistan issue as well, the communications between Pakistan and the Central Asian states have repeatedly emphasized the need for the restoration of normality in Afghanistan and have made pleas to the Afghan leaders to agree on some consensual power-sharing formula. Pakistan has tried to rally support for its Afghan policy from the Central Asian states. In fact, one of the main reasons for Pakistan to shift its Afghan policy from one of supporting the hard-line Islamic groups like Gulbuddin Hekmatyar's Hizb-i Islami to advocating a diverse coalition perceived to be more moderate has been its desire to expand its influence in Central Asia.

In political-strategic terms, Pakistan wishes to develop the ECO countries as a counterweight against India at the regional level. An official document on Central Asia stresses that '[our relationship with the] Central Asian states can provide Pakistan the strategic depth that we lack'.[10] It is unclear how far the Central Asian states will be willing to cooperate with the political and strategic objectives of Islamabad because their priorities appear to be regime survival and economic restructuring; foreign policy considerations are relevant only if they enhance these objectives. The Central Asian states would not like to risk the potentially beneficial relationship with India which they developed earlier through their Soviet connection. India had substantive trade relationships and active collaboration with nearly all of the Central Asian states, in fields like construction, management, consulting and hotel management.[11]

Economic

Pakistan had from the beginning emphasized the economic dimension of its relationship with the Central Asian states. Prime Minister Nawaz Sharif, inaugurating the ECO foreign ministers' conference in Islamabad on 30 November 1992, declared:

> Our organization now corresponds to the boundaries of the ancient region which had brought prosperity and civilization to its people through fruitful exchanges along the historic silk route. The people of these lands have a shared history and common spiritual and cultural values.[12]

He listed four common objectives: (1) to facilitate mutual trade and economic cooperation and to develop commercial and financial institutions; (2) to develop human resources and cooperation in science, technology and communication; (3) to establish an infrastructure of road, rail and air links to support growing economic activity within the ECO; and (4) to intensify interaction among the ECO peoples through cultural and media exchanges. President Ghulam Ishaq Khan also emphasized institutionalized cooperation in all sectors of the economy, stating that the ultimate objective should be two-fold: to create a common market for the free flow of goods and services among the Muslim countries, and to develop the ECO's capital and financial markets to provide financial security and balance of payment support to member countries. He said that Pakistan was ready to offer the Central Asian republics the use of its port facilities, access to Pakistani markets on a reciprocal basis and training in moving to a free market economy.[13] The Pakistani officials have stressed that the ECO was not a 'Muslim bloc' but merely an 'economic bloc'.[14]

Pakistani economists have discovered a number of complementarities between the economies of the two regions. The Central Asian republics can supply oil, gas, electricity and such minerals as copper, iron, chromium and lead to Pakistan while Pakistan, in return, can supply textiles, cement, medicines, shoes, machinery and telecommunication equipment. A high-level delegation led by Sardar Assef Ahmed Ali, the Minister of State for Economic Affairs, visited Russia and the Central Asian states between 24 November and 15 December 1991 and concluded several bilateral economic agreements with Uzbekistan, Azerbaijan, Tajikistan, Kyrgyzstan and Kazakhstan. Pakistan initially extended a $30 million credit to each of the states, proposing to establish joint ventures in cotton, textiles, garments, pharmaceuticals, engineering goods, surgical instruments, telecommunications and agroindustry.[15] Pakistan also agreed to provide training in banking, customs, income tax, scientific education and management, and to construct hotels in each of the Central Asian republics.

It was also agreed that Tajikistan, which ranked second in the former Soviet Union in terms of absolute hydro-energy reserves, would supply 4000 megawatts of electricity to Pakistan; Pakistan would provide $500 million for the two power-generation projects, and the cost of the transmission line between Pakistan and Tajikistan. This project is likely to mature by 1997.[16] Tajikistan has also entered into a barter agreement with Pakistan for the supply of tea, wheat, rice and meat from Pakistan in exchange for cotton and aluminium from Tajikistan.

Pakistan has given special significance to Uzbekistan in its bilateral diplomacy. On Nawaz Sharif's visit to Uzbekistan in July 1992, a leading national daily newspaper said in an editorial:

> It was a shrewd move that the beginning in Pakistan's high level bilateral diplomacy should have been made with Uzbekistan. It is the largest Muslim republic of the ex-USSR in terms of population with 40

million people – boasting a high literacy rate and education standard – Uzbekistan is rich in natural resources such as cotton, rice, oil, copper and gold and is highly industrialized. It constitutes a major part of the 80 billion dollar export market that the six Muslim ex-Soviet republics offer to the world.[17]

On 8 July 1992, Pakistan signed an agreement with Uzbekistan for the establishment of a satellite communications link, construction of highways, joint production of telecommunications equipment and the manufacture in Pakistan of rolling stock for Central Asian Railways.[18] Pakistan also agreed to set up joint ventures with Uzbekistan in agriculture, mining, industrial manufacturing and other economic sectors such as water resources, power generation, irrigation and land reclamation.

Pakistan has signed several agreements with Kazakhstan: on trade, communications and banking services; on scientific, technical and educational exchanges; for textiles, medicines, shoes, machinery and cement plants; and an agreement to purchase natural gas from Turkmenistan.

Communications

The major advantage Pakistan offers to the land-locked Central Asian states is that it provides the shortest access to the port facilities at Karachi. According to an analyst, 'calculated from the Tajik capital Dushanbe, Vladivostok on the Pacific Ocean is some 9,500 kms away; Rostov-Na-Donu on the Black Sea, 4,200 kms; Abadan and Bandar Abbas on the Gulf, around 3,200 kms and Karachi on the Arabian Sea, about 2,700 kms. Estimates of other routes put the distance between Muslim Central Asia and the Arabian Sea (Pakistan) at barely 2,000 kms',[19] and between Dushanbe (Tajikistan) and Peshawar (Pakistan) only 650 kms.

There are several routes from Pakistan to Central Asia. The shortest trade route is via the Karakoram Highway, from Rawalpindi and Gilgit through Khunjrab Pass and the Chinese Turkestan town of Kashghar to the Kazakhstan capital of Alma Ata. The major communication routes, however, lie through Afghanistan – one running from Peshawar through Jalalabad and Termez on the Oxus to Tajikistan; the other from Quetta and Chaman through Kandahar and Herat over the Oxus into Central Asia. A fourth possible route runs from Chitral across the Wakhan corridor into Tajikistan, and a fifth goes via Iran, from Quetta through Koh-i-Taftan and Zahidan to Ashakabad in Turkmenistan. The routes through Afghanistan, however, remain blocked because of chaotic internal political conditions in Afghanistan. Most of the agreements between Pakistan and Central Asia will remain unimplemented until Afghanistan returns to normal.

Pakistan has also agreed to construct four highways in Afghanistan and one in Uzbekistan to improve its links with Central Asia, and is in the process of building the Indus Highway on the west bank of the Indus River, which will reduce the distance between Peshawar and Karachi by 400 km. It is also developing a double railway track from Peshawar to Karachi and a new seaport at Gawadar in Baluchistan and additional facilities at the Karachi port to handle cargo for Central Asia,[20] and there have been various proposals to build railway links with Central Asia through Afghanistan. Kazakhstan has proposed a grand North–South railway, linking the Central Asian states with Pakistan as far as Pasni on the Arabian Sea through Afghanistan. The Pakistani finance minister, Sartaj Aziz, noted that a 480-km railway link between Chaman (Pakistan) and Kuska (Turkmenistan) passing through Kandahar and Herat (Afghanistan) would link Karachi to the rest of the Central Asian states.[21] This would enable the Central Asian states to handle the bulk of their exports to Africa, the Middle East, South-east Asia and other countries. Feasibility studies for such a project are being conducted by Pakistan and the Central Asian states.

Pakistan International Airlines (PIA) has already begun flights to Tajikistan and Uzbekistan. A joint plan to form an ECO airline has also been agreed upon at the ECO Foreign Ministers' Conference held in Islamabad in November 1992.

Cultural

Pakistan has signed several agreements to promote cultural exchanges with the Central Asian states, involving scientific and technical exchanges, training programmes for personnel in banking, customs, income tax and other services, and scholarships at the Pakistani universities. 'Memoranda of Understanding' with several Central Asian states have also been signed for the exchange of students, professors and textbooks in the universities.

The multilateral level

The Economic Cooperation Organization (ECO) came into existence in 1985 as a successor organization to the Regional Cooperation for Development (RCD) formed in 1964 among Iran, Pakistan and Turkey.

The organization remained largely dormant until 1985, when it was renamed. After the collapse of the Soviet Union, the Central Asian republics showed their interest in the organization and their representatives participated in ECO meetings at the Tehran summit (16–17 February 1992) attended by the presidents of Turkey and Iran and the prime minister of Pakistan. At the Tehran summit a protocol was signed establishing a preferential tariff structure, the first step towards building a common market among the member countries. Further progress was made at the Ashkabad summit held in May 1992, which resulted in an agreement to construct a new railway along the ancient silk route, a highway and a gas pipeline.[22] Seven new members – Afghanistan, Uzbekistan, Turkmenistan, Kazakhstan, Kyrgyzstan, Azerbaijan and Tajikistan – were formally inducted as new members of the ECO at the extraordinary session of the ECO Council of Ministers held at Islamabad on 28 November 1992. Its objectives included the expansion of trade, promotion of joint ventures, cooperation in shipping, air services, railways, roads, postal services, telecommunications, tourism and consolidation of cultural and spiritual ties. Nawaz Sharif, highlighting the economic objectives of the ECO, declared:

> The aspirations of 300 million people who share a common heritage and culture have been realized.... Together our nations can build a prosperous and vibrant society. The ECO should embark on a comprehensive strategy for cooperation. The most important and dynamic mix seems to consist of massive investments in infrastructure and the encouragement of the private sector which can bring together resources and act as a multiplier for development.[23]

The ECO has taken several concrete steps towards creating a common market for the member countries. It was decided at the ECO Council of Ministers to establish an ECO Chamber of Commerce, an ECO Development Bank, an ECO Airline and a preferential tariff structure for the member countries. It will be years before a common market can be realized, but the first steps in that direction have been taken. In the short run, the ECO framework will also help mute the nationalist rivalries among Iran, Pakistan and Turkey.

Constraints

Economic limitations

Pakistan's primary economic limitation is that it does not have adequate financial resources to translate the dream of building a bridge to the Central Asian states and bringing the goal of a unified ECO community into reality. The credits offered by Pakistan to the Central Asian states have largely been symbolic in nature. Merely developing an effective infrastructure for communications would require huge sums of investment, which Pakistan can hardly afford; the Central Asian states themselves are badly in need of foreign exchange and are unable to contribute significantly to this project. However, Pakistan may persuade Arab countries, who also appear to be watching the developments in Central Asia, to invest in developing a basic communications infrastructure.

The economic feasibility of many of the joint ventures signed between Pakistan and Central Asia has been seriously questioned by economists. For example, it has been pointed out that the cost of a transmission line from Tajikistan to Pakistan would be so high that the electricity supplied would be far more expensive than producing it at home.[24] In fact, the economic rationale of many such joint ventures has not been seriously thought through; a practical implementation of the agreements would probably bring the planners to more realistic conclusions.

The Afghanistan factor

Another and probably the most significant limitation, however, is the unsettled nature of political conditions in Afghanistan. It has already been pointed out that Pakistan's major communications routes to Central Asia lie through Afghanistan. Therefore, until and unless normalcy returns to Afghanistan, Pakistan's vision of building an effective relationship with the Central Asian states will remain unrealized.

The situation in Afghanistan continues to be highly unstable, with recurrent civil conflict among the principal resistance groups which had fought against the Soviet Union. The victory of the mujahedin in the wake of the collapse of the Najibullah regime in Kabul in April 1992 raised expectations that the mujahedin would be able to settle their internal political differences amicably, but these expectations have yet to be fulfilled. In fact, as the prospects of a peaceful settlement recede, the spectre of the Balkanization of Afghanistan along ethnic lines appears to dominate the political horizon of the war-ravaged country, with potentially serious consequences for both Southwest and Central Asia.

The crux of the problem has been the lack of agreement between the two major resistance parties, Gulbuddin Hekmatyar's Hizb-i Islami and Burhanuddin Rabbani's Jami'at-i-Islami, on a basic power-sharing formula. On the eve of the collapse of the Najibullah regime, his Uzbek commander, General Abdul Rashid Dostam of northern Afghanistan, made an alliance with Akhmed Shah Masud of Jami'at-i-Islami which precipitated the coup against the Najibullah regime.[25] This Uzbek–Tajik alliance led the Pashtun generals of the Najibullah regime to side with Hekmatyar's Hizb-i Islami, which has its stronghold in predominantly Pashtun areas of southern and eastern Afghanistan. The Najibullah regime's remnants, in an attempt to save themselves, accentuated the hitherto dormant ethnic rivalries within the Afghan resistance. Sibghatullah Mujaddedi, who had been appointed the first interim president of Afghanistan for two months under the Peshawar Agreement, quickly realized the capability of the Dostam militia to make or break any regime and tried to appease it, further aggravating the differences between the two major parties. Rabbani took over as president on 28 June 1992 and agreed to disband the Uzbek militia from Kabul, which was the major point of contention between him and Hekmatyar. However, after a brief, uneasy truce with the Hizb-i Islami, during which Hekmatyar's Tajik representative, Ustad Farid, served as prime minister, Rabbani like his predecessor preferred to rely on the support of Dostam's Uzbek militia to maintain his fragile regime. Rabbani extended his tenure as president for another two years through a hand-picked Shura Hal-o-Aqad (council of wise men) on 30 December 1992, further alienating the Hekmatyar group.[26] Now a civil war is raging in Afghanistan with little prospect of subsiding soon.

The external parties to the conflict, Pakistan, Iran, Saudi Arabia and the USA, lack an effective coordination of policies. With a view to improving its relationship with the Central Asian states, Pakistan decided to bypass Hekmatyar on 25 January 1992 and built a coalition of all other elements within the Afghan resistance; this was formalized under the Peshawar Agreement signed among the various mujahedin groups on 24 March 1992.[27] However, this led to the exclusion of the major Pashtun groups, which constitute more than 45 per cent of Afghanistan's population and have traditionally been the rulers of the country. The Pakistani policy had the unintended effect of further strengthening Hekmatyar's position, bringing all splinter Pashtun groups to his side, and further deepening the ethnic

divide in the country. Iran and Saudi Arabia have been more interested in promoting their sectional interests by supporting smaller
groups, thus further complicating the process of reconciliation. Iran
has been arming the Hizb-i-Wahdate, which consists of Shi'ites from
Hazarajat, and Saudi Arabia has been financing the Itihad-i-Islami,
an extremist Sunni group led by Abdul Rasool Sayyaf, which has
twice led to serious Shi'ite–Sunni clashes inside Kabul since the
mujahedin take-over. The United States appears either to have lost
interest in Afghanistan since the disintegration of the Soviet Union
or to prefer to work though its proxies, such as Pakistan or Saudi
Arabia.

Pakistan, Iran and Saudi Arabia, in an unusual concerted effort,
helped to broker the 7 March 1993 Islamabad Accord among the
warring Afghan mujahedin leaders. According to the agreement, the
principal Afghan mujahedin leaders consented to a power-sharing
formula, elections within 18 months, creation of a national army and
machinery to implement the agreement. However, continuing differences among the Afghan leaders coupled with a lack of direction from
Pakistan due to its own internal political crisis led to the breakdown
of the agreement and the outbreak of war among the principal resistance leaders.

The highly volatile situation in Afghanistan could lead to any of
the following possibilities: (1) a coordinated effort among the external
parties, leading to an agreement on power-sharing among the mujahedin groups; (2) prolonged civil war and Lebanonization of Afghanistan; (3) disintegration of Afghanistan along ethnic lines. In the first
scenario, there are serious indications that Pakistan, Iran and Saudi
Arabia are making concerted efforts to get the mujahedin to agree to
a plan which would bring about a general election in the country and
the formation of a loosely federal government based on the electoral
mandate.[28] The second possibility is one of a prolonged civil war in
which various ethnic, religious or tribal warlords would carve out
their separate fiefdoms without any central authority, in which case
Afghanistan would fragment like Lebanon or Yugoslavia. The third
possibility is the disintegration of Afghanistan along ethnic lines, with
the Uzbeks, Tajiks and Pashtuns carving out their own states or
merging with their adjacent states. Some elements within these
communities have begun to think along these lines, and have started
some tentative diplomatic efforts to that end.[29] It is difficult to predict
which scenario is going to materialize, but it is certain that Pakistan's

meaningful contacts with the Central Asian states will be delayed until the conflict in Afghanistan is resolved.

The transitional character of Central Asian regimes

Another major hindrance to the evolution of stable relationships is the transitional nature of most of the Central Asian regimes. These are the states where a communist élite is still ruling, with merely a change of names of the political parties. A mass politics has yet to emerge which could lead to genuine change in either domestic or foreign policies. The recent events in Tajikistan which led to a change of the communist élite to a coalition consisting of moderate communists, liberals and Islamist élites, and the hard-line communists' take-over in December 1992 (with the help of the Russian army) shows the political fragility of these regimes. The Foreign Minister of Tajikistan, due to unstable conditions at home, could not even attend the joining ceremony of the ECO held at Islamabad. Furthermore, 80,000 Tajik refugees, fleeing from the communist forces, have crossed the Oxus River into Afghanistan, with potentially serious consequences for both countries.[30] It has been reported that these Tajik refugees are seeking help from the Afghan government to assist them in their struggle against the communist take-over in Tajikistan, but it is unlikely that the Afghan government, due to its own internal difficulties, will be able to give them any meaningful help in the short run, although if Afghanistan consolidates itself, it could help them overthrow the regime in Tajikistan. However, this seems to remain a distant possibility.[31]

Besides the question of the political survival of these regimes, the Central Asian states lack their own currencies, monetary systems, financial institutions, armies, embassies or trade missions. Their economies are still linked to the valueless ruble, which has discouraged private investors from making major investments, although limited barter trade agreements have been signed.

Other external factors

The presence of Iran, Turkey, Russia, the Western powers, India and Israel presents the Central Asian states with multiple choices. Turkey considers Central Asia a natural cultural extension of the 'Anatolian heartland', and dreams of establishing a 'Turkish common market'. It has concluded several major agreements with the new states aimed at providing education, trade, commerce, military training and satellite links. Similarly, Iran is also building links with Central Asia, especially focussing on constructing mosques and providing religious education, besides economic and political relations.[32] Russia is still very influential in the Central Asian states and there is concern in Russia that Central Asia might move out of Russia's traditional sphere of influence. Tass, the Russian news agency, commented on the formation of the ECO:

> Now we can say that Central Asia will be influenced more powerfully by its Muslim neighbours than by the Commonwealth of Independent States. As a result, Russia will have at its southern frontier a dynamically growing union of independent Muslim states rather than separate republics that seek cooperation with Moscow.... the Muslim republics are rapidly moving out of Russia's sphere of influence and into the sphere of influence of the power-houses of the Islamic world.[33]

The United States, the Western powers, the Arab countries, India, Israel and many other countries are interested in Central Asia and have greater economic capability to woo these states than do the regional states. However, the geographic proximity and the historical, cultural and religious ties between Central Asia and South-west Asia give a natural edge to Turkey, Iran, Afghanistan and Pakistan, though it is unclear whether they will prefer to coordinate their policies under the ECO framework or will adopt individual policies.

Notes

1. Ghani Eirabie, 'The promise ECO holds', *Dawn* [Karachi], 19 December 1992; Mushahid Hussain, 'ECO: A bloc is born', *The Nation* [Lahore], 29 November 1992; Shameem Akhtar, 'Relations with Central Asian states', *Dawn*, 14 August 1992; S. Rifaat Hussain, 'Political economy of Pak relations with CARS', *Regional Studies* [Islamabad], Autumn 1992.

2. V. A. Jafarey, 'Economic Relations between Pakistan and Central Asia', *The Muslim* [Islamabad], 13 December 1992; Eqbal Ahmad, 'Prospects in Central Asia', *Dawn*, 6 December 1992.

3. Tahir Amin and Mohammad Islam, 'Pakistan–United States aid deal: a Pakistan perspective', *Pakistan Journal of American Studies*, ii/1 (March 1984).

4. Shameem Akhtar, 'Relations with Central Asian States'.

5. Mohammad Ali Siddiqi, 'Whither US–Pakistan ties?' *Dawn*, 19 January 1993.

6. Abida Hussain, the Pakistani Ambassador to the USA, made these remarks at a seminar held at MIT, Cambridge, in January 1992. See also the report of Robert B. Oakley, the former US ambassador to Pakistan, *Afghanistan and Post-Soviet Central Asia* (Washington, DC: USIP, 1992).

7. Excerpts from the Pentagon's report published in the *New York Times*, 8 March 1992; for a background see Tahir Amin, *The Tashkent Declaration: Third Party's Role in the Resolution of Conflict* (Islamabad: Institute of Strategic Studies, 1981).

8. *Dawn*, 28 June 1992.

9. *The News*, 29 November 1992.

10. *Economic Report on the Visit of Pakistan's Delegation to the Central Asian Republics* (Economic Affairs Division, Government of Pakistan, Islamabad, 1992).

11. *India and Central Asia: Past, Present and Future* (Islamabad: Institute of Regional Studies, 1992).

12. *Dawn*, 30 November 1992.

13. *The Muslim* [Islamabad], 29 November 1992.

14. Ibid.

15. *Economic Report on the Visit of Pakistan's Delegation to the Central Asian Republics* (Economic Affairs Division, Government of Pakistan, Islamabad, 1992).

16. Ibid.

17. *The Frontier Post* [Peshawar], 4 July 1992.

18. Based on the text of the agreement between Pakistan and Uzbekistan.

19. Ghani Eirabie, 'The Promise ECO holds', *Dawn*, 19 December 1992; 'The peril ECO faces', *Dawn*, 20 December 1992; and 'New calculus of Muslim power', *Dawn*, 21 December 1992.

20. Ibid.

21. *The Muslim*, 1 December 1992.

22. Syed Riffat Hussain, 'The Ashkabad summit', *Strategic Perspective* [Islamabad], i/3, 1992.

23. *Dawn*, 29 November 1992.

24. Khalid Saeed, 'Power generation in Central Asia', *The Frontier Post*, 26 May 1992.

25. For a useful analysis, see Rahimullah Yusufzai, 'More troubles ahead for Afghans', *The News*, 2 January 1993.

26. *The News*, 31 December 1992.

27. For details of the shift in Pakistan's Afghan policy, see *The News*, 28 January 1992.

28. A preliminary agreement was in fact signed among the mujahedin groups. See *Dawn*, 1 January 1993.

29. See the insightful report in *The Nation* [Lahore], 8 September 1992.

30. See 'Central Asia: the Silk Road catches fire', *The Economist*, 26 December 1992.

31. See 'The new domino game', *The Economist*, 19 December 1992.

32. See Shireen T. Hunter, 'The Muslim Republics of the Former Soviet Union: Policy Challenges for the United States', *Washington Quarterly*, Summer 1992.

33. Cited in Elizabeth Schogran, 'ECO ties with Central Asia', *Dawn*, 12 May 1992.

PART IV

Rethinking the Role of the Great Powers

10

Russia and the Emerging Geopolitical Order in Central Asia

MIKHAIL KONAROVSKY

Russia's foreign policy options in Asia

Having proclaimed loyalty to all the former USSR international commitments, Russia has inherited the bulk of what remains of the former Soviet global policy. Referring to its 'particular responsibility conferred on it by history',[1] Moscow has confirmed that the country 'will not cease to be a great power'.[2] Such an approach is determined, *inter alia*, by strategic dimensions of its territory, significant human and natural resources, and its nuclear status.[3]

But Moscow's inheritance is also a heavy burden. Possible geopolitical advantages in being a bridge between the West and the East will most likely be outweighed by numerous problems. Central among them are Russia's relations with its CIS partners. Their mutual ties are considerably burdened by the other CIS members' suspicions and concerns about Russia's intentions to inherit the former USSR's ambitions. A few ill-considered and short-sighted steps taken by Moscow before and after the creation of the CIS have resulted in the rise of such anxieties, and in many cases justify such an approach. There is an urgent necessity to dispel such prejudices and concerns in order for Moscow to strengthen the 'belt of good-neighbourliness' along the entire perimeter of its borders. This is one of the main tasks of ensuring national security.

Russia's external policy conception is based on the necessity to create a favourable international environment for the country's economic revival. That is why relations with the new immediate

neighbours, including those in the south, are of special importance to
Moscow, despite Russia's own comprehensive Westernization in economic and social life.

In its present configuration Russia may be considered predominantly an Asian nation. The bulk of its borders, both with foreign and
CIS nations, are in Asia and the Pacific. The eastern regions (despite
the industrial potential and ascendant part of the population which
still remains in the European areas) might in the long run ensure
Russia's economic revival and its political fate. Given the present
geopolitical conditions, the country's leap to the West will occur to a
marked degree through its East, starting with the Asia-Pacific.

Dimensions of foreign policy in general and towards Asia in particular became a matter of intense discussion in parliament and in the
media just after the CIS was born. Having expressed anxiety about
Moscow's 'overly close' relations with the West at the possible expense
of its ties with strategically important neighbours in Asia, analysts
were concerned about the fact that a long-term vision of policy in the
East, including the neighbouring Islamic world in the Southern Tier,[4]
has not been clearly outlined. President Yeltsin's visits to South Korea,
China and India in 1992–3 were to a considerable extent aimed at
dispelling such doubts. But such concerns are quite evident and
natural, since dealing with 'more distant' states means for Moscow, in
the first place, the large Muslim zone along the southern border of
the former USSR. Developments in that region over the last decade,
including the dramatic changes in Afghanistan, Iran, Turkey and
Pakistan, have had an enormous impact on Soviet foreign and domestic
policies. There are two urgent and interdependent considerations
prompting Russia to pay special attention to the region now. The new
geopolitical situation there may exert a further dramatic influence on
the Central Asian and Transcaucasian republics, which are Russia's
immediate neighbours in the south. These countries' swift turn to the
Islamic world makes it more urgent that attention be paid to the
region. The emergence of new regional economic associations, a
process that embraces Central Asia and Transcaucasia, makes it particularly important for Moscow to watch developments here carefully.

Furthermore, developments in the southern republics might in due
course affect stability in the Russian Federation itself. This pattern
has special significance for the country, since, in its present unstable
situation, domestic issues have a crucial impact on the country's foreign policy options in general and with respect to this part of Asia in

particular. The painful transformation to a completely new socio-
economic structure is significantly burdened in Russia by deep
economic and social crises and political instability. Moves towards
disintegration are significantly fed by the rise of pan-Turkic activities
and Islamism in several economically important parts of the country,
a trend also seen in neighbouring Central Asia.

A new Federation Treaty did not eliminate doubts about the
country's future as an integral state. Tatarstan, one of the most
industrially advanced parts of the federation's central regions, producing 26 per cent of its total oil and having the second largest populated area, with an approximately 50–50 Turkic–Slavic population,
confirmed its independence from Russia. Having declined to join the
Federation Treaty, Tatarstan insists that its bilateral relations with
Moscow be built on a separate agreement. It maintains that it does
not want secession from Russia, but such moves may be only a first
step in that direction.[5] Disagreements with another large territory with
significant industrial capacity such as Turkic Bashkortostan were
watered down at the last moment before the treaty was initialled.
North Caucasian Muslim Chechenya, having unilaterally proclaimed
its independence from Russia, also refused to participate in the accord.
To counter Moscow's pressure, it called on Tatarstan, Bashkortostan,
Azerbaijan and Turkmenistan for religious and ethnic solidarity, encouraging them to pool their efforts to oppose 'the anti-national policy
of the Russian leadership'.[6] Uncertainties in these areas, as well as the
newly emerging Muslim and pan-Turkic movements among Siberian
Tatars, where separatist motions are being directly fed by extracts of
religious and nationalistic sentiments, are all factors which will for a
long time be a matter of deep concern to the Russian leadership. The
constitutional crisis in Russia in 1993, resulting from different approaches to basic reforms, has encouraged such autonomist groups to
demand more economic and political independence from Moscow.

Further instability in the country may in the long run significantly
hinder implementation of basic reforms, causing irritability and un-
predictability in both domestic and foreign policy. In such domestic
circumstances, Moscow is and will be very sensitive to any undesirable
and distracting outside influence that may worsen the situation. The
Southern Tier countries on Russia's borders, with the newly born
Central Asian nations as a main political, economic and ideological
'battlefield' in the region, seems to be one of the most vulnerable
areas in this regard.

Central Asia: a new geopolitical image

The creation of the CIS, followed by the swift diplomatic recognition of the Central Asian states by their Near East and South-west Asian neighbours, has given new impetus to further expansion of their relations with the region. Political, economic and cultural cooperation with Turkey, Iran and to a certain extent Pakistan are at the core of the moves that started in the late 1980s, on the eve of the political disintegration of the USSR.

With respect to economic ties, special emphasis is placed on the reconstruction of infrastructure, the exploitation of mineral resources and – in Kazakhstan, Turkmenistan and Uzbekistan – the production of oil and gas. Hard currency revenues from sales abroad are considered one of the main sources of self-sufficiency in local economic and social programmes. Kazakhstan extended cooperation to the Gulf Arab states.[7] In spring 1992 Oman mediated a $20 billion oil development agreement with Chevron Corporation, the biggest partnership by mid-1992 between an American firm and any CIS state.[8] Uzbekistan is seeking similar support from the West and the Arab oil-producing world to exploit its oil fields. Turkmenistan has come to an agreement with Ankara and Tehran for the construction of a pipeline which will supply its natural gas to Turkey through Iran, and which might in the future be extended to Europe.

All regional players, both traditional and new, are drawing up the framework of a broad new common economic space, embracing existing structures. In February 1992 both Central Asia and Transcaucasian Azerbaijan were admitted to the Economic Cooperation Organization (ECO) that earlier included Turkey, Iran and Pakistan. Ankara has no doubt been a driving force in these efforts. During visits to Central Asia by high-ranking officials from Turkey in 1992–3, a sort of 'Turkic Common Market' was on the agenda. To bolster these efforts, Ankara has put forward an idea to create a Development Bank for Central Asia and to incorporate the Turkic republics in the recently established Black Sea economic zone.[9] Total Turkish loans to the new republics are estimated to be $600 million, with $250 million to Azerbaijan. Ankara took the initiative to hold under its auspices regular summits of regional Turkic nations to discuss economic and other issues of mutual concern. On the other hand, in May 1992 a high-level meeting of representatives from Central Asia, Turkey, Iran and Pakistan discussed measures to implement joint projects. These efforts, against the background of the earlier understanding to link regional railways to provide Central Asian access to the Persian Gulf, Pakistan and China, indicate the impending emergence of a new, large Asian economic community based on a strong ethnic and religious identity.

The interest of the regional South-west Asian states in Central Asia may have a 'nuclear component' as well. Though the principal plants for producing plutonium and enriched uranium are in Russia,[10] the bulk of the uranium mines in the former USSR were concentrated in Central Asia, especially in Kazakhstan and Kyrgyzstan, and the major facilities for heavy water production were in Tajikistan.[11] Experts suggest that uranium enrichment plants were also in operation in Uzbekistan and Kyrgyzstan.[12] Kazakhstan was also the main nuclear testing and space missile launching site. In the light of Iran and Pakistan's intentions to speed up nuclear cooperation among the Muslim countries, not only for economic but also for political reasons, Central Asia, rich in strategic mineral resources, may in the long run become one of their main targets. Historical, religious and ethnic ties might bring a new ideological impetus to such a cooperation.[13] The major CIS nations signed a multi-lateral Export Control Agreement, with Central Asian Kazkhstan, Uzbekistan, Tajikistan and Kyrgyzstan also as participants. It is aimed at coordination in nuclear export deals as well.[14]

Against the above background further Turkish–Iranian competition for influence in the region is also under way. It is taking place against the backdrop of the rise of two main ideological and ethnic (Islamic and pan-Turkic) tendencies. The rise of Muslim fundamentalist sentiments, bolstered by Iran and Pakistan, as well as the mujahedin movement in Afghanistan before and after the overthrow of the Najibullah regime in April 1992 is a distinguishing feature of developments in the region. The 'Struggle for Islam' in Central Asia has been gaining momentum since the mid-1980s, when the republics first started moves towards obtaining greater sovereignty and independence. These tendencies have spiralled upwards since the dissolution of the USSR, having significantly tinged the domestic political make-up of Central Asia.

The emergence of Islamic parties in Central Asia, such as the Islamic Renaissance Party in Tajikistan, which are strongly bolstered by the growing influence of 'non-official' mullahs among both rural and urban populations, indicates that Islam is on the political agenda of Central Asia.[15] The official clergy nevertheless seems to exhibit a careful approach to its prospective role in politics. Its leaders, with the exception of those in Tajikistan, emphasize that the time for this has not yet come, and that the main objective today is 'to let Islam reemerge as a belief'.[16] But inevitably, due to the nature of the situation in Central Asia during the many years of Soviet power, a next step after such a reemergence would be an increased Islamic involvement in the *realpolitik* of the region.

Official communist ideology had been embraced only by the transparent, superficial layers in social structures; traditional institutions, having had a predominant influence on the local way of life, remained in fact untouched. Soviet power was urged only to adjust itself to reality.[17] Its gradual decline since the mid-1980s, parallel to a growing social openness, generated popular appeals to return to historical, cultural and religious 'roots'. Severe economic deterioration over the years of perestroika gave extra domestic impetus to a revival of traditionalism as well, since a considerable part of the population regarded traditionalism as the only moral formula to overcome all-round economic and social crises. The dissolution of the USSR, the extension of comprehensive ties with neighbouring Muslim Iran, Pakistan and Turkey, and the geographically more distant, but religiously and culturally close Arab world, have speeded up the process.

An alliance between the clergy and local intellectuals is encouraged by the tendency of both to overstress national traditions, mores and customs. Most Central Asian intellectuals, being humanists, also have deep family and clan ties with the clergy.[18] Such an alliance seems to be natural, given the present conditions, but in the near future it will inevitably be destroyed in favour of traditionalism. The secular intelligentsia is small in number, and its influence extends to only part of the urban areas, while religious institutions, both official and unofficial, have a widespread network extending throughout the region.

The political and cultural sphere is one of the principal battlefields between Iran and Turkey, and to some extent Pakistan. Turkic nationalism in policy and secularism in economy, on the one hand, and Iranian Islamism backed by the country's rich historical heritage on the other, are weighty arguments in each of the two parties' dealings with Central Asia. Revival of that region, where the Muslim population remains predominantly Turkic[19] and where the movement has 'the strongest links between the Turkic and Turkestani Muslim ethnic groups in a seeming affirmation of pan-Turkic regional tendencies'[20] determines a more favourable position for Turkey in such long-term competition. Turkey promised help in implementing the regional Turkic states' transformation of their alphabet from Cyrillic to Latin. Ankara expressed its readiness to educate foreign service personnel and to lift visa barriers after national passports are instituted, and has expanded its participation in the mass media. Uzbekistan is discussing possible representation by Ankara of its interests in some foreign states and international organizations. The Turkish economic and political breakthrough to Central Asia and Azerbaijan is significantly backed by increasing pan-Turkic sentiments both in Ankara and the newly established states.

Tehran, to prevent the Turkish influence, in particular in Turkmenistan (Iran's only immediate neighbour in the north-east), has provided $50 million for the purchase of Iranian goods at prices lower than those established by Russia.[21] Mass media, education and the introduction of the Islamic juridical system in a new region are matters of Tehran's special attention, too, particularly in ethnically and linguistically close Tajikistan. Tehran and Islamabad render support for Central Asia to join the Organization of Islamic Conference (OIC). Kazakhstan, having participated in its sixth summit meeting in December 1991 as part of the Iranian delegation, was admitted to the OIC as an observer. Iranian efforts in this field are also focussed on preventing the enhancement of Islamic institutions by the religious and cultural influence of Saudi Arabia and other Gulf states, who provide Central Asia with significant assistance.[22]

The establishment of ties between the Central Asian republics and their neighbouring South-west Asian nations, beginning even before the collapse of the Soviet Union, is unlikely to result in immediate economic advantage, though the rapid extension of religious and cultural ties with these countries may exert additional influence on Central Asia's shaky domestic political equilibrium. The growing shift in mass-consciousness towards Islam and pan-Turkism probably favours 'back-to-traditionalism'.

The future of Russian minorities in Central Asia is one of the main causes of Moscow's general concern in relations with the new neighbours in the south. Despite the steady decrease in numbers over the last three decades, the Russian-speaking population in Central Asia still remains significant, numbering about 6 million.[23] An increase in Russophobia and intolerance of 'infidels' all over the region might hamper good relations in the long run. The open and latent discrimination against the Russian-speaking population in other CIS countries prompted Moscow to regard the protection of the Russians outside the federation as 'a top priority' in relations with newly established states.

The tendency of non-Muslim minorities in Central Asia to leave the region has increased since 1986–7. But in the case of their leaving as a result of nationalist intolerance, not only Russia, but also the Central Asian nations may find themselves in a difficult and ambiguous political and economic situation. Russia is already facing the problem of settling and providing jobs for them. In the present conditions of drastic budget deficits and impending mass unemployment (estimated at 12 million by the end of 1994), it will be extremely difficult for Moscow to meet this challenge without risk of serious new social problems. A massive influx of people from Central Asia and Kazakhstan, a process now under way, might swing the public opinion pendulum in Russia towards nationalistic tendencies and isolationism, strengthening an ultranationalist party such as Zhirinovsky's LDP. This may fuel the general debates about the wisdom of continuing the traditional ties with the regions, where 'by any objective criteria, the imperial masters were subsidizing their reluctant subjects' during both the tsarist empire and Soviet rule.[24] For their part, the Central Asian nations might face a further recession in their economy, since the Russian-speaking population forms the bulk of the skilled labour force in local industries, management and business administration.

Still, serious economic dependence on Russia is nevertheless at the core of Central Asia's long-term interest in maintaining close ties with Moscow. Regional leaders are proponents of further 'institutionalization' of the CIS as well. Their efforts to design a new Central Asian Common Market, which led to an agreement in January 1993, seems not to be a dramatic shift from CIS structures. On the contrary, such moves seem to have been intended predominantly to compel Russia to take an even more active stand on the matter. Yeltsin reaffirmed Moscow's long-term commitments to the CIS in mid-March 1993.[25]

Being interested in a radically reshaped economy, Central Asian leaders call their drive a 'Turkish-style' drift towards a market economy. But this term is being used mainly for political reasons. It means, first and foremost, a strong desire to build up a nationalistic and secular – as opposed to a religious, 'Iranian-style' – state structure. In reality, it is hardly likely that a market economy in Central

Asia will be a 'pure' Turkish-style economy. It will have its own specific features, and its deep-rooted interdependence with Russia, rather than Turkey, may exert additional influence on its future shape. Most probably Ankara is now more realistic in reviewing such a reality. Its unilateral breakthrough to Central Asia is likely to have got bogged down, due mainly to Turkey's domestic economic challenges, the aggravation of its social and national problems and the growing determination of Central Asian leaders not to find themselves in the strong hands of a new 'elder brother'.

Both Russia and Central Asia, in building their post-Soviet relations, should show mutual discretion and consideration. A transfer of the intolerance and suspicion shown by all of them towards 'the Centre' over the years of perestroika to their new mutual relations, would not only prevent their solving their own complex domestic and bilateral problems, but also would create new dilemmas. Moscow must be supremely conscious of the political, cultural and economic expediency and appropriateness for Central Asia to extend and strengthen relations with the Near East and South-west Asia, and to maintain a reasonable balance with these areas and Russia. The maintenance of influence here might significantly protect Moscow from aggressive intolerance from the Southern Tier.

For their part, the present nationalistic leaders of Central Asia, both former communist apparatchiks and Westernized democrats, should realize Moscow's sensitivity to developments in the region. Close relations with Western-orientated Russia directly corresponds with the republican leaders' interests as well. A politically realistic understanding with Russia might help prevent increasingly radical pan-Turkic notions from arising both inside and outside Central Asia.

For Russia's long-term regional strategy, close relations with Kazakhstan seem to be in this respect a matter of particular importance. Such a conclusion stems from a number of considerations. The country's longest southern border is with Kazakhstan, which possesses the third largest industrial capacity (after Russia and Ukraine) in the CIS, still retains nuclear capacity, and owns strategically important space-launch sites. In Kazakhstan's northern regions, the bulk of its heavy industry, in essence an integral part of the largest Ural-Siberian economic zone of the former USSR, is now on Russian territory. This fact determines their continuous economic interdependence, as well as the necessity for transparent borders. Kazakhstan's specific demographic situation, with more than 40 per cent of its population non-Turkic, urges the government to pursue a more cautious and balanced policy with respect to ethnic and religious issues, a policy which still enjoys the support of the official clergy, who maintain a negative view of the direct involvement of Islam and pan-Turkism in domestic politics.[26]

Like Russia, Kazakhstan is a driving force in strengthening the CIS. The two nations are also the largest successors of the former Soviet Union in Asia. President Nazarbaev's address to the 47th General Assembly in October 1992 indicated that country's interest in playing a more salient role in Asian security arrangements. The Kazakh proposals, having been reviewed with some scepticism because of their evident diffusiveness, may nevertheless form a new groundwork for the two countries' closer cooperation in the CIS's southern tier.

Kazakhstan's intention to expand political and strategic relations with the West as a new linchpin in ties between Asia and Europe may not only influence Kazakhstan's more efficient bilateral regional co-ordination with Russia, but also might determine tripartite cooperation beetween Russia, Kazakhstan and the USA. Rapprochement of Almaty with Beijing is important for Russia as well, in order to coordinate the principal approaches to developments in the region with these two nations.[27] Desire to overcome a sort of ethnic inferiority in the eyes of the rest of the Central Asian nations, and in particular the Uzbeks and Tajiks,[28] is an invisible historical and psychological aspect conditioning Kazakhstan's aspiration to pursue a broader policy than other Central Asian republics.

Nevertheless, a hidden process similar to that in other Central Asian republics is also under way in Kazakhstan.[29] The changes in status of language and citizenship were considered by many non-Kazakh residents here as 'discrimination', and they requested more rights for themselves in governmental bodies in the country's northern areas where the predominantly non-Kazakh population is concentrated in local enterprises.[30] As a result of complex bargaining in parliament, a newly adopted constitution has declared the official language to be Kazakh, with Russian as a language of international communications. Simultaneously, it was only the energetic *démarche* of President Nazarbaev that made it possible to evade the intention of many deputies to place in the constitution a provision that the country's president could be a Kazakh only by birth.

Having drawn up a bilateral Treaty of Friendship and Mutual Assistance, Russia and Kazakhstan initiated a Collective Security

Treaty, signed in mid-May 1992, with three Central Asian republics (minus Turkmenistan) and Transcaucasian Armenia. It provides that all national armed forces be included in the new bloc (which still has joint CIS frontier troops),[31] and calls for the members to render military support if one of them is being attacked.

Disengagement among the three Slavic founders of the CIS might make the new treaty (if it survives) a precursor to the emergence of a new Eurasian political, military and economic association to replace the CIS. In spring 1994 President Nazarbaev of Kazakhstan (known as a consistent advocate of the CIS's comprehensive integration) put forward an idea to create a Eurasian union, with both economic and political ties to be more close and compulsory than those in the CIS. The new dimensions of economic integration – the Black Sea economic zone, an enlarged ECO, the Caspian Council – gaining momentum in the vast space from the Black Sea and the Near East to South-west Asia, may favour such a move. The process, embracing newly post-Soviet Central Asia and Transcaucasia as well as Russia, might lead to the emergence of new regional structures, with traditional economic ties among the CIS members as only one of their integral parts.

On the other hand, the differences in specific economic policies, in starting-points and pace of implementation of economic reforms, may torpedo the mutual efforts of a newly emerging Slavic–Turkic, Christian–Muslim, identity in terms of introducing a market-orientated economy. The possible future differences in views on building up political relations of regional dimensions might well be a stumbling-block to the drawing up of joint security strategy. In the short term, such differences may emerge in the approach to the state of affairs in Transcaucasia in general and to the Armenia–Azerbaijan dispute over Nagorno-Karabakh in particular. Muslim Azerbaijan, with its uni-lateral shift towards Turkey, did not join the treaty. Christian Armenia did, as a guarantee for its political survival in predominantly Muslim surroundings – Azerbaijan, Turkey and Iran. It is unlikely that the Central Asian Muslim nations will show enthusiasm for being deeply involved in bolstering Christian Armenia in its conflict with Azerbaijan. Being interested in having the CIS's common security umbrella, with joint peace-keeping forces, the Central Asian nations are nevertheless very cautious about sharing the real security burden. Strong commitments are being avoided, even if developments in neighbouring areas may affect prospects for stability in some of them. An example is the low profile of Kazakhstan and Kyrgyzstan's peace-keeping measures in Tajikistan, even though it was these two countries that, together with Russia and Uzbekistan, initiated the process in November 1992.

Persistent domestic instabilities also will cause uncertainties for the bloc in the long run. The present secular regimes in Central Asia might fall, to be replaced by a combination of Islam-orientated traditionalist or nationalist governments. As a result, significant new shifts in their foreign priorities may emerge, leaning further to the south. In this case, their interest in strong military-political ties with other members of the treaty, and particularly with Russia, may be called into question. Moscow for its part will face political dilemmas in continuing close ties with Central Asia in such circumstances.

Russia and Kazakhstan are essentially at the core of the hexahedron. The state of relations between them will significantly determine the military, political and economic fate of the new Eurasian body. At the same time, due to its population of 17 million, rich resources and historical heritage as a dynamic Turkic nation, Uzbekistan will be the principal challenger to Kazakhstan in playing a key role in Central and possibly in neighbouring South-west Asia. A remarkable example is Tashkent's interest in developments in Tajikistan. Uzbekistan, formally backing the intra-Tajik dialogue begun in Moscow in April 1994, nevertheless expects to see in power in Dushanbe those who are traditionally close to Tashkent. The particular attention paid by President Karimov to Uzbek-populated northern Afghanistan and especially to its principal leader, General Dostam, must be seen against this background. This makes it necessary for Moscow to build up smooth relations with Tashkent, which will be important in dealing with this vast, predominantly Turkic, region as a whole. Tashkent's growing ambitions in neighbouring areas might sooner or later cause grave concern, not only in Tajikistan but also among Tajiks in Uzbekistan and Kyrgyzstan, as well as in such regional capitals as Almaty and Ashkhabad.

South-west Asia and the Near East

Iran, Turkey and Pakistan are the main regional players, exerting increased influence on the Central Asian nations and their internal and foreign policy. This accounts for Russia's special attention to those nations.

Iran

In December 1991 Russia conducted the first talks in Tehran on how to adjust Moscow's relations with Iran to the new political realities in regional and intra-regional dimensions. Expert committees were established to follow up, reaffirm or review the previous Soviet agreements with that country, and to seek new spheres of cooperation to maintain their continuity. Relations between Russia and Iran were designed on principles of political, cultural and scientific cooperation, in the memorandum signed in November 1991. The two sides expressed their intention to maintain the ties that had existed between the former USSR and Iran, and to continue the implementation of projects of bilateral cooperation. Negotiations on the controversial political legacy of the past determined the destiny of the Russian–Persian Treaty of 1921, concluded before the USSR was created, which has long since become *de facto* outdated. In 1979 the USSR showed no official reaction to Iran's decision to abolish the treaty's two articles (Numbers 5 and 6) that justified the intervention of Russian troops in case of hostile anti-Russian activity in Iranian territory. A draft of Basic Principles for Bilateral Relations, as part of the new situation resulting from the dissolution of the USSR, was initialled in Tehran in March 1993.[32]

Soviet–Iranian economic relations were predominantly focussed on industrial cooperation. Trade was centred on the export of raw materials, metal, machinery and military equipment, mainly from Russia. The 1989 programme on long-term economic cooperation included new spheres such as space and the use of nuclear energy for peaceful ends with the possible sale to Iran of light water reactors.[33] But today new dilemmas arise in this respect, since the principal former Soviet space installations are deployed not in Russia but in Kazakhstan. In May 1992 the CIS heads of state agreed in Tashkent on the joint use of space-vehicle launching sites in Baykonur. That understanding might provide Russia's and Kazakhstan's cooperation in implementing the 1989 agreements with Iran.

At the same time Russia's nuclear cooperation with Iran, and its supplying arms to that country, a policy the USSR resumed in 1989, are matters of particular sensitivity in view of Moscow's new relations with the West. In August, 1992, the US Senate adopted a resolution making economic aid to Russia conditional upon Russia's not providing arms to Iran. The consensus between the executive and legislative bodies in Washington on the need for more support for Russia's reform movement may for a while put aside these concerns. But the anxiety of the White House about Iranian ambitions does not seem to have lessened. The Clinton administration, like Bush's, considers Tehran a principal 'spot of instability' in the region, a 'driving force' of terror, and a centre for the diffusion of Islamic radicalism. Such concerns are being fuelled by a new outburst of fundamentalist movements in the region, which have affected even 'safe' Middle East nations such as Egypt. The continuing supply of arms from Russia has been confirmed by both sides,[34] which again was seen by the USA as encouraging Iranian ambitions. Restraining such ambitions is at the core of Washington's 'dual containment' policy in the Persian Gulf.

But Russia is unlikely to give up such deals, and, in reviewing Moscow's relations with Tehran, the West should keep in mind their special features. Despite differences on some aspects of world development, long-term understanding and cooperation with Iran is a matter of expediency for Moscow. This stems from a number of economic and political considerations, of which the Iranian presence in Central Asia and its influence in the Caucasus are only two. Stable relations with Iran are necessary for the country to maintain a regional balance; even more than others in the area, Russia is interested in seeing its Southern Tier stable and secure for the long run. An imbalance here might affect its transparent borders with Asia, and thus Moscow's policy cannot be focussed on the unilateral reinforcement of Iran, which explains Russia's caution in building military ties with Iran by providing defensive weapons.[35] On the other hand, now that Moscow has lost many of its foreign markets for arms, such deals are of particular commercial benefit for a country in serious economic crisis. Principal regional markets are 'distributed' among leading Western suppliers, who seem unwilling to make concessions to their former Cold War adversary, despite the understanding at the Vancouver Summit in April 1993 between Russia and the USA on Moscow's access to high-technology world markets.

There is another consideration that encourages Russia to make arms deals with Tehran. China and North Korea, until the 1990s the main arms suppliers to Iran, may not be as sensitive to maintaining an equilibrium as Moscow, being farther from the region. Continuous intensive missile deals between Tehran and Pyongyang are significant in this respect. Russia's arms supplies could provide the leverage in case of need to restrain Tehran's regional ambitions; the same holds true for bilateral cooperation in peaceful uses of nuclear energy (for which China has similar arrangements). Iran, having used in its favour the tensions in political and economic relations between Russia and Ukraine, has concluded a long-term agreement with Kiev that provides for the supply of Iranian oil and gas to Ukraine in exchange not only for machinery and industrial equipment, but also possibly for weapons from Kiev.[36] This and Kazakhstan's intention to enter the world arms market may significantly limit the scope of Russia's economic and military ties with Iran, giving Tehran more flexibility in striving for influence in Central Asia, without taking into account Russia's concerns.

Pakistan

The new political make-up in Central Asia and recently in Afghanistan has opened new possibilities for Pakistan in South-west Asia.[37] If its relations with the region are significantly developed, Islamabad may strengthen not only its western flanks in political and military competition with India in South Asia, but also its positions on a more global scale.[38] While Turkey in Central Asia focuses attention mostly on economic spheres of relations, Islamabad tries to make its ties more politically orientated. Its proposal to set up a regional 'Union of Ten' (Pakistan, Afghanistan, Iran, Turkey, Azerbaijan and the five Central Asian states), an idea stemming from its previous concept of 'strategic consensus' (Pakistan, Iran and Afghanistan) is aimed at such a union's domination of the region. But today, in comparison with Turkey and Iran, Pakistan's chances in the region seem considerably limited. The main obstacle is the continuous turmoil in Afghanistan and now in Tajikistan, which are the geographical linchpins for the new Central Asia.

Despite the fact that Afghanistan is not now a principal obstacle to extending Moscow–Islamabad relations, Russia's anxiety about Islamabad's and Tehran's increased influence in Central Asia might to some extent restrict its relations with these two countries. The prospect of putting into effect new ties with Pakistan's defence establishment is a sensitive question as well, since this may cause grave concern in India. Political relations with New Delhi, despite differences in approach to some regional as well as global issues (Delhi is not happy with Russia's support for Islamabad's stand on the nuclear-free zone in South Asia), will likely remain one of Moscow's top priorities in the region in the long run. A new treaty signed in Delhi in January 1993, providing for close contacts and coordination in favour of the 'elimination of threat' in the region, reaffirms that long-term objective.[39] In such circumstances the new prospects of cooperation with Pakistan will require maximum flexibility from Russia. Attention should be focussed on drawing up a comprehensive formula, which might not only improve the emergent balance in Moscow's relations with both Islamabad and New Delhi, but also restrain new Pakistani ambitions in Central Asia.

Turkey

The evident necessity to expand relations with Ankara is connected first of all to Russia's vital considerations in both European and Asian dimensions, and to Turkey's specific role in Europe and in the Near East. That the two nations have Eurasian geopolitical scope structures the strategic problems they are facing now and will continue to face in the future. Their long-term socio-economic strategies have similar objectives, having been focussed on joining the developed Western world. Russia shows specific interest in cooperating with European (now Eurasian) political structures, as well as with the EU and NATO. Having established a close partnership with the West, Moscow has thereby strengthened its bonds with neighbouring Turkey, which is a member of the principal military-political and economic structures of the West, let alone its status in the Conference on Security and Coopearation in Europe (CSCE). That is why it seems logical that Turkey was the first among all Moscow's neighbours in the Near East and South-west Asia with which Russia signed a Treaty on Fundamentals of Relations in May 1992.

Both Turkey and Russia express concern over developments in South-west Asia and in the Near East. A point for close contact might be a shared view on introducing Turkey's secularist model of market economy to Muslim Central Asia, an option that is evidently being backed by the West, especially the USA. Understanding and close cooperation between them seem to be quite reasonable in the interests of resolving regional conflicts that concern both countries.

Both bilateral and multi-lateral cooperation with Turkey might have a particular importance for Moscow with regard to using appropriate Turkish experience in building up a market economy. Turkey's economy, however, is obviously served by continuing to import raw materials from Russia, including oil products, as well as metals and machinery. In May 1992 a Declaration on Black Sea Economic Co-operation, proposed by Ankara in the late 1980s, was initialled by Turkey, Russia, Ukraine, Georgia, Bulgaria and Romania at the Istanbul Summit. Three non-coastal republics of the former Soviet Union – Azerbaijan, Armenia and Moldova – joined the project as well. With the gradual emergence of a sort of 'Asian Common Market' (ACM), patterned after the recently enlarged ECO (with the incorporation of Azerbaijan and five Central Asian republics), and with the possible future inclusion in the ACM of the recently formed Caspian Council (Iran, Russia, Azerbaijan, Kazakhstan and Turkmenistan), Russia might be induced to enhance and deepen the coordination of its regional economic policy, not only with Iran and Pakistan, but also with the more advanced Turkey. Nor should Russia's future entry in the ECO be ruled out, given its diverse bilateral economic ties with practically all regional nations. An understanding with Ankara in this regard would be of significant importance.

But relations between the two countries will most probably remain controversial and ambivalent. The prospects of their bilateral and multi-lateral cooperation in the Black Sea zone might be lessened by distrust and differences among the various members of that new regional organization (Turkey–Bulgaria; possibly Turkey–Georgia and Armenia; Russia–Ukraine and Moldova as well as possibly Russia–Romania; Armenia–Azerbaijan; Georgia–Azerbaijan, etc). There have been differences in approach to Bosnia; the problem of the Crimea seems to emerge again. As it was in the eighteenth century, it might be turned into a hot debate in relation to the Black Sea. The problem is still a matter of controversy between Russia and Ukraine. But in the near future the Crimean Tatars (who total about 400,000 in the former USSR, including about 135,000 in Crimea) seem to play a more significant role in the peninsula's fate. In June 1991 their congress (*kuroultay*) adopted a declaration on sovereignty aimed at establishing a Crimean Tatars' national state.[40] There is little doubt that the movement will seek Turkey's direct support in dealing with both Kiev and Moscow.

Ankara's present policy in Central Asia might still be considered by Moscow as not as strongly ideologically orientated as that of Iran, or to some extent that of Pakistan. This attitude influences the existing mutual understanding between Russia and Turkey. But having developed extensive ties with Azerbaijan and Central Asia, Ankara is expanding its relations with the Russian Federation's economically advanced Turkic-populated areas as well, at the same time keeping an eye on political trends there. Until now, Turkey has repeatedly stressed its formal negative view of the revival of any Islamic or pan-Turkic political movements in the former USSR including Russia, a stand that corresponds with Moscow's interests. But growing pan-Turkic notions in Turkey, supported to a certain extent officially, as well as Islamic activities during local elections in Turkey in the spring of 1994 mainly as a result of the country's economic decline, might cause anxiety in Moscow. A matter for concern may also be persistent attempts to draw the Russian Federation's Turkic republics and autonomous regions into establishing a confederation of all regional Turkic nations. These moves may be seen as additional outside provocations to cause Russia's disintegration. Ankara's manoeuvres towards a higher profile in reviewing the conflict between Georgia and Abkhasia, as well as developments in the Russian North Caucasus, may become another matter for concern to Moscow.

At the same time, any formal dramatic shift to pan-Turkism in Ankara's policy would have a negative impact on its major goal of joining the EU. On the other hand, pan-Turkic and fundamentalist pressures on Ankara from both the outside and inside, as well as serious doubts in Europe on the wisdom of accepting Turkey as a full EU member (a policy that is motivated by several considerations including ideological ones) may cause public opinion inside the country to swing towards radicalism in its regional policy.

Afghanistan

In late April 1992 the Najibullah regime in Kabul was overthrown by the mujahedin, and Afghanistan was proclaimed an Islamic republic. This event has significantly strengthened regional Islamism and ethnic controversies, and exerts new pressures on Central Asia, particularly on Tajikistan. The new instability in Kabul, a result of the struggle for power-sharing, may bring in a long period of uncertainty in the country, with ethnic rivalry at its core, and seriously worsen the situation in the region, eventually involving neighbouring Pakistan and Iran. Proceeding from different considerations, both Pakistan and Iran agree on the necessity to prevent any serious aggravation in Afghanistan, since that might create problems in their own domestic affairs and in their regional strategy for a 'soft breakthrough' to Central Asia

and Transcaucasia. Uzbekistan, the largest and potentially most powerful of Afghanistan's immediate neighbours in Central Asia, as well as
Tajikistan and Turkmenistan (all with populations related to that
country's northern areas) are all preoccupied with economic crises
and domestic uncertainties. But if ethnic rivalry in the Pashtun–Tajik–
Uzbek triangle in Afghanistan were to increase, Central Asia would
not be able to avoid an involvement in the conflict. Mutual suspicion
between Uzbekistan and Tajikistan might arise, embroiling other
Central Asian nations such as Turkmenistan, Kyrgyzstan and possibly
Russia's immediate neighbours such as Kazakhstan, which would be a
matter of grave concern to Moscow.

The situation outlined above also calls for Moscow to have, to a
marked degree, a high profile in the new Afghanistan. But its influence
on developments in that country is now seriously limited. Afghanistan
is now not only politically but geographically a 'distant state' to Russia,
which will probably lead to significantly diminished bilateral relations
in the long run. Moscow's principal approach to Kabul will very
probably be drawn up through a focus on Russia's relations with
Central Asia, as well as with Iran and Pakistan. Nevertheless, it is in
Russia's long-term interest to take part in curbing any new rise of
general instability in Afghanistan.

During talks in Moscow in November 1992 the mujahedin insisted
that all Soviet–Afghan agreements signed after the April 1978 coup in
Kabul be regarded as invalid. As a result of bargaining it was agreed
that they would be reviewed by the Islamic government now in power,
but revisions may pose many problems for Russia. Kabul's main target
will be the 1978 Soviet–Afghan Treaty, under which Soviet troops
had been brought to Afghanistan. With the treaty abolished, the
former mujahedin may again raise the question of repayment of the
damages inflicted upon the country during the eight and a half years
of Soviet occupation. Given Moscow's heritage, the burden would in
this case fall predominantly on Russia. But given Russia's present
economic crises, it seems unrealistic for Kabul to expect massive
compensation from Moscow. Russia made this quite clear, having confirmed that it 'does not consider itself responsible for the sufferings
and destruction caused by Soviet intervention in Afghanistan.'[41] The
Central Asian and other republics of the former USSR may take the
same stance as well. The former Soviet POWs might nevertheless
remain the mujahedin government's lever to exert necessary pressure
on Moscow. To break the possible joint efforts by Russia and Central

Asia to release POWs, Kabul might again embark on its previous practice of dividing them between Muslim and non-Muslim.

These regional and domestic considerations will prompt Russia, despite its preoccupation with internal problems, to participate in post-war reconstruction in Afghanistan. The former USSR's massive economic assistance to that country was shared by several union republics including Central Asian ones. Thus it seems expedient for Moscow to cooperate closely with them in the reconstruction of Afghanistan. Such a cooperation would not only assist Russia to have its POWs released, but it would also help build a common stand with Central Asian republics in establishing long-term relations with Afghanistan.

But the situation in Afghanistan, despite efforts by Pakistan, Saudi Arabia and Iran to reconcile the former mujahedin, remained uncertain. There is no visible consensus among them on power-sharing, a trend that may continue for a long time. Instability and ethnic quarrels may result in the country's *de facto* disintegration, with northern, predominately Uzbek- and Tajik-populated areas seeking unity with their kinsmen in the former Soviet south. Such a scenario is unlikely to be approved by regional players, not only in Central Asia but also in South-west Asia. Tripartite efforts were evidently not enough to defuse the stand-off, since each player has its own latent part in Afghanistan. The international community, and for the first time the UN, seem ready to tackle the mediation process, too. Russia is more likely to be cautious in taking unilateral peace-making steps in Afghanistan. Against the background of the situation in that country, Moscow will probably be urged to render more border control assistance to Tajikistan, Uzbekistan and Turkmenistan.

Possible cooperation with the USA

Strategic changes in East–West relations since 1985 in general and in Europe in particular have caused the diminution of Russia's political and military presence there in comparison with that of the former USSR. This fact may logically determine Russia's gradual shift to paying more attention to its new début in the West through the geographical East. Since the Transcaucasian republics of Azerbaijan and Armenia as well as Central Asian nations joined the CSCE institutions in early 1992, the all-European process has turned towards Asia. This may favour Moscow's involvement in the European process from its 'Asian angle' too. Accordingly, the geographical dimensions of Russia's relations with the USA, now that the two countries 'do not regard one another as potential adversaries',[42] and after the Vancouver Summit declared their 'democratic partnership', might be shifted to Asia, as affirmed at the January 1994 Moscow Summit. The strategic coincidence of the two parties' interests in Pacific Asia, South and South-west Asia, and the Near East is obvious. Growing concern in the USA about its political and economic future in the Pacific and its decreasing influence in South Asia are factors that urge it to realign policy and to breathe new life into its strategy in the regions where Russia has historically had vital interests. In the Pacific, where Washington is determined to 'remain a key factor of reassurance and stability',[43] Moscow (against the background of Japanese demands for the return of four small Kuril islands) especially needs to have an understanding with the USA in order to play an active role in establishing new security arrangements 'from Vancouver to Vladivostok'.

At the same time, the two sides are rethinking their priorities in South Asia in terms of that region's new strategic situation. Having inherited a Soviet stand on nuclear non-proliferation in the region, having signed a new more balanced Friendship Treaty with Delhi, and having initiated an analogous document with Pakistan, Moscow is paving the way towards equilibrium in its relations with both India and Pakistan. The encouragement of Indo-Pakistani rapprochement and adoption of confidence-building measures[44] is also Washington's regional goal. A lessening of the predominant orientation on Pakistan and a move towards realignment of relations with India indicate that the USA is seeking smooth relations with both as a possible fresh start in South Asia.[45] The nature of Moscow and Washington's views on non-proliferation in the region, the necessity to restrict the supply of sophisticated weapons, the two sides' need to agree on parameters and limits of nuclear non-military ties and on the supply of missile technology to regional states, their mutual concern about the possible emergence of radical imbalances in neighbouring South-west Asia as well as in Central Asia, which the USA has reluctantly 'discovered', are all factors that create real grounds for significant coordination of the two parties' policies in South and South-west Asia.

Until 1994 Washington seemed not to pay special attention to the new trends in the policies of Russia's new neighbours in Central Asia. Its general approach to the region seemed to be similar to the traditional one (before 1978, and after 1989) on Afghanistan as a region out of the sphere of US political and economic priorities. Immediately after the emergence of new Central Asian states American specialists predicted that the US presence there would be 'relatively modest' and suggested that the USA be cautious in its dealings with Central Asia.[46] But the new world situation, characterized by the growing conflict between the North and the South, a phenomenon which might ultimately take the shape of a conflict between the West and the Muslim world, has gradually changed Washington's view of that region. Among the main factors of such a shift is the dynamism of Central Asian nations, which are rapidly establishing formal ties with the world, intending to build up relations not only with their southern neighbours and the Pacific rim but also with the West in order to benefit from their own geopolitical advantages in a badly-needed economic revival. A cause of the US concern may be that the newly emerged regional nations might become embroiled in a regional arms race, or that nuclear instability might emerge here as a result of Islamic Iran or Pakistan gaining access to the Central Asian uranium mines. By the end of 1993 Washington's Central Asian strategy had weathered a period of hesitation, and by mid-1994 the administration had formulated its goals in the region, now considered to be of great strategic importance to the USA. Most important are its unique geographical location as a linchpin between the Far and the Near East, Russia and the Muslim south, and its vast natural and human resources. Washington's objectives in Central Asia include support for the development of market democracy there through encouraging US trade and investments in order not to lose newly emerged opportunities in the global competition with other Western, Pacific and Muslim countries.[47]

The USA's basic objectives in the region seem not to be in contrast with those of Russia; on the contrary, they may well be complementary to each other. In this case the USA might attach more political significance to coordinating its regional policy with Russia, for whom Central Asia is a vital sphere of interest, a fact that seems to have been taken for granted by Washington. A key factor in both the Russian and the American approaches to developments in Central Asia is the similarity of their views on stability in the region. Thus it is in both sides' interest to show more dynamism in encouraging a new prominent profile for each other in Central Asia, so that the struggle for the region does not end with the defeat of secularism.

Politically the two nations might coordinate monitoring hidden deep-seated trends in overall developments in the region. Economi-

cally, they may set up joint ventures and joint regional programmes
after the example of the now operating US–Israeli, US–Turkey and
US–Japan ones. It seems, however, that any direct attempts by either
Russia or the USA to impose its perceptions of democracy or its
values upon the region – whose leaders, each in an individual style,
see their nations' drift to a market economy and democracy through
a lens of 'enlightened authoritarianism' – will most likely fail. A
dynamic, coherent and rational approach in dealing with the Central
Asian nations seems to be the wisest course of action for both Russia
and the USA.

Notes

1. A. Kozyrev (Minister of Foreign Affairs of Russia), 'Russia: chance for
survival', *Foreign Affairs*, vi (Spring 1992), p 12.

2. Ibid. p 10.

3. By the end of 1991, 51 per cent, or 148 million of the total USSR
population, lived in the Russian Federation. At the same time, Russia produced more than 90 per cent of the oil, 80 per cent of the timber, more than
60 per cent of the electricity, about 60 per cent of the steel and more than 50
per cent of the coal, grain and meat (*The Economist*, 2 November 1991, p 44).

4. In this chapter the 'Southern Tier' refers to the Near East and South-
west Asia (Turkey, Iran, Afghanistan, Pakistan) and the Central Asian republics of Kazakhstan, Uzbekistan, Tajikistan, Turkmenistan and Kyrgyzstan (i.e.
excluding Transcaucasian Azerbaijan, Armenia and Georgia).

5. In February 1992 the vice-president of Tatarstan, Viktor Likhachev,
while on a visit to Florida, obtained the Tatar diaspora's confirmation of its
'readiness ... to facilitate the republic's recognition by the international community'. *Interfax* [Moscow], 1 March 1992. FBIS-SOV-92-043, p 30.

6. *Interfax* [Moscow], 6 March 1992. FBIS-SOV-92-046; 9 March 1992,
p 33.

7. The Bilateral Memorandum on cooperation with Kuwait in the field of
petroleum provides Kazakhstan with 'technical know-how in the drilling for
oil and its refining'. *KUNA* [Kuwait], 1 March 1992. FBIS-SOV-92-044; 5
March 1992, p 72.

8. *Washington Post*, 19 May 1992, pp C-1, C-2.

9. Interview with Demirel, *Time*, 10 February 1992, p 40.

10. Robert S. Norris, 'The Soviet nuclear archipelago', *Arms Control Today*,
xxii/1 (January–February 1992), p 27.

11. William C. Potter, 'Exports and experts: proliferation risks from the
new commonwealth', *Arms Control Today*, xxii/1 (January–February 1992),
p 37.

12. Ibid.

13. Ibid, p 34.

14. *Sodrugestvo Nezavisimio Gosudarstv: Processy i perspecivy*, Study Report, Centre for International Studies, Moscow Institute of International Relations (Moscow: September 1992), Appendix 5, p 31.

15. According to the public opinion poll carried out in October 1991 by the National Public Opinion Studies Centre in Moscow, more than 60 per cent of those who were questioned in Central Asia considered installation of an Islamic government in their republic quite possible in the near future (FBIS-SOV-91-0219, 13 November 1991).

16. Interview with the Chairman (mufti) of Kazyat of Muslims of Tajikistan, Kazi Kolon Khodzi Akbar Turajonzoda, *Berliner Zeitung*, 22 November 1991, p 7 (FBIS-SOV-91-229, 27 November 1991, p 73).

17. 'The Soviet regime in Central Asia represented itself as a sort of de-formed tangle of Communist ideas and ways of governing, and customs and rules of local khans, let alone tribe relations and religious forms' (*Izvestiia*, 13 September 1991, p 3).

18. 'The overwhelming majority of the national intelligentsia are human-ists, mostly historians and philologists who study the history of their peoples and contiguous nations. Perceptions that "everything which is ours, is the best" prevail in their approaches. Hypertrophied over-emphasis of cultural values, created by this or that respective nation, determines the nutrient me-dium for nationalism.... A significant part of humanist intellectuals ascend those segments of society which in the past have possessed a monopoly on religious titles and posts' (S. Polyakov, 'Traditionalism v sovremennom sredneasiatskom obshestve' [Traditionalism in Central Asian Society Today], *Znaniye* [Moscow], 1989, pp 88–9).

This research, disclosing a traditional way of life in both urban and rural areas of the Soviet Central Asian republics, seems to have been one of the most reliable sources ever officially issued in the USSR. The author, head of the Moscow State University's Archaeological Mission in Central Asia, worked in that region for about 30 years. When I met him in May 1991, Polyakov told me that this research caused dissatisfaction in the republics and was banned for distribution in Central Asia.

19. In Central Asia only Tajiks are non-Turkic. Among the total popula-tion of 56.4 million in Central Asia and Azerbaijan, ethnic Turks make up an estimated 33 million; Tajiks, who constitute only 60 per cent of the popula-tion in Tajikistan itself, about 3 million; and 13.5 million are 'Russian speak-ing'. Compiled from data issued by the *Washington Post*, 24 November 1991.

20. Thomas S. Szayna. 'The ethnic factor in the Soviet armed forces: the Muslim dimension', RAND R-4002-A, 1991, p 5.

21. Moscow, *Postfactum*, 5 March 1992. FBIS-SOV-92-045, 6 March 1992, p 57.

22. *Izvestiia*, 16 March 1992, p 1.

23. By the 1980s it comprised in Kazakhstan about 41 per cent, in Kyrgyz-

stan about 26 per cent, and Turkmenistan about 13 per cent, and in both Uzbekistan and Tajikistan about 11 per cent of the total population. *The Nationalities Question in the Soviet Union*, ed. G. Smith (London and New York: Longman, 1992), Appendix 3, Table 3.

24. Dimitri Simes, 'Russia reborn', *Foreign Policy*, no. 85 (Winter 1991–2), p 49.

25. President Yeltsin's message to the leaders of the CIS nations, *Nezavisimaia gazeta*, 18 March 1993.

26. Mufti of Kazakhstan R. Nysanbaev strongly opposed the idea of the creation of an Islamic party in the country, since 'if it were established, the republic would certainly be swept by pan-Turkic ideas which could inflame hostility between the adherents of various religious convictions.' FBIS-SOV-91-221, 15 November 1991, p 88.

27. In March 1992 the prime minister of Kazakhstan, Sergei Tereschchenko, visited China. A joint communiqué outlined the principles of bilateral political relations and stressed the necessity to develop economic ties. Agreements on cooperation in economics, transport and in setting up a joint economic and technological commission were signed. The two sides positively assessed the results of Soviet–Chinese border talks and decided to continue their discussions (TASS International Service, 28 February 1992. FBIS-SOV-92-048, 11 March 1992, p 59).

28. Statement by Prof. G. Mirsky, Congressional hearings on US policy towards Central Asia, 28 April 1992. *Central Asia Monitor*, no. 2 (1992), p 30.

29. It should be remembered in this respect that it was the ethnic–religious rioting in Almaty as far back as December 1986, after the ouster of the corrupt republican Communist Party chief Dynmuhammad Kunaev and his replacement by an ethnic Russian, that essentially became the first challenge to Gorbachev's domestic policy.

30. *Rossiiskaia gazeta*, 29 February 1992, p 7.

31. *Izvestiia*, 16 May 1992, p 1.

32. *Nezavisimaia gazeta*, 31 March 1993.

33. William C. Potter, op. cit., 1992, p 33.

34. Joint press release after Kozyrev's visit to Iran. Ibid.

35. Anthony Lake, Assistant to the President for National Security Affairs, 'Confronting Backlash States', *Foreign Affairs* lxxiii/2 (March–April 1994), pp 52–5.

36. News conference in the Ukrainian Foreign Ministry after First Vice-President K. Msyk's visit to Iran. Kiev Radio, 4 March 1992. FBIS-SOV-92-045, 6 March 1992, p 42.

37. Rodney W. Jones, 'Old quarrels and new realities: security in Southern Asia after the Cold War', *Washington Quarterly*, xv (Winter 1992), p 114.

38. Shahid Javed Burki, 'Pakistan's cautious democratic course', *Current History* (March 1992), p 122.

39. 'Treaty of friendship and partnership between the Russian Federation and the Republic of India', Art. 3, *Diplomaticheskiy vestik* (Diplomatic Re-

view), Foreign Ministry of the Russian Federation, no. 3–4 (February 1993), p 20.

40. *Izvestiia*, 7 July 1991.

41. *ITAR TASS*, Moscow, 14 May 1992. FBIS-SOV-92-095, 15 May 1992, p 14.

42. 'On the principles of new mutual relations: the Camp David declaration by President Bush and President Yeltsin', *Rossiiskaia gazeta*, 3 February 1992, p 3. FBIS-SOV-92-022, 3 February 1992, p 26.

43. 'National security strategy of the United States', President Bush's Report to Congress: The White House, August 1991, p 9.

44. Ibid., p 10.

45. Selig S. Harrison, 'South Asia and the United States: A chance for a fresh start', *Current History*, March 1992, p 98.

46. Graham E. Fuller, *Central Asia: the New Geopolitics* (Santa Monica, CA: The RAND Corporation, R-4210-USDP/1992), p 77.

47. Remarks by Strobe Talbott, Acting Secretary of State, US–Central Asia Business Conference, Washington, 3 May 1994.

I I

Central Asia:
Issues and Challenges for
United States Policy

NANCY LUBIN

The new Central Asian states that emerged from the former USSR pose a range of opportunities and challenges for the United States. Central Asia's vast resource base – including the largest gold mine in the world, enormous reserves of copper and other non-ferrous metals, and among the world's largest reserves of oil and gas – has made the region increasingly attractive to foreign investors, including the US business community. Uzbekistan is the eighth largest gold producer in the world, and the fourth largest cotton producer; Turkmenistan is the world's third largest producer of natural gas; some believe Kazakhstan's rich oil and gas reserves will make it 'another Kuwait'.

But the five new countries that comprise formerly Soviet Central Asia – Kazakhstan, Uzbekistan, Kyrgyzstan, Tajikistan and Turkmenistan – also pose serious challenges. With a mostly Muslim population of 50 million bordering Afghanistan and Iran; with a vast area more than half the size of the continental United States and as large as East and West Europe combined; with governments that are already unstable, if not in the midst of local wars; and with a large arsenal of nuclear weapons, it seems likely that events in Central Asia will reverberate far beyond the republics' borders. Further instability in the region could hinder the already precarious reform process in Russia, complicate the shifting alliances in the Middle East, exacerbate regional conflict and increase the outflow of narcotics and nuclear materials from the former Soviet Union that has already begun to occur.

These dangers are not hypothetical. Civil war in Tajikistan has already claimed tens of thousands of lives, more than have been lost in all the combined postwar internal conflicts of the former USSR. The acts of cruelty committed there are as inhuman as those in Bosnia-Herzogovina, and the number of refugees from Tajikistan topped 0.5 million out of a population of little over 5 million. Weapons flow or military involvement has expanded from Russia, the other Central Asian states and Afghanistan. Other countries, like Iran, Turkey and Pakistan, are vying for influence in the region and are concerned that the conflict may spread.

In the past, Western attention has focussed on questions of Islam and ethnicity as the main catalysts for conflict in Central Asia, and thus the key to any Western response. This analysis has been misleading. Certainly since its introduction in the seventh century, Islam has in many ways formed the basis of life in the region, whose people are more akin to the neighbouring Persians and Turks than to the Russians to the north. Russian conquest in the 1860s and Moscow's subsequent efforts both to eradicate and coopt Islam not only sharpened differences between Muslims and non-Muslims, but also greatly distorted the population's understanding of Islam and created competing Islamic ideologies among the Central Asians themselves. Likewise, although the major ethnic and national groups in the region – as well as the borders of these former republics – are essentially creations of the Soviet period, they too have acquired a life of their own, forming the basis for competing claims and rivalries. By now thousands of people have died in territorial disputes and what have been called inter-ethnic and religious conflicts, and the number continues to grow.

Although these issues are important, and while grievances may well be expressed under the banner of ethnicity or Islam, historical, ethnic or religious animosities do not adequately explain the causes of conflict in the region. Indeed, the most vicious conflicts that have already occurred in Central Asia have been *among* Muslims, *between* Central Asians and *within* individual ethnic groups themselves. The civil war in Tajikistan did not erupt as a result of Tajiks fighting other ethnic groups, but because of rival Tajiks fighting one another. The other major conflicts that have erupted in Central Asia – such as the Uzbeks versus the Meskhetian Turks, the Uzbeks versus the Kyrgyz, or even the Uzbeks versus each other – have overwhelmingly pitted Muslims against each other rather than against non-Muslims, and Islam has not been their root cause. A broad mix of other factors – economic, military, environmental, social and political – may become even greater sources of instability in the region and require a more coordinated and effective response.

It should be stressed that there are large differences among these new states. Although most of the republics have seen little violence so far, Tajikistan has witnessed the outbreak of full-fledged civil war. Turkmenistan, Kazakhstan and Uzbekistan are well-endowed with energy or other resources attractive to foreign investors; Tajikistan and Kyrgyzstan are relatively resource-poor. In Kazakhstan, the Russian proportion of the total population is large; in Tajikistan, Uzbekistan and Turkmenistan it is small and continues to decline. Although it is still unclear where democratic institutions may ultimately take root, Kyrgyzstan and Kazakhstan have been more tolerant of opposition groups on their territory than have the other Central Asian states.

Despite the differences among the five Central Asian states, the broad issues that follow are relatively common to the region, and will demand more coordinated and informed attention if we are to respond effectively to events that may challenge Western interests.

Economic challenges

Growing poverty, unemployment and economic inequality are viewed by Central Asians as among the key causes of the tragic conflicts that have already occurred in that region, and as potentially explosive catalysts for conflict in the future. These republics were long the poorest in the Soviet Union. According to official statistics, the vast majority of Kyrgyzstan's population lives below the CIS poverty line, a standard that is exceptionally low to begin with; and Kyrgyzstan is by no means the worst-off of these new states. By the beginning of 1994, total output in Kazakhstan – among the better-off of these new states – had fallen by a quarter relative to two years earlier. Price rises have already triggered serious riots in Uzbekistan and Kyrgyzstan, and the economies of most of these new countries continue to deteriorate against rising social needs.

Likewise, increasing competition *among* the newly independent Central Asian states over scarce resources is likely to trigger not only internal disturbances but also serious inter-state armed conflicts. Although Central Asian leaders recognize that they must work together if their republics are to survive as viable states, more often the new countries have been competitors rather than partners. Today, competing claims to water resources, arable land, energy and mineral resources and the like are viewed as some of the most likely areas of serious conflict among the fledgling states in the near future. Water is plentiful, for example, in the two states where it originates, Kyrgyzstan and Tajikistan, but it barely reaches the western parts of Turkmenistan, Uzbekistan and Kazakhstan; now that water allocation among the new states is no longer centralized in the hands of Moscow, it is being used as a political lever among the new countries. Kyrgyzstan and Tajikistan have made veiled threats to divert this water, the lifeline of the other states, to China and elsewhere in response to pressures from its former Soviet neighbours.

All of these problems are exacerbated by rapid population growth. With population growth rates in some of these countries estimated as high as 3 per cent per year, demographic pressures on increasingly scarce resources will place greater strains on governments to gain control of important resources and could intensify popular discontent.

Narcotics trafficking and organized crime

Widespread poverty and corruption, as well as the weakening of law enforcement and customs control, have fuelled the expansion of 'organized crime' networks and narcotics trafficking. Many Central Asians fear that this could become a major source of instability, greatly hindering democratic reform. In a region where natural resources have not been exploited to benefit local economies, for example, narcotics are a readily available source of hard currency. Indeed, the amount of land under opium poppy cultivation in Central Asia has exploded over the past few years, making it potentially one of the largest opium producers in the world. Russian sources estimate that the opium poppy grows today on roughly 300,000 acres of land in this region. Although this has not been independently verified, the figure would rank Central Asia with Myanmar (Burma) as the two largest opium poppy growers in the world; Afghanistan, at only 30,000 acres, would be a distant third. Opium production and trafficking into Western Europe and elsewhere have likewise increased dramatically. As one Central Asian put it, 'we may well be witnessing the emergence of the new "Colombia" of Europe – only this time with nuclear weapons.'

Because of the poverty of Central Asians, opium products are viewed as providing quick profits otherwise impossible to attain. Indeed, two of these new countries, Kyrgyzstan and Kazakhstan, decided in the winter of 1991-92 to legalize the growing of opium for 'licit', or medicinal, purposes. Although Kyrgyzstan rescinded the decision within weeks, Kazakhstan – geographically the largest state after Russia to emerge from the former USSR and the possessor of a huge arsenal of nuclear weapons – did not. Kazakhstan, a major opium producer, boasts an additional 10 million acres of hemp, whose dried flowers are used to make hashish and marijuana.

Central Asians seem to acknowledge the near impossibility of stopping illegal production of these drugs once even a portion has been legalized, as well as the increasingly limited legitimate world market for opium products. Several locals have expressed apprehension that organized crime, 'narco mafias' and home-grown cartels will assume more influence in Central Asia. Many fear this could lead to further instability at home, as it has in Latin America, as well as to a surge of heroin on the Western market.

Military challenges

Economic hardship and widespread corruption have made the role of the military and the presence of nuclear weapons reasons for greater concern. Some Central Asians have questioned the reliability of Russian and Kazakhstani troops – where disaffection, frustration and personal hardship are growing – to safeguard the more than 1400 nuclear warheads on Kazakh territory and the large amounts of nuclear materials there. The recent seizures in Germany of nuclear materials likely from facilities in Russia have heightened concerns that protection of nuclear weaponry or its components in the entire former Soviet Union may be much more tenuous than commonly thought. This concern has been difficult to verify and demands serious investigation.

Less ambiguous is the likelihood that the present proliferation of conventional arms throughout Central Asia will provoke further conflagration. Enormous quantities of weapons have become widely available in Central Asia, mainly from Afghanistan and the former Soviet military. Local leaders on both sides of the civil war in Tajikistan have cited this situation as a serious impediment to ending the carnage in Tajikistan, and some have urged Western assistance in disarming the region's population before an even greater bloodbath ensues.

Such concerns are fuelled by the discrimination and harassment directed towards Russian military personnel in these new sovereign states, where over 90 per cent of the officer corps are Slavs and where the republics' independence has increased resentment towards the continued presence of Russian soldiers there. Local ministers of defence have repeatedly stated that the majority of Russian military personnel – many of whom did not want to be in Central Asia in the first place – would like to return to Russia, but most cannot. This has been confirmed in public opinion surveys taken within the military ranks. Some find it darkly humorous to say that there is nothing more explosive than a population who are increasingly frustrated in their daily lives, find mounting difficulties in feeding and clothing their families, face hostility and discrimination as well as personal hardship – and are armed.

All of this is exacerbated by the ambiguous control of governments over local military affairs. Although a large portion of the forces located in Central Asia now fall under local budgets, it remains unclear who has authority over these troops and what role Russian forces should play in the region. Interviews in Central Asia have suggested that the bilateral agreements of Russia with several of these states do not fully clarify these roles. Another disconcerting source of tension for local leaders has been the repeated statements from Moscow, and apparent popular sentiment in Russia, that Russia should be prepared to intervene militarily to protect the rights of Russians in the former republics.

Environmental issues

Devastating environmental problems are also serious sources of discontent around which angry grassroots groups have started to form, among which the Aral Sea is perhaps the best-known environmental disaster. To supply a new crop, cotton, water has been siphoned off since the 1960s from the two main rivers that feed the Central Asian region, and the Aral Sea – once the fourth-largest inland sea in the world – has now shrunk to about a third of its 1960 volume, and half its 1960 geographical size. Huge salt and dust storms, heavy salinization of the surrounding land and water, and soaring rates of intestinal and respiratory disease now abound in what was once a relatively healthy area.

But the Aral Sea problem is only the beginning. Heavy use of chemicals and pesticides on the land has massively contaminated local drinking water supplies. With few water treatment plants, Turkmenistan's minister of health stated in the mid-1980s that much of the population drank from contaminated irrigation ditches and canals or from the Amu Darya river itself – in his words, from 'nothing better than a sewage ditch'. Today, the situation is worse; severe air pollution has been identified in public opinion surveys as an even greater concern. Serious air quality problems are created by factories and auto emissions as well as by the prevalence of salt and dust storms and the spraying of pesticides and defoliants for the cotton crop. The economic effects of these environmental disasters have been enormous. Carried long distances by wind, the salts from the Aral Sea have reportedly ruined hundreds of thousands of hectares of once arable land. Because of increasing salinization, even during the 1980s planners were pumping more investment into farms and sustaining greater losses. Today about 44 per cent of irrigated land is strongly salinated in Uzbekistan alone. The cumulative result has also been a dramatic rise in death and disease. Frequently cited in the press are increasing occurrences of typhoid, paratyphoid and hepatitis due to contaminated drinking water, rising rates of intestinal disease and cancers; and increased frequency of anaemia, dystrophy, cholera, dysentery and a host of other illnesses. The average life expectancy in some villages in the Aral Sea region is roughly 38 years.

Infant mortality is often considered the most comprehensive indicator of a population's health. In the Central Asian states it has risen by as much as 50 per cent over the past twenty years, to levels among the highest in the world. In some areas, infant mortality has officially reached as high as about 111:1000 – meaning that more than one child in ten does not live to reach his first birthday. Most informal estimates are almost double that figure. As Central Asians watch their loved ones die in greater numbers than before, the legitimacy of those in power begins to dwindle.

Social and political issues

All of this has been compounded, of course, by the enormous upheaval that has so fundamentally affected Central Asians' everyday lives. It is often difficult to fathom the degree to which the social fabric of the former Soviet Union has been rent in the chaos, dislocation and frustration caused by the breakup of the USSR.

Tensions have certainly surfaced between Russians and Central Asians. By the end of 1992, well over 100,000 Russians, many of whom were valued specialists, had already left these new Central Asian states. A 1993 public opinion survey conducted by this author among 2000 respondents in Uzbekistan and Kazakhstan, under the auspices of the United States Institute of Peace, suggests that the number may continue to grow. When asked whether, given the opportunity, they would like to leave Central Asia to live in another place, well over 90 per cent of our Central Asian respondents said no; but 43 per cent of the Russians in Kazakhstan, and over one third of the Russians in Uzbekistan, replied in the affirmative, despite the fact that many likely had roots in Central Asia going back two or three generations and had established their own communities there.

In many ways the situation is typical of other countries that have undergone decolonization, as Russian 'colonizers' have been reluctant to learn local languages or adapt to local control. Another survey in 1992 indicated that a full 80 per cent of the 1.5 million Russians living in Uzbekistan felt more insecure and fearful than they did before Uzbek independence, and 86 per cent opposed the creation of an Uzbekistan armed force. These figures have reportedly not diminished.

Sources of unrest, however, have also emerged from the turmoil among Central Asians themselves. Multiple and mixed identities – Muslim and atheist, Soviet and Asian, Turkic and Slav, clan and regional, and individual ethnic identities – have long coexisted within Soviet Central Asian society, if not within individual Central Asians. Many people viewed themselves as both Eastern and Western, modern and traditional, 'believers' and good Soviets simultaneously, depending on context. With the collapse of the old system, individuals are re-asserting old identities and seeking new ways of defining themselves. This is an enormously difficult personal as well as societal transition, leading to frustration and conflict in many parts of Central Asia. 'I am 100 per cent Uzbek', said one Uzbek, 'but I also feel 98 per cent Russian. Who am I?' 'My children speak only Russian', lamented a Kyrgyz official, typical of many of his compatriots, 'where do they fit in a world where, overnight, that has become scorned?'

The dislocation that has emerged throughout Central Asia has been reflected in a breakdown of social control. In some of these Asian states, soaring crime and homicide rates have rocked small communities, as have more heavyhanded official crackdowns on emerging independent groups. On the whole, the social dislocations in Central Asia today are massive. Many people no longer know where they fit, creating fertile ground for the growth of social and religious organizations antithetical to either the interests of local governments or to those of the West.

Challenges for the West

All these issues present increasingly important challenges not only to the Central Asians, but to US policymakers. Perhaps more than in other regions, the USA must walk a tightrope in Central Asia between competing and often contradictory goals in its own policies. In these new countries, where authoritarian leaders and centralized economic and political control are still the norm, US policy-makers must balance the goal of maintaining stability with that of promoting measures for democratic reform that are likely to bring instability in their wake. In a broader region where Russia is still the first US priority, balancing Russian interests with those of the Central Asians and of the USA has also been difficult. And in a region where economic opportunity for the foreign investor is potentially great, combating the obstacles to successful investment – lack of infrastructure, rampant corruption etc – has proved formidable.

In the short time that these former Soviet republics have been independent states, the United States has made significant efforts in terms of humanitarian and technical assistance. According to the US Agency for International Development (US AID), as of December 1993 the USA had provided roughly $379 million in humanitarian assistance to the new Central Asian states – $55 million to Kazakhstan, $17 million to Uzbekistan, $124 million to the Kyrgyz Republic, $73 million to Tajikistan and $110 million to Turkmenistan. Millions of dollars' worth of food and medicines have been sent to these countries to alleviate some of the immediate crises facing their populations. US AID boasts that its initiatives to encourage democratic and market reform in these countries have included technical assistance and training programmes in a wide range of fields, such as privatization, small business development, financial and tax policy, labour and management relations and rule of law. Again, as of December 1993 about $64 million had been provided for technical assistance to these countries – $32 million to Kazakhstan, $13 million to Uzbekistan, $12 million to the Kyrgyz Republic, $4 million to Tajikistan and $3 million to Turkmenistan. Major corporations have set up offices throughout Central Asia on US government-supported projects to offer local governments advice and assistance in financial planning, privatization etc, while groups such as the Peace Corps have sent volunteers to teach English and provide expertise for small business development. A number of trade agreements and bilateral assistance arrangements between all of these countries and the USA have been aimed at providing legal protection and assurances for US investors. Agreements with lending institutions such as the Overseas Private Investment Corporation (OPIC) and US Eximbank complement these efforts by providing direct loans and guarantees, assisting with project-investor financing and, in the case of Eximbank, providing short-term insurance coverage to projects in these countries.

But the effects of these efforts have been mixed. Some projects have been praised as constructive and useful by locals and Western assistance agencies themselves. Many of these have been carried out on low budgets by US non-governmental organizations such as ISAR, Mercy Corps, and others, who have had a good deal of prior experience on the ground. Other major projects in all these new states, however, have been widely criticized for being misguided, redundant, ill-fitted to Central Asian realities and costing the US taxpayer millions of dollars to generate few significant results. They have been criticized for empowering the very government or corrupt structures the USA hopes to reform; for promoting policies and projects that may be appropriate for other parts of the developing world but do not fit here; for becoming tools of authoritarian governments which use the spectre of Islamic 'fundamentalism' or political unrest to garner Western support for controversial policies; or simply for being an ineffective waste of money.

In thinking broadly about the role the USA can play in efforts to diminish the potential for future unrest and to assist these countries in their move towards democratic reform, three points might be useful. First, these issues must be made a priority. This does not necessarily require greater allocation of already limited resources, but rather requires a more sober approach in defining the most serious challenges in Central Asia and shaping the way in which US resources are used. Instead of magnifying a potential Islamic threat, for example, it would be useful to understand in what ways Islam may play a constructive role in Central Asia in the midst of upheaval and change, and in what ways other factors may trigger unrest. In applying US resources to the region, humanitarian and technical assistance must be accompanied by a greater degree of follow-through in terms of oversight, accountability and constant reassessment of US efforts. The twisted economic, social and political legacy of Soviet rule means that the experience gained from other parts of the developing world cannot be readily applied to Central Asia; what worked in Africa, Asia, the Middle East or South America will not necessarily work here. Specialists more familiar with navigating the particular Central Asian political and economic systems must combine with technical specialists to create policies and projects that address the interests of all sides. The work of NGOs – who tend to have longer on-the-ground experience, more cost-effective budgets and a long-term presence – should be expanded.

Second, these issues must be addressed in a coherent, coordinated and interdisciplinary manner; none of them can be viewed in isolation. Nuclear proliferation, organized crime or narcotics trafficking, for example, cannot be viewed as purely legal or law enforcement issues in societies in which 'organized crime' is often part and parcel of local and national governments, law enforcement is intentionally selective and weak, accountability and oversight of government officials has been non-existent and corruption and illegal economic activity have been the norm for decades. Likewise, the Aral Sea and other environmental problems cannot be addressed apart from questions of water allocation and resource management, health care delivery, economic and political reform, organized crime and relations with the other Central Asian states. The visit of Vice President Gore to the Aral Sea several years ago sent a powerful message that the United States regards the Aral Sea tragedy as an important environmental, political and human problem meriting world attention. Today, coordination and coherence are needed if Western follow-up efforts are to have any impact.

Most importantly, the motivation behind US policies in this region should not be, as has often been the case, to offer benevolent or humanitarian assistance to an exotic, faraway region that has little relevance at home. Instead, it should stem from the stark reality that many of these practical issues – narcotics trafficking and organized crime, control of nuclear weapons, environmental devastation and regional instability – will directly affect US national security interests. As these new countries grapple with creating new systems, new priorities and new directions, it is much cheaper and easier to help address these issues early on than to wait until they have ballooned out of proportion and are far more difficult to control.

Acknowledgements

This chapter was written while the author was a fellow at the United States Institute of Peace and Associate Professor at Carnegie Mellon University, and is an expanded version of her 'Dangers and Dilemmas: The Need for Prudent Policy Toward Central Asia', published in the *Harvard International Review*, vol. xv/3 Spring 1993, pp 6–9. Reprinted with permission. She greatly appreciates the support of the United States Institute of Peace and the National Council for Soviet and East European Research.

Notes on the Contributors

Tahir Amin received his Ph.D in political science from the Massachusetts Institute of Technology and is an associate professor in the Department of International Relations, Quaid-i-Azam University, Islamabad. His research interests include theories of international relations, ethnic conflict in South-west and Central Asia and Pakistani politics. His most recent publications include *Ethno-national Movements of Pakistan: Domestic and International Factors* (1989) and *Nationalism and Internationalism in Liberalism, Marxism and Islam* (1991).

Muriel Atkin is an associate professor of history at George Washington University. She is the author of *The Subtlest Battle: Islam in Soviet Tajikistan* (1989) and *Russia and Iran, 1780–1828* (1980). Her current research deals with the recent upheavals in Tajikistan.

Ali Banuazizi is Professor of Social Psychology and Modern Iranian History at Boston College and a research fellow at the Center for International Studies at MIT. He served as the editor of the *Journal of Iranian Studies* from 1968 to 1982 and has published widely on the culture and politics of Iran and the Middle East. With Myron Weiner he is the co-editor of *The State, Religion, and Ethnic Politics: Afghanistan, Iran, and Pakistan* (1986) and *The Politics of Social Transformation in Afghanistan, Iran, and Pakistan* (1994).

Graham E. Fuller is currently a senior political scientist at RAND in Washington, DC, where his primary work is on the Middle East, Central Asia and ex-Soviet nationality affairs, Russian–Middle East relations, Islamic fundamentalism and problems of democracy in the Middle East. He has written a RAND study on the Kurdish problem, a study on the survivability of Iraq, and has written on problems of democracy and Islam in the Middle East. He is co-author of *Where Civilizations Meet: The Geopolitics of Islam and the West* (Westview 1994).

Henry Hale is a Ph.D candidate in government at Harvard University. After conducting research for a year and a half in Russia, Uzbekistan, Ukraine and Kazakhstan from 1992 to 1994, he is writing his dissertation on relations between the former Soviet republics. He is the author of 'The Politics of Sovereignty: the 1993 Russian Parliamentary Elections in Bashkortostan', due to be published by the Brookings Institution in 1994 in a volume on the 1993 Russian elections edited by Timothy Colton and Jerry Hough.

Mikhail A. Konarovsky is presently a counsellor on Middle East, Southwest and Central Asian affairs at the Russian Embassy in Washington, DC. He received his Ph.D at the Institute of Oriental Studies, Academy of Science, Moscow and has been a fellow at the Center for International Affairs, Harvard University.

Nancy Lubin is currently President of JNA Associates, Inc and an adjunct professor at both Carnegie Mellon and Georgetown Universities; she has been an associate professor at Carnegie Mellon and a fellow at the United States Institute of Peace. She has published widely on Central Asian affairs, including *Labour and Nationality in Soviet Central Asia: An Uneasy Compromise* (Macmillan and Princeton University Presses, 1984), congressional testimony, and a range of scholarly and popular articles, among which the most recent is 'Central Asians Take Stock: Democracy, Corruption, and Ethnicity' (United States Institute of Peace, forthcoming, 1994).

Martha Brill Olcott is a professor in the Department of Political Science at Colgate University and a senior fellow at the Foreign Policy Research in Philadelphia. She is the author of *The Kazakhs* (Hoover Institution, Stanford University Press, 1987) and the editor of *The Soviet Multinational State* (M.E. Sharpe, 1990), and is currently completing *Central Asia in Modern Times* for Cambridge University Press.

Boris Z. Rumer is a fellow at the Russian Research Center of Harvard University. He is the author of *Investment and Reindustrialization in the Soviet Economy* (1984), *Soviet Steel Industry* (1989), *Soviet Central Asia: A Tragic Experiment* (1989) and numerous articles.

Seyed Kazem Sajjadpour received his Ph.D in political science from George Washington University in 1991. He was a post-doctoral fellow at The Center for Middle Eastern Studies at Harvard University from 1991 to 1993. He currently teaches at Tehran University, and is a senior research fellow at the Institute for International and Political Studies in Tehran. He is a member of the editorial board of the *Iranian Journal of*

Central Asian and Caucasus Studies. His major areas of interest include the foreign policy of Iran, Russian politics and the relationship between the post-Soviet republics and the Middle East.

Sabri Sayari is the Executive Director of the Institute of Turkish Studies, Inc, in Washington, DC, and an adjunct professor of political science and international affairs at the George Washington University. Previously he was a senior staff member at the National Academy of Sciences' Nation Research Council (1992–94) and a consultant at the RAND Corporation (1985–92). His publications include 'Politics and Economic Policy-Making in Turkey', in *The Economics and Politics of Liberalization in Turkey* (1992), 'Turkey, the Changing European Security Environment, and the Gulf Crisis', in *The Middle East Journal* (1992) and 'Democracy in Turkey: Problems and Prospects' (with Ilkay Sunar), in *Transitions from Authoritarian Rule* (1986).

Tadeusz Swietochowski is Professor of Soviet/Russian and Middle Eastern Studies at Monmouth College, New Jersey. His articles have appeared in journals and publications in France, Germany, Azerbaijan, Turkey and Poland. He is author of *Russian Azerbaijan 1905–1920: The Shaping of National Identity in a Muslim Community* (Cambridge University Press, 1985), and *Russia and a Divided Azerbaijan: Foreign Conquest and Divergent Historical Development* (Columbia University Press, forthcoming).

Myron Weiner is Ford International Professor of Political Science at the Massachusetts Institute of Technology. From 1987 to 1992 he was the director of MIT's Center for International Studies. He is the author of numerous books and articles on South Asian politics and problems of international migration, including *The Child and the State in India* (1991) and *The Global Migration Crisis: Challenges to States and to Human Rights* (forthcoming, 1994), and the editor of *International Migration and Security* (1993). He is a member of the American Academy of Arts and Sciences.

Index

Abdolrazaqov, Obaidollah, 211
Adbulhamid II, Sultan, 120
Abdurahmanov, Erik, 47
Afghanistan, 7, 8, 9, 10, 13, 20, 36,
  38–9, 63, 68, 69, 70, 74, 75, 76,
  83, 91–117, 123, 154, 159–60,
  161, 164, 165, 166, 168, 216–31,
  236, 249, 252–3, 254, 255, 261,
  262, 264; border troubles,
  110–11; civil war in, 226, 227;
  invasion of, 105; Tajik refugees
  in, 109
Aghazadeh, Gholam Reza, 209
agriculture, 25; claims to land, 76
aircraft industry, 55
Akaev, Askar, 31, 46, 47, 48, 50, 52,
  58, 59, 60, 62, 73, 83, 129, 152,
  212
Al-Hoda bookstore, 97, 210
Ali, Sardar Assef Ahmed, 161, 221
Aliyev, Haidar, 123, 130, 131, 188,
  203
alphabet question *see* script
Ambartsumov, Evgenii, 71
Andropov, Yurii, 123
Ankara Doctrine, 157, 158
Arab world, 41–2
Arabic language, 12
Arabic script, 32, 42, 93, 94, 97,
  127, 184, 190
Aral Sea, devastation of, 7, 32, 266,
  267, 271; revival of, 151
Armenia, 10, 14, 23, 31, 35, 36, 130,
  147, 148, 154, 176, 187, 197, 198,
  200, 203, 204, 207–8, 245, 251;
  blockade of, 131
Armenians, 1, 4, 23, 51, 119, 124,
  186, 201, 202; attacked, 126
Asian Common Market (ACM), 251
Association of South-east Asian
  Nations (ASEAN), 163
Ataturk, Kemal, 33, 156, 177, 178
atheism, 100
Avicenna, 199
Azat (Freedom) movement
  (Kazakhstan), 60
Azerbaijan, 4, 5, 8, 13, 14, 25, 31–2,
  34, 35, 36, 42, 103, 104, 118–35,
  147, 148, 176, 177, 178, 179, 180,
  182, 183, 184, 185, 187, 189, 191,
  192, 193, 197, 198, 200, 203, 204,
  216, 221, 224, 245, 249, 251;
  artificial division of, 125;
  declaration of independence, 128;
  external influences on, 33–43;
  re-entry into CIS, 132; relations
  with Turkey, 127; treaty with
  Iran, 121; withdrawal from CIS,
  130
Azerbaijani Democratic Party, 122
Azerbaijanis, 10, 11, 22, 31
Azerbaijanism, 122, 123, 124
Azeri language, 9, 122, 126
Azeris, 1, 118, 119, 120, 121, 123,
  124, 130, 148, 181, 186, 201, 202,
  205, 208; Persianization of, 130;
  Russianization of, 124, 127;
  separatism of, 36
Aziz, Sartaj, 223

Babri mosque, destruction of, 218
Baker, James, visit to Central Asia,
  85
Bangladesh, 63, 161

276